2000
99BB

Sourcebook for Training in Clinical Psychology

Contributors: ELTON ASH
HAROLD BASOWITZ
LEONARD BLANK
HENRY P. DAVID
GORDON F. DERNER
ARTHUR KOVACS
LUCIANO L'ABATE
MARTIN MAYMAN
CECIL P. PECK
LESLIE PHILLIPS
KARL E. POTTHARST
WILLIAM SCHOFIELD
JOSEPH C. SPEISMAN
GEORGE J. WISCHNER

SOURCEBOOK for TRAINING in CLINICAL PSYCHOLOGY

edited by

LEONARD BLANK, Ph.D.
Director of Psychology Training
New Jersey Neuro-Psychiatric Institute
Department of Institutions and Agencies
Princeton, New Jersey

HENRY P. DAVID, Ph.D.
Associate Director
World Federation for Mental Health
Geneva, Switzerland

SPRINGER PUBLISHING COMPANY, INC.
NEW YORK

Contributors

DR. ELTON ASH
Chief Consulting Psychologist
Department of Medicine and Surgery
Veterans Administration
Washington, D.C.

DR. HAROLD BASOWITZ
Psychologist, Training Branch
National Institute of Mental Health
Bethesda, Maryland

DR. LEONARD BLANK
Director of Psychology Training
New Jersey Neuro-Psychiatric Institute
Princeton, New Jersey

DR. HENRY P. DAVID
Associate Director
World Federation for Mental Health
Geneva, Switzerland

DR. GORDON F. DERNER
Director, Clinical Psychology Training Program
Adelphi University
Garden City, L.I., New York

DR. ARTHUR KOVACS
Clinical Psychologist
Western Psychological Center
Encino, California

DR. LUCIANO L'ABATE
Associate Professor and Chief Psychologist
Children's Clinic, Department of Psychiatry
School of Medicine
Emory University
Atlanta, Georgia

DR. MARTIN MAYMAN
Director, Psychology Training
Menninger Foundation
Topeka, Kansas

DR. CECIL P. PECK
Chief, Psychology Division
Psychiatry, Neurology, and Psychology Service
Department of Medicine and Surgery
Veterans Administration
Washington, D.C.

DR. LESLIE PHILLIPS
Director, Psychology Department
Worcester, State Hospital
Worcester Massachusetts

DR. KARL E. POTTHARST
Co-Director
Western Psychological Center
Encino, California

DR. WILLIAM SCHOFIELD
Professor of Psychology
University of Minnesota
Mayo Medical Center
Minneapolis, Minnesota

DR. JOSEPH C. SPEISMAN
Training Specialist in Psychology
Training Branch
National Institute of Mental Health
Bethesda, Maryland

DR. GEORGE J. WISCHNER
Chairman, Departmental Committee on Clinical Training
Psychology Department
University of Pittsburgh
Pittsburgh, Pennsylvania

Preface

Fostered by massive governmental support, clinical psychology in the United States mushroomed in the years following World War II when social demands for mental health services outdistanced all available resources. In the nearly two decades since, much time and energy have been devoted to spirited discussions of persistent problems in clinical training. It is the purpose of this sourcebook to review past recommendations, consider current programs and issues, and suggest implications for future modifications and innovations.

Years of experimentation with the *Shakow* Report and with the *Boulder* Conference recommendations for graduate training in clinical psychology were followed by reconsideration at *Miami*. The shortage of mental health workers, underscored in the Report of the Joint Commission on Mental Illness and Health, stimulated more discussion and meetings, including the 1962 *Princeton* Conference on Manpower and Psychology Training.

For those who train clinical psychologists, for those who develop professional services, and for the training aspirant himself, this book offers a summary of evolving trends in clinical psychology training since World War II.

The text is divided into three parts. Part One begins with a distillation of the salient features from the *Shakow* Report and the *Boulder, Stanford, Miami,* and *Princeton* Conferences,* focussing on curriculum structure, practicum and field experience, and related issues. This is followed by a review of the growth of training resources from 1945-1962, supported by the United States Public Health Service and the Veterans Administration. The first part concludes with a survey of the development and impact of professional evaluation and social control, the function of the American Board of Examiners in Professional Psychology, and state certification and licensing. Part Two discusses issues. University clinical psychology programs, ranging from tradi-

---

* Dealing specifically with training in clinical psychology, the book does not directly refer to such specialty conferences as the Northwestern Conference on the training of counseling psychologists in 1951, the Thayer Conference on school psychology in 1954, and the Estes Conference on research in 1958.

tional research-oriented training to a practitioner orientation, are noted. In this section, postdoctoral training and specialization in psychotherapy, psychodiagnosis, and research are considered. Part Three presents resources, commentaries, and conclusions. Training in a state system and training abroad are reviewed. Feedback after years of clinical practice is presented by graduates of an accredited program.

Referent points for the reader, as they have been for the contributors, are these *general* issues: vast social demand and more encompassing roles for clinical psychologists; training within a tradition of dual scientific and professional orientation. *Specific* issues, considered wherever applicable, are: curriculum structure; sub- and postdoctoral programs; practicum and field training; specialization; quality of professional services in universities, agencies, and private practice.

Clinical psychology is faced with an identity crisis. In posing our questions, we are asking whether and how psychologists will respond to the opportunities of our time.

The editors wish to extend their appreciation to the following agencies that have been helpful in the preparation of this manuscript: the United States Public Health Service, the Veterans Administration, New Jersey Department of Institutions and Agencies, the New Jersey Neuro-Psychiatric Institute, and the World Federation for Mental Health. The American Psychological Association has been unstinting in its generous supply of pertinent training data and permission to quote from articles published in APA publications. The participants and sponsors of the conferences at *Boulder, Stanford, Miami,* and particularly *Princeton* (where the idea for this book germinated) are owed a debt of gratitude. Virginia Erdman and Dr. Cyril M. Franks spent many hours in critical review of drafts of the manuscript.

<table>
<tr><td>LEONARD BLANK</td><td>HENRY P. DAVID</td></tr>
<tr><td>*Princeton, New Jersey*</td><td>*Geneva, Switzerland*</td></tr>
</table>

The following abbreviations are used in the book:

ABEPP	American Board of Examiners in Professional Psychology
APA	American Psychological Association
CTCP	Committee on Training in Clinical Psychology
ETB	Education and Training Board
NIMH	National Institute for Mental Health
USPHS	United States Public Health Service
VA	Veterans Administration

Contents

Part One: Overviews

1   Clinical Psychology Training, 1945-1962:
Conferences and Issues   *Leonard Blank* ...   1

Conferences

    A. The Shakow Report   2
    B. The Boulder Conference   2
    C. The Stanford Conference   3
    D. The Miami Conference   5
    E. The Princeton Conference   6

Major Training Issues

    I.   Undergraduate Program   8
    II. Graduate Program   10
    III. Field Training   17
    IV. Subdoctoral Training   26
    V. Specialization in Training   28
    VI. Training for Psychotherapy   30
    VII. Training for Research   32
    VIII. Staff Training   35
    IX. Relations with Other Professions   36
    X. Selection of Students   37
    XI. Accreditation and Licensing   40

2   Program Support for Training by the National Institute
of Mental Health: 1947-1963
    Harold Basowitz and
    Joseph C. Speisman   43

3   Training in the Veterans Administration
    Cecil P. Peck and *Elton Ash*   61

Supplement: An Example of Training in the Armed
Services   *James L. Hedlund*   82

4   Standards for Clinical Psychology: Origins and
Evaluation   *William Schofield*   86

Part Two: Issues

5   Clinical Psychology Training in the University
    George J. Wischner   115

6   Postdoctoral Professional Training: How and Why?
        Martin Mayman   140
7   Specialized Training and Innovations in
    Psychodiagnosis
        Conventional Training Considerations
            Leonard Blank   152
        Innovations for Training
            Luciano L'Abate   157
8   Training for Psychotherapy
        Gordon F. Derner   175
9   Specialized Training for Research
        Leslie Phillips   185

Part Three: Resources and Commentaries

10 Training Within a State Program
        Leonard Blank and
        Henry P. David   205
11 Graduate Training Abroad
        Henry P. David   219
12 The Crisis in Training Viewed by Clinical Alumni
        Karl E. Pottharst and
        Arthur Kovacs   278
13 Conclusions and Implications
        Leonard Blank and
        Henry P. David   301

Part Four: Resource References

Bibliography on Clinical Training, 1955-1963
        Martin Mayman   311
Appendixes
    A Criteria for Evaluating Training Programs in Clinical
       or in Counseling Psychology   322
    B APA Approved Doctoral Programs in Clinical and
       in Counseling Psychology, 1963   325
    C Internships for Doctoral Training in Clinical
       Psychology Approved by the APA   328
Index   333

1

Clinical Psychology Training, 1945-1962: Conferences and Issues

LEONARD BLANK

Introduction

World War II gave great impetus to the growth of modern clinical psychology. Psychologists were in considerable demand for screening of military personnel, psychodiagnosis, and psychotherapeutic procedures. The immediate postwar period stimulated extensive training of clinical psychologists, particularly in the VA and the USPHS (*see* Chapters 2 and 3).

In 1957, it was estimated that 847 clinical psychologists would be required by 1965 for mental health clinics in addition to those employed in 1955. In 1953, the Veterans Administration alone was short 800 psychologists and estimated a further need for 500 by 1960.

Recognition of the need for guidelines produced the pioneering *Shakow* Report in 1947. The *Shakow* and the subsequent *Boulder* Conference Proceedings have had, and still are having, a strong influence on the course of clinical psychology. In the past decade, however, changing needs have stimulated additional conferences and recommendations at *Stanford* (1955), *Miami* (1958) and *Princeton* (1962). It is the purpose of this chapter to present an overview of the history and major themes of clinical psychology training from the 1947 *Shakow* Report to the 1962 *Princeton* Conference. After a brief description of the deliberations at each convocation, the most significant issues are reviewed as amended from one meeting to the next. The reader may identify the specific issue referred to at a particular conference by the coding system illustrated in the Table of Contents. (For example, IIB refers to discussion of Graduate Programs at *Boulder*.)

CONFERENCES

A. *The* Shakow *Report*[7]

In March 1947, the Board of Directors of the APA appointed the Committee on Training in Clinical Psychology, with David Shakow as Chairman, to perform the following tasks:

1. Formulate a recommended program for training in clinical psychology.

2. Formulate standards for institutions giving training in clinical psychology, including both universities and internship and other practicum facilities.

3. Study and visit institutions giving instructions in clinical psychology, and make a detailed report on each institution.

The report limited consideration to training programs at the four-year doctoral level and recommended that further training of clinical psychologists at the M.A. level be discontinued. The *Shakow* Report, in its detailed recommendations for curriculum, field experience, and discussion of training issues, has served since as a guideline for American clinical psychology and still wields considerable influence.

B. *The* Boulder *Conference*[5]

In August of 1949, a conference supported by the NIMH convened at Boulder, Colorado, to consider problems connected with the training of clinical psychologists. Seventy-one representatives from training universities, mental health service agencies, and allied professions participated. (Of these, 2 represented state hospitals and 1 a community clinic. The VA was represented by 3, USPHS by 6, and the Army by 1.)

At *Boulder*, it was frequently reiterated that *training in clinical psychology should be broadly professional in the doctoral program, leaving most specialization to postdoctoral experience.* (The issue of specialization is discussed later in this chapter and also in Chapters 6,7,8, and 9.)

The Conference called for clinical psychology training programs that reflect the changing needs of society as well as the theoretical and technical changes taking place within the profession of psychology and its related fields. Diversified university training programs were encouraged, although a basic core of general and clinical psychology was believed necessary to provide uniformity of background.

Recommended almost unanimously by the Conference was the limitation of the term "clinical psychologist" to those persons who have received the doctoral degree based upon graduate education in clinical psychology at a recognized university.

C. *The* Stanford *Conference*[8]

A *Boulder* Conference recommendation had been to hold a follow-up conference after five years. In August, 1955, an Institute on Education and Training for Psychological Contributions on Mental Health convened at Stanford University. The participants represented 37 universities with accredited training programs in clinical and counseling psychology and 14 field agencies, together with representatives of the USPHS, the VA, and the APA. Unlike the *Boulder* meeting, this conference passed no resolutions but rather discussed issues raised by papers on several topics. The *Stanford* Conference stressed professional contributions of psychologists, particularly as mental health workers, in contrast to the *Boulder* emphasis on training and concomitant university responsibility.

University representatives complained that agencies too frequently looked on interns as "cheap slave labor"; that service was emphasized to the exclusion of training or research; and that the attitudes of agency personnel were too frequently anti-theoretical, tending to diminish the student's interest in his academic work. From the standpoints of all three parties involved —the university, the field agency, the student—these criticisms indicated an unsatisfactory state of affairs. There was general agreement that closer integration must be established.

Among the suggestions were: Consultant appointments on the agency staff for university faculty and fuller utilization of such resource personnel not only for training but also for case, staff, and research consultations. The belief was expressed that it would be equally important to have university appointments for agency staff members. An opportunity to participate in a program of formal instruction, in discussions of training, and in periodic evaluation of interns was deemed likely to enhance the agency's interest in the integration of theoretical and practical issues while reinforcing commitment to the training function. (Practicum training is discussed in detail later in this chapter.)

Heated discussion was precipitated by the suggestion that the term "clinical psychologist" be extended to include counseling and school psychologists. One point of view stressed the medical connotation of the term "clinical." It was argued that clinical psychology should be synonymous with medical psychology; that training and practice should be restricted to a medical setting. This could include, as in medicine, concern with normal personality development and with the prevention of maladjustment. It would serve to designate the clinician engaged in public health activities as well as the individual working in a traditional clinical or hospital setting. It would have the advantage of maintaining the distinction between the clinical psychologist and counseling or school psychologists.

Surveys of opinion concerning reorganization of the divisional structure of the APA, it was averred, leave little doubt that the majority of members in the school, counseling, and clinical divisions wish to maintain their separate professional identities. Extension of the term "clinical" to include the other two fields was not believed likely to meet with approval in any of the divisions concerned.

It was also maintained that distinctions among areas of professional specialization did not require separate doctoral training programs. If a broader doctoral program could provide basic professional training for the various specialties, it would be useful to have some descriptive term, just as the M.D. degree signifies completion of basic medical education. No generally satisfactory term was suggested during the discussion. "Applied" was considered too broad, since it includes training, interests and practices outside the areas common to the counseling, school, and clinical fields. The term "professional," which is used in the title of the ABEPP, while almost synonymous with "applied" psychology, was thought to be a somewhat more acceptable term.

D. *The* Miami *Conference*[6]

The *Boulder* Conference called for periodic examination of the concepts and programs of graduate education. The *Miami* Beach Conference on Graduate Education in Psychology did not focus on training in any single specialty but dealt with the whole field of graduate education in psychology. The 122 participants came from 65 colleges and universities in the United States and Canada; from 6 governmental organizations; 8 hospitals, clinics and special schools; 3 public school systems; 1 foundation; and 1 accrediting agency. They met February 1958.

In contrast to *Boulder,* the Miami conferess were not predominantly involved in clinical psychology per se—there were far fewer field agencies represented and the universities sent department heads who, with few exceptions, were not clinical psychologists. It is not surprising that the *Miami* Conference emphasized research, with the internship seen more as an appendage than an integral aspect of training.

The *Miami* Conference agreed that serious attention must be given to preparing persons for some of the functions which are basically psychological in nature by means of training programs which are less costly in time and personnel than in a doctoral education. It expressed the conviction that for some roles appropriate and adequate training could be given in one or two years of graduate work.

The recommendation of the *Miami* Conference that emphasis be placed on subdoctoral training needs careful explication. It was not an endorsement of the then present M.A. programs in psychology. Rather, it asked psychologists in all specialties to examine their practices and to identify those skills and techniques which could be learned adequately in a shorter time, applied effectively without the background knowledge and research training which the *Miami* Conference unequivocally supported as essential for doctoral training in psychology. It was expected that persons trained in such techniques would function in limited situations or under supervision of broadly trained professionals of an appropriate discipline.

The recommendation of training subdoctoral "psychologists" was a major departure from the *Shakow, Boulder,* and *Stanford* suggestions for training. Although not significantly implemented, it has stirred up considerable controversy. A similar recommendation in the keynote address at the *Princeton* Conference occasioned lively debate with generally negative reactions. This issue will be discussed more fully later in this section under the topic "subdoctoral training," as well as in Chapter 13.

E. *The* Princeton *Conference*[1]

The ever-growing demand for professional psychological services since World War II led to the conferences concerned with clinical psychological training and its changing goals. The Joint Commission Report on Mental Illness and Health (1961) and its implications for the crisis in clinical psychology training provided impetus for the conference on "Manpower and Psychology: Joint Responsibilities of States and Universities," which met at Princeton in June 1962.

The *Princeton* Conference brought together, for the first time, directors of university clinical psychology training programs and state-level psychologists in the ten northeastern states with colleagues from the USPHS and VA and with consultants from other sections of the country. While the previous conferences focussed largely on defining university responsibilities, at *Princeton* the *joint* responsibilities of states and universities received primary consideration, with particular emphasis on the nature and quality of the internship experience.

There was substantial, though not unanimous, agreement that the production of people called psychologists, who would be trained only at the M.A. level, was not desirable for the development of state or other programs. This was not a suggestion, however, that there should not be many non-doctoral mental health workers of varied kinds. The roles for some of these were seen as emerging and other roles would still have to be defined. Psychologists, along with members of other professions, would have functions in selecting and training the less than doctorally trained persons.

There was acknowledgement of the considerable contributions of the VA, but there were questions as to whether the VA provides an adequate model. It was noted that 5% or less of hospitalized mental patients are in VA facilities and that the VA itself is experiencing difficulties in recruiting psychologists. (Psychology in the VA is discussed in Chapter 3.) State mental health programs are rapidly expanding beyond the confines of mental hospitals, and concentrating on manpower logistics (more people doing more of the same) may no longer be pertinent.

In discussing these issues, it was observed that not enough clinical psychologists were being trained and that training for a "generic" psychologist was unfeasible since no program was so inclusive as to train a student in all the skills. It was argued that it was as deceptive to describe diagnosis and therapy as limited and technical procedures as to consider experimental psychology unlimited and non-specific. There were opinions that therapy and research may both be "generic" to the practice of psychology.

There was also discussion about establishing professional schools, oriented to training for clinical service and providing opportunities for clinical research with clinical problems in clinical settings. While there was some question of the validity of the skills to be taught, it was conceded that experimentation was indicated and that methods of training might be further diversified rather than aimed in any one direction.

Related to the quality of training of clinical psychologists was the question of what constituted adequate preparation for field experience. One conclusion of the *Princeton* Conference was the desirability of closer cooperation between university psychologists and state-level psychologists in training—for example, through joint appointments of clinical coordinators and training supervisors in both universities and state agencies.

As for possible solutions to the shortage and the quality of training clinical psychologists, several alternatives were suggested at the *Princeton* Conference: 1) expand present university training programs. 2) Add to present training facilities, for example, by retooling current Master's programs, and by utilizing state colleges for doctoral training. 3) Experimentally develop professional schools that would concentrate on clinical doctorates, perhaps de-emphasizing less essential elements of the traditional doctoral program but including firm grounding in basic psychology.

MAJOR TRAINING ISSUES

I. *Undergraduate program*

IA. The *Shakow* Report presented the following basic requirements for clinical psychology students:

Clinical psychology seeks to acquire systematic knowledge of human personality and to develop principles and methods by which it may use this knowledge to increase the mental well-being of the individual. If we recognize that clinical psychology is both a science and an art calling for scientific rigor tempered by personal and social sensitivity, we can specify these goals fairly clearly. The preparation of the clinical psychologist must combine applied and theoretical knowledge in three major areas: *diagnosis, therapy,* and *research.* A specialized background in only one or two of these areas is inadequate for functioning as a clinical psychologist.

1. *Psychology.* Approximately 20 semester hours acquainting the student with the field of psychology both in its general and in its laboratory aspects. The main emphasis should be on courses in dynamic psychology ("fundamental theories of motivation, conflict, and resolution of conflict applied to the understanding of normal and abnormal behavior") which consider crucial human problems at a fairly rigorous scientific level.

2. *Biological and physical sciences.* Approximately 20 semester hours of which the major part should preferably be in biology, including genetics, and the balance in physics and chemistry. Satisfactory secondary school preparation in the latter two subjects would reduce the amount required at the college level.

3. *Mathematics and statistics.* Approximately 9 semester hours in mathematics and statistics, with special emphasis on their logical principles.

4. *Education.* Approximately 6 semester hours in the fundamentals of educational philosophy as well as experimental didactics in the form of practice teaching, if this can be arranged.

5. *Social sciences.* Approximately 12 semester hours in sociology, anthropology, and economics. (Political science or history might be substituted for the last.)

6. *History of culture.* Approximately 9 semester hours in history of civilization, comparative literature, comparative religion, philosophy, etc.

7. *Psychology as revealed in literature.* Approximately 6 semester hours, if this can be arranged.

8. *Languages.* Reading knowledge of French and German. (Some consideration should, however, be given to the desirability of substituting other languages, for example, Spanish and Russian.)

IB. At *Boulder,* it was resolved that the undergraduate curriculum should approximate that recommended in the *Shakow* Report. The consensus was that courses and training in diagnostic and other clinical skills and techniques should be offered only at the graduate level. Furthermore, it should be offered only to students whose education would give reasonable assurance that the use of such skills would be made with proper regard for the best interests of clients or patients and with proper regard for problems of validity and the limited applications of the data derived from such techniques.

Specifically, the resolution urged that courses should not be offered at the undergraduate level in the Stanford-Binet, the Wechsler-Bellevue, or the projective techniques. Even at the graduate level, enrollment in such courses should be restricted to students who would have a legitimate use for them and who could be trusted to understand the limitations of the techniques themselves. Courses designed to train students in psychotherapy fall into the same category.

IC. The recommendations with respect to undergraduate programs made at the *Stanford* Conference were general rather than specific. Greater emphasis was placed on courses dealing with social factors. The participants considered that there was a growing interest in the influence of social factors on perception, learning, motivation, personality, and psychopathology. They suggested that psychology students should become familiar with psychology as a social as well as a biological science. The content of undergraduate and graduate courses in experimental psychology, they thought, ought to be broadened accordingly. In courses in statistics, the *Stanford* Conference recommended that more emphasis be given to construction of tests and scales, descriptions and analyses of social phenomena, nonparametric methods, transformations, matrix analyses, and machine techniques.

ID, IE. The *Miami* Conference, in its avowed purpose to discuss "graduate education in psychology," did not address itself directly to the undergraduate program. This was also true of the *Princeton* Conference.*

I. SUMMARY

The emphasis in undergraduate preparation for clinical psychology appears to have shifted from specific course requirements to a broadly based liberal arts program with increasing recognition of social phenomena. Currently, there seems to be stress on the student learning *who* people are and what they do, have done, and can do.

II. *Graduate program*

IIA. The *Shakow* Report was specific and comprehensive in its recommendations with respect to graduate program. Since these suggestions continue to wield considerable influence, many of the details are presented here.

1. Preparation should be broad and include at least a four-year program which combines academic and clinical training throughout; it should include intensive clinical experience in the form of an internship; it should be directed to research and professional goals.

2. The program should stress basic courses and principles rather than techniques. *A broadly based psychologist rather than a technician is the primary goal.*

3. The specific program of instruction should be organized around a careful integration of theory and practice, of academic and field work, by persons representing both aspects.

---

*A suggestion for teaching abnormal psychology in a general psychology class is offered by Tyler. The students spend two months in a state mental hospital where their service duties are incidental. The topics covered in class assignment include: classification of disorders, various therapies (i.e., shock and drug therapy, psychotherapy), cognitive disorders, the psychoneuroses, the affective disorders, schizophrenia, motivational and "ego-function" abnormalities, etc.[10]

4. Through all four years of graduate work, the student should have contact, both direct and indirect, with *clinical material*, e.g., illustrative cases with which the instructor has had personal contact. The student should, from the first year, be provided with opportunities for contact with human material in naturalistic, test, and experimental situations.

5. The student needs to have contact with *normal material* in order to become acquainted with the range of normal and borderline persons who never establish clinic contacts.

6. A systematic plan ought to be initiated to use the representatives of related disciplines for teaching the trainee in clinical psychology, and opportunities for joint study with students in these disciplines should be provided.

7. Throughout the training there should be emphasis on the research implications of the phenomena with which the student is faced.

8. The above requirements call for study in six major areas: a) general psychology, b) psychodynamics of behavior, c) diagnostic methods, d) research methods, e) related disciplines, and f) therapy.

a) *General psychology.* 1) General, physiological, and comparative psychology. 2) History of psychology and contemporary schools of thought. 3) Developmental psychology—fundamental theories of genetic development: child, adolescent, and adult; individual differences. 4) Social psychology.

b) *Psychodynamics of behavior.* 1) Fundamental theories of personality and motivation of normal and abnormal behavior. 2) Experimental dynamic psychology—conferences and laboratory work: classical experiments in general psychology, theory and design of clinical research and experiments on personality characteristics and dynamics, critical analysis of published studies and applications of experimental techniques to actual problems in the clinical field. 3) Psychopathology—the consideration of symptoms and symptom complexes in various mental disorders, with emphasis on nosology to some extent, but more particularly on the mechanisms and dynamics behind symptoms. The course should be organized largely around actual case presentations.

c) *Diagnostic methods.* 1) Students should be trained first in observation and reporting. For this purpose, one-way screens, paired observers, and recording devices of both sound and visual types should be used in settings where individuals and groups are under observation in free and controlled situations. Constant checking of the observers' reports against each other, against supervisor's observations, and against the mechanical devices should be standard practice. 2) Survey of clinical psychology to provide student with a perspective of the whole field of clinical psychology. 3) Method of case study, case analysis, and interviewing. 4) Theory and practice of psychological diagnostics: theory of testing and test construction; verbal "intelligence" tests; non-verbal ability tests of sensory and perceptual function; educational achievement test; vocational tests; clinical tests of psychological deficit, aphasia, conceptualization, etc; projective and other personality procedures; clinical analysis and integration of diagnostic devices.

(The recommendations concerning therapy and research, (d) and (f), are discussed separately in sections VI and VII of this chapter.)

e) *Related disciplines.* The program of the *first year* of graduate work should include: 1) physiological sciences (lectures and demonstrations). Selected aspects of physiology and anatomy, especially neurophysiology, neuroanatomy, autonomic nervous system, and endocrinology. 2) Introduction to clinical medicine (lectures). Introductory course in clinical medicine to acquaint the psychologist with the major characteristics of the clinical pictures of various diseases and with technical medical procedures which he will hear about in the settings where he works. Special attention should be given to those diseases which today are usually referred to as psychosomatic. 3) Social organization and social pathology (lectures and field visits). A course to acquaint the psychologist with social structure, the pathological aspects of this structure as seen in crime, poverty, etc., and the agencies set up to take care of these. The major part of this course could most effectively be given by psychiatrically oriented social workers rather than sociologists. 4) Influence of culture on personality (lectures): what cultural anthropology contributes to the understanding of personality.

The program of the *second year* of graduate work is directed mainly at providing the student with the background in the experimental, diagnostic, and therapeutic approaches to the problems of clinical psychology. Although some teaching may still be in the form of lectures, the emphasis is on direct contact with patients, clients, or other persons, either in the diagnostic or in the experimental setting. Practicum courses and clerkships in different clinical settings are essential elements of this program.

The *third year* consists of an internship whose content is discussed in detail in a later section. The Committee believed that the third year spent in an internship and the fourth, and final, year at the university was the most desirable arrangement, although other patterns should be experimented with. The advantages are many: 1) the student is enabled to complete the analytic and final work on his dissertation at the university. 2) The sequence permits final integration of the experiences acquired during the internship with the more theoretical principles emphasized by the university. Otherwise the internship may be considered as an appendage. 3) The return of graduate students with internship background to the university should have an influence on the unity of the course of training provided by the university and the internship center. 4) The student is placed geographically close to the agency which has an established placement service.

The program of the *fourth year* should be elastic and could include most of the following: 1) final work on dissertation. 2) Cross-disciplinary seminars (attended by representatives of psychology, anthropology, sociology, social work, psychiatry, etc.) devoted to the discussion of psychology's relation to the other sciences concerned with the adjustment problems of the individual and the group. 3) Seminars on professional problems—standards, ethics, etc. 4) Courses in psychology needed to round out the individual student's program. 5) Additional courses in related fields as needed. 6) Advanced therapeutic work, if indicated. 7) A program of self-evaluation, if indicated. g) *Dissertation.* Whenever possible, the dissertation ought to be related to clinical problems such as encountered in the internship, during which the intern will usually collect data. Supervision of his project should continue a joint responsibility of the university and field training center. h) *Integration of academic and field program*. The problem of integration arises with respect to three aspects: 1) content, 2) supervision, and 3) accrediting and certification.

IIB. The *Boulder* participants decided that training should prepare students for both research and practice. The core of the *Shakow* Report was endorsed, but more as a guide than a listing of requisite courses. (No agreement was reached in *Boulder* with regard to foreign language requirements. Strong opposition to the status quo—two modern languages, particularly French and German—was expressed.) Fields or contents were recommended for consideration rather than courses which imply a specificity. Such specificity was, however, not really intended by the *Shakow* Report.

A subcommittee agreed that the following 12 fields (*not courses*) should be included in a core curriculum:

1. *Human physiology*. The sub-group included in this material has explicit recognition of the prerequisite training ordinarily required for course work in physiology, endocrinology, neurophysiology, and neuroanatomy.

2. *Personality theory*. This area should include both cross-sectional and genetic theories.

3. *Developmental psychology*. As used here, the term refers to psychological development and change throughout the life span. Training in this area should deal with the biological, sociological, and cultural determinants of psychological development.

4. *Social relations*. The term refers explicitly to material in social psychology, sociology, economics, and anthropology.

5. *Psychopathology*. It is not intended that work in this area should be concerned primarily with the gross abnormalities found in mental illness (*see* 7 below). It should cover the psychology of deviant personality.

6. *Personality appraisal*. This area includes all the methods available to the clinical or nonclinical psychologist for evaluating the individual and groups of individuals. In addition to testing methods, it also refers to interviewing, observation techniques, and the like.

7. *Clinical medicine and clinical psychiatry*. It is here that training concerning the nature of kinds of mental illness is to be

included, together with such basic information in clinical medicine as is appropriate and necessary for the nonmedical clinician.

8. *Psychotherapy and remedial procedures.* The latter half of this designation is added, not as an attempt to differentiate remedial procedures from psychotherapy, but to indicate that training in such areas as relearning and remedial reading should be included.

9 *Clinical research methodology.* There are enough research problems peculiar to the clinical situation to require special training in this area. The usual training in research methodology does not necessarily cover this area.

10. *Professional and interprofessional relationships.* This area involves explicit attention to the nature and functions of allied professional groups, relationships with one's own professional colleagues, and all other phases of professional ethics.

11. *Community resources and organization.* The clinical psychologist must know a great deal about the resources, agencies, and institutions of the community. He must be familiar with their operations and the protocol involved in working with them. With respect to methods of training in this area, much can be learned from the experience accumulated by psychiatric social workers.

12. *Practicum and internship experiences.* (Discussed in detail in Section III.)

IIC. Discussions at the *Stanford* Conference "brought out agreement that there is, in effect, a common core, but the Conference refused to specify this in terms of course content, preferring to leave it to each department to select, from the totality of psychological knowledge, whatever sampling best fitted the needs of its program and the capacities of its faculty."

IID. Two primary conclusions derived from the *Miami* Conference discussions. First, there is a common core. Second, we should not specify what this is lest we in any way discourage imaginative innovation in graduate training. (In fact, the deliberations concerning the graduate curriculum became focussed on inculcating research interests in the student.)

Although several groups considered lists of areas that might be included, the participants were not willing to specify the common core in terms of course content. There was, however, strong acceptance of the idea that the defining characteristic of the Ph.D. psychologist was his research training. This agreement did not imply that professional, applied work was inappropriate for psychologists. It meant that the *Miami* Conference expressed the view that applied psychologists should be educated to practice with inquiring minds.

It was proposed also that universities consider making fuller use of practitioners as additional faculty members under conditions which would insure the practitioners' genuine participation in the educational process. This might mean, for example, providing space and equipment, or appropriate research facilities. It might also facilitate taking students into an apprenticeship relation. A probable corollary would be further development of the participation of faculty members in extramural activities, with consequent feedback.

IIE. Many participants at the *Princeton* Conference stressed that efforts to train students simultaneously as a researcher and practitioner often have proved less than satisfactory. The field representatives particularly were concerned that students assigned for internship had little or no coursework in abnormal psychology, personality and psychopathology theory, tests, and projective techniques.

II. SUMMARY

The recommendations of the *Shakow* Report still serve as guidelines for graduate curricula in clinical psychology. There has been a tendency to de-emphasize the specificity of the *Shakow* recommendations, conceding greater flexibility to individual psychology departments. The stress on research versus practice has swung back and forth, suggesting a double problem: 1) all clinical psychologists should be *acquainted* with the methodology of both areas. 2) Students wishing to do primarily research ought to receive concentrated training by the university in this area with the opportunity of clinical experience in the field, perhaps related to research problems; students, aspiring primarily to practice, ought to receive concentrated training by the university in this area but be inculcated, as well, with an investigative attitude and acquire some facility for researching clinical problems.

III. Field training

IIIA. The *Shakow* Report paid particular attention to the philosophy of field experience.

1. Extensive and intensive experience with people is held to be essential if the student is to acquire a proper perspective and the ability to apply effectively the scientific facts and techniques which he has acquired in the academic setting. The internship is not a "repair shop" in which the failures of the academic center are taken care of. The university must adequately carry out its function of providing the necessary training in *tool subjects* so that the student may take full advantage of what the internship is set up primarily to provide, namely, material on which to use these tools. A "good" internship provides opportunities for diagnosis, research, and therapy, with a reasonably varied population under adequate supervision where a variety of disciplines, such as psychiatry, social work, nursing, as well as psychology, play a part.

2. For the program to be most effective, the content provided by the two teaching centers (field and university) must be *integrated*.* In this respect, faculty members have been quite lax, leaving it largely to the student to correlate and integrate the material from the variety of courses he has taken at the university. The integration of university and field center activities has been neglected even more. If training is to be optimally effective, the two leading groups must become essentially *one* faculty. Arrangements for reciprocal visits and conferences between staffs should be made to discuss such problems as the points of view to be emphasized, the techniques of teaching, and the avoidance of overlap.

3. In the matter of *supervision,* an integrated program must also be achieved. The supervisor at the internship center must be held responsible for the major part of the student's activity.

---

* This idea of *integration* is a leitmotif reiterated from conference to conference, but application has not followed the repeated affirmation.

If the candidate is to use the research time available to him at the institution to work on his dissertation, an agreement as to the division of supervisory responsibilities must be reached by the two groups, e.g., the university may consider appointing several of its instructors as field supervisors on a rotating basis.

4. To meet the obvious need for *combined responsibility* in setting and maintaining standards, the internship center must be accepted as an institution of comparable status with the university and in some respects a part of it. This can be achieved primarily through an interchange of staffs. The teaching staff of the university should be encouraged to spend time at the institution on guest appointments. The staff of the institution should be given temporary full-time or permanent part-time appointments at the university on a regular faculty or lectureship basis.

IIIB. Three levels of field training were defined at the *Boulder* Conference:

1. *Laboratory*. This pre-field work setting serves the primary purpose of developing a refinement in the use of basic tools and techniques.

2. *Clerkship*. This experience serves the following purposes: a) developing a feeling of responsibility for the client and a sensitivity to the clinician-client relationship. b) Developing an initial competence in the use of psychological techniques in a clinical setting. c) Familiarization of students with a wider range of techniques. d) Teaching of the nature and meaning of service. e) Beginning of integration of university course content with the clinical viewpoint and with procedures in a service setting. f) Introducing the interdisciplinary approach to clinical problems; learning to cooperate with colleagues of other disciplines. g) Applying professional ethics. h) Learning to communicate by the writing of case reports for clinical use. i) Providing a wide range of clinical contacts at a relatively superficial level.

3. *Internship*. This is differentiated from the clerkship in the following respects: a) supplying intensive and long-term clinical experience (especially through close follow-up of clinical courses). b) Developing a degree of professional competence at a level comparable to that of junior staff members. c) Providing

intimate contact with clinical problems in which the intern's activities have a bearing on the handling and disposition of a case. d) Developing responsibility in the management of a case through semi-independent handling of psychological examination and treatment. e) Developing confidence in operating in a service setting, particularly in the matter of assuming responsibility. f) Establishing close working relationships with trainees and staff members of other professions by working intensively as a member of a clinical team—i.e., application of the interdisciplinary approach to clinical problems. g) Offering intensive training in the techniques of communicating clinical information to colleagues on the clinical team. h) Imbuing the intern with the spirit and values of the field institution. i) Providing a learning experience for the intern in a setting in which he contributes to service because competent and essential provision of service is one of the best contexts in which to learn.

The term "internship" was found unsatisfactory by the *Boulder* participants because of its variable usage, but the term "practicum" suggested in its stead implied too much of practice rather than on-the-job training. (The VA use of the term "trainee" may meet these objections.)

It was recommended at *Boulder* that the APA study the problem of setting *standards for field agencies* (*see* Chapter 4 on Social Controls). It was further resolved that the choice of field agencies should be made primarily on the basis of quality and amount of supervision available, and secondarily on the basis of kinds of clinical experience. Field training should be so planned as to provide a variety of functioning with persons of varied ages and socio-economic levels—including normal individuals, the maladjusted, and persons of various degrees of psychopathology. When specialization is desirable for particular students, the variety of clinical experience may be correspondingly reduced, but such specialization should not be given before the third year.

Representatives from field work agencies and institutions reported that universities sometimes demand of the agency too much teaching in the use of tests and other techniques that could well be taught in the university laboratory courses. Universities, on the other hand, reported that some supervising psychologists in the agencies expect students to be finished clinicians or, more specifically, to be well versed in tests or interpretative techniques favored by the agencies.

The *Boulder* participants reached a fairly clear-cut agreement on one point: The university department has the responsibility of teaching the administration, scoring, and elementary levels of interpretation of some tests for clinical use and of certifying to the practicum agency the student's readiness for clinical (practicum) use of such tests.

Field placements on the third- and fourth-year levels of training should be at least 9 months of full-time work or 18 months of half-time work. The recommendation for *full-time work* was based upon the arguments: that full-time internships are necessary to provide continuous, intensive experiences in the follow-up of patients; to develop a sense of clinical responsibility; and to permit the intern to take advantage of the full range of staff conferences, teaching seminars, and informal case discussions provided by the training center. One suggestion given some consideration was that, since a children's agency, an outpatient neuropsychiatric clinic, and a hospital for psychotic adults seemed to represent indispensable areas of the training program, a student might profitably divide six months between two of them on a part-time basis and devote another six months full-time to the third.

IIIC. At *Stanford,* the report on field training was presented by Dr. Shakow. He made the following points:

1. The greater the degree of integration achieved between theory and practice and between university and field center, the more effective the program. The major responsibility for achieving unity falls upon the university since it is the degree-granting institution.

2. Each year would offer theory and practicum, provided either by the university or the field center but usually by both. In the first year there would be emphasis on theoretical courses at the university. At the same time the university would provide laboratory practice in observation and tests, and laboratory work in experimental psychodynamics or similar courses. In the second year, the university would provide additional advanced theory, and the field would provide the clerkship with

theory directly relevant to practice. In the third year, the first internship year, the field station would be required to provide theory related to the field work as well as the field work itself. The fourth year was to become a second internship year during which the dissertation work is carried out at the field center. During this year *both* the university and the field station take the responsibility for the theoretical work connected with the dissertation and any other aspects of the training. Although, during each year, one of two agencies would carry the major responsibility, the other agency would still carry some responsibility for the program.

3. Local institutions will have to be developed. This would permit the close interaction required between the university and the field center. Some of the advantages of mixing students from different universities might be maintained where there are several universities in one area. Although there are advantages to "captive" (in the good sense) centers, the gains are greater all around if there is no exclusive relationship with one university.

As regards the major issue raised by Dr. Shakow- -integration of theory and practice of the university and the field agency—representatives of both groups agreed that, with the exception of a few programs, a satisfactory degree of *integration* had not yet been attained. Agency representatives complained that, too frequently, there was little or no communication between the university and the agency; that the university showed little interest in the teaching program of the agency or in the progress of the student during the internship; that the university seemed to consider theoretical training to be its prerogative; that the university's bias in favor of "critical research" and elegance of experimental design tended to discourage interest and participation of students in research in the agency setting; in short, that the university frequently made little or no effort to help the student function outside its ivory tower.

IIID. 1. At *Miami,* there was agreement that the university department was primarily responsible for the selection of the internship facility, for maintaining close contact with the students while they were there, and for working with the facility to assure that the training was not only adequate in terms of specific skills but could also be integrated into the student's general experience.

2. It was noted that the *choice of internship centers* sometimes seemed to be dictated by such expediencies as service, the theoretical orientation of the training center, politics, and the possibility of consultantships for university faculty.* These considerations were regarded as irrelevant and generally inimical to good training. The choice should be dictated by the best interests of the students. Even geographical locations should not be a prime consideration.

3. It was agreed that the internship should be viewed primarily as a *learning experience rather than a service function.* Objections came from several people on the grounds that service is an essential part of an internship, that the student himself should feel that he is rendering service because it is the one experience he has to learn the feeling of responsibility which must be carried in future jobs. It was believed that there are instances in which the facility, to obtain service ends, will exploit the trainee, and that both university and facility should guard against this. But it was held that the student must develop attitudes of responsibiliy in the application of his specialty, and that such attitudes are not incompatible with maintenance of a controlled and systematic observational set. It was noted also that responsibility is not engendered in a student by exploitative behavior on the part of his mentors.

4. The consensus was that, during the internship, the student should be able to maintain *contact with the university,* whether or not it is geographically distant, or whether the internship is pre- or postdoctoral. This is essential since the internship is viewed as an integral part of the student's training. It was felt that part of practicum training should be the development of a hypothesis-generating attitude towards his experience, and that this can best be fostered by acquaintance with research going on at the university and at the internship center. It was not considered essential that the intern be doing research at this period.

5. It is clear that there was at *Miami* considerable dissatisfaction, both explicit and implicit, with the degree and kind of *cooperation prevalent between university and intern center.* The same kinds of dissatisfaction had been expressed at *Stanford.*

* The editors in their survey of intern assignments in the Northeastern states reached a similar conclusion as to reasons for intern assignments.

It remained doubtful to the *Miami* participants whether the situation had improved or deteriorated in the intervening four years. (The *Princeton* Conference participants of 1962 expressed the perennial unhappiness on this point.)

6. There was some *dissatisfaction with the Boulder model*. The *Miami* participants did not deny that the procedure had produced large numbers of effectively functioning clinical psychologists. Some participants pointed out that the training model created problems for the university and the trainee. Perhaps because of the poor integration between the training centers and the university departments, the internship year was generally viewed not as broadening the student's horizons but as interrupting his academic work and interfering with his research and dissertation. In addition, many felt that the training did not prepare the student adequately to carry out all functions of a clinical psychologist, including research, diagnosis, and therapy. In particular, there was strong objection to the use of young, inadequately trained Ph.D.'s to supervise the training of interns.

The inadequacy of Ph.D. training as sole preparation for a career in psychotherapy was stressed, and it was generally assumed that postdoctoral training was essential. Nevertheless, the conference was not willing to go on record as recommending an additional year of supervised internship, either pre- or postdoctoral. The feeling seemed rather to be that both the new Ph.D. and his employers should be aware of his limitations and of his need for continuing consultation and supervision.

7. When the issue of the *timing* of the internship period was raised, the proposition that it should be (only) predoctoral received a split vote. The major discussion on this topic followed upon the presentation, the following day, of a proposal for an experimental revision of clinical training, drawn up by an *ad hoc* committee. It will be recalled that, at the time of the *Boulder* Conference, the training program approved for a degree in clinical psychology required one year of predoctoral internship. This became the pattern which was generally instituted in universities, and this is the pattern which has been accredited.

8. The modification proposed by the *ad hoc* committee was to introduce a *2-year internship following the Ph.D.* The student would have a 3-year (or 4-year) program with a con-

centration in personality research or some related area. This would include practicum experience, especially in the areas of assessment and therapy. Ideally it would attempt some integration of theory and practice. It would provide research experience (hopefully, somehow coordinated with the practicum) with an emphasis on direct participation in personality research and on acquisition of the skills necessary for such research (e.g., naturalistic and systematic observation, interviewing, case study, as well as certain laboratory procedures). The graduate would be a Ph.D., but would not be designated "clinical psychologist." He would then enter a two-year residency program, given at an accredited postdoctoral training center, which were to include work in diagnostic evaluation, psychotherapy, and clinical research under the direct supervision of highly qualified staff members, and he would be ready, after two years, for "minimal certification" as a clinical psychologist. The *Miami* report suggested, however, that because of the problems of controls, and the administrative and financial burdens involved in the development of residency training centers at this level, such a program should be introduced very gradually. (The issue of specialization and postdoctoral training will be discussed in Chapters 6-9.)

There was disapproval of any moves to formalize postdoctoral training as a requirement. Some participants, who had had experience with both predoctoral and postdoctoral internships at university and internship centers, pointed out that, other things being equal, training effectiveness seemed to be about the same.

9. The issue of a *professional doctoral degree* (i.e., a non-research degree) was raised, but the group reaction was one of indifference with some negative overtones. There was no disagreement that the Ph.D. is a research degree and should be retained as such. (The *Princeton* participants were divided on the advisability of a professional school, but they were nearly unanimous in favoring experimentation.)

IIIE. The *Princeton* conferees particularly emphasized the shortage of qualified candidates for internships. They recommended joint state and university internships as well as federal and state support for such training.

Data relevant to field training was gathered and discussed at

Princeton. To the student shortage, it was noted, is added the problem of quantity and quality of clinical psychology internships. The number of intern assignments made by all 19 northeastern universities during the past five years averaged 163 per year. If this figure was correct, it was twice the number of Ph.D's graduating each year, suggesting considerable delays in completing all university requirements or a high attrition rate. Non-APA accredited universities supplied 20% of interns around the country (report of the *ad hoc* committee, 1961), with training opportunities also provided for students from subdoctoral programs. What controls and what training as psychologists, other than the internship, these people had and what impact they had on the mental health field and on the profession of psychology, was found to be a serious issue.

A related matter was the assignment of interns to centers accredited by the APA Education and Training Board. Of the 69 approved independent agencies in 1959-60, 26 were in the northeastern states. According to the *Princeton* survey, 21 interns, fewer than half of those assigned by universities, were assigned to accredited agencies. Indifference was expressed frankly by several coordinators of clinical training programs. It was considered likely that such factors as geographical location, available funds for stipends and consultation, and relations between particular agencies and universities frequently play a deciding role in assigning interns. Accreditation has been initiated, however, to insure objective standards for qualified intern training.

III. SUMMARY

The plea for coordination between university and field agency has been made consistently since the *Shakow* Report but has not been acted on to an appreciable degree. While the predoctoral internship, usually at the third or fourth year of graduate school, has been the rule, innovations have been suggested periodically. The most popular suggestion has been the postdoctoral internship, including specialization in therapy, diagnosis, or research. Utilization of state and community agencies for field assignments has won increasing favor. Further innovations appear indicated. (*See* reference to practicum training in Chapter 4, especially the suggested innovations.)

IV. *Subdoctoral training*

IVB. While the *Shakow* Report did not address itself to the issue of subdoctoral training, the *Boulder* Conference did make recommendations on it. Concern was expressed that subdoctorally trained persons would not make a maximum contribution to mental health. The demand for personnel, however, would make it necessary to fill many positions with partially trained persons, it was argued, who might function with adequate supervision.

One group of *Boulder* participants recommended establishing a two-year subdoctoral training program. This would be terminal in nature, not composed of the first two years of current Ph.D. training, but designed for the training of workers who would handle the technical routine and service functions of clinical psychology. Supervised field experience would be part of this program.

IVC. The *Stanford* Conference did not make any specific recommendations as to subdoctoral training.

IVD. The *Miami* Conference tangibly grappled with the problem of subdoctoral training: "The considerations point to the conclusion that we must now give serious attention to preparing persons for some of the functions which concern us by means of training programs which are less costly in time and personnel than is doctoral education. One of these is the conviction that for some roles appropriate and adequate training can be given in one or two years of graduate work. The other is that the supply of doctoral psychologists will be limited. Psychology departments now participating in subdoctoral programs, either under their own auspices or in collaboration with other departments, should be encouraged to continue. Newly established graduate programs in psychology should, if they request it, receive the assistance of the APA staff in contacting psychologists who might advise them on the establishment of subdoctoral educational goals. (This statement is, of course, not intended as a blanket endorsement of subdoctoral training regardless of the functions to be performed.)"[6] (p. 68)

There was no discussion at *Miami* of the details of non-doctoral programs in particular psychological service subspecialties. The Conference participants felt that such discussion would be premature. It was agreed that for service-oriented students supervised field experience could be as important as a thesis, that a thesis need not be required of them, and that the faculty should include service-oriented psychologists who, in part, were to provide models for the student. The Committee of the Education and Training Board (ETB), in 1955, had recommended a core curriculum, technique courses with laboratory practice, and supervised practice in appropriate work settings.

There was also agreement at *Miami* that nondoctoral training should be provided only in those specialty areas in which doctorally trained personnel are available to supervise and direct the training and, whenever possible, the services as well.

The problem of status and professional affiliation for persons in nondoctoral specialty programs and in M.A. teaching programs was admittedly a difficult one. For the technical specialty groups, the recommendation was that there should be appropriate job titles which would not include the term "psychology." The 1955 Committee of the ETB had proposed "psychological technician." For those with M.A. training who are to teach psychology, the participants agreed, the issue becomes a particularly difficult one, and no resolution was achieved.

IVE. At the *Princeton* Conference, Professor Schofield offered recommendations to meet the crisis of scarcity in supply and quality of clinical psychologists by innovating and carrying the *Miami* recommendations for subdoctoral training one step further. Some of his points were:

1. Instruction and supervised field work could be designed within the framework of a two-year M.A. program. Students would be selected for such technical training on the basis of specific interests, motives, and aptitudes—*not as doctoral rejects.*

2. Equal recognition should be given to the specialties of diagnosis, therapy, and research. All could be taught adequately in a two-year graduate program, although a student in psychodiagnosis, for example, would then not be as competent in therapy or research.

3. The M.A. specialty training program should be an experience of "total impact" (e.g., therapy training would include

exposure to group therapy, tapes, reading, discussion, observation, etc.).

4. Such concentrated, two-year specialty training courses would produce psychodiagnosticians and psychotherapists more competent than the average doctoral graduate.

The majority of the *Princeton* participants, however, strongly expressed the opinion that on the M.A. level one should not train psychologists but mental health workers of various kinds.

IV. SUMMARY

Although experimentation with subdoctoral programs has been suggested several times in the past two decades, today's trend toward specialization and the increasing demand for psychologists are underscoring the need for innovations in training.

V. *Specialization in training*

VA. The *Shakow* Report was not addressed in detail to specialization in training.

VB. The participants of the *Boulder* Conference agreed that narrow specialization, such as psychodiagnosis or psychotherapy, was unwise for graduate students. They believed that specialities within clinical psychology had not crystallized but that this was imminent and would require a decision as to postdoctoral or doctoral training.

VC. It was felt at *Stanford* that it was quite feasible to arrange a curriculum which would provide for adequate attention to the major problems and techniques in the three areas of mental health with which psychologists are primarily concerned: disorders in adults, disorders in children, and the vocational and emotional problems of the relatively normal. The common core of such a program would then be the training in research procedures and in mental health problems and techniques. The opportunity for specialization would still remain and might well be encouraged in advanced seminars, in dissertation and internship experiences.

Such a plan would obliterate to a large extent the boundaries *at the training level* between clinical, counseling, and school psychology. The recommended training programs for the Ph.D. for all three subdisciplines, as established at the *Boulder* Conference (clinical psychology), the Northwestern Conference (counseling psychology), and the Thayer Conference (school psychology), are very similar in basic outline except for perhaps one-fourth of the material in each of the three fields. In all three programs, training for research is regarded a necessity. All three pay some attention to general psychology, to normal and abnormal personality, and to psychometric and projective techniques. All three require some proficiency in assessment and treatment procedures.

The advantages of a Ph.D. program which distinguishes but minimally among these three areas would be: first, breadth of training could be obtained with sacrificing an opportunity to specialize. Second, the vocational mobility within the field of psychology as applied to mental health could be preserved. Third, such a program would make more sense to university departments of psychology which now have great difficulty in distinguishing among the three areas in question.

Similarity of the *training* programs would continue to permit a psychologist to join two or even all three divisions, although his employment would still depend upon his qualifications rather than his divisional affiliation.

Discussion of the trend toward increased specialization in psychology revealed widespread concern that this might encourage technological training rather than broad, scientifically oriented professional training. Technological training tends to become obsolescent. The capacity to adapt to changing techniques, changing needs, and changing functions is dependent on a professional education and outlook, The opinion at *Stanford* was overwhelmingly in favor of broadening the scope of the present training programs in psychology and of attempting to define a "basic professional core" that would provide an adequate foundation for specialization in various areas.

The current training programs in clinical, counseling, and school psychology require essentially the same basic preparation in general psychology. Similarly, they have a common "basic professional core." This includes personality theory, development and dynamics; psychological assessment, including the use of interview techniques and the construction, administration, and interpretation of tests; and some of the general principles and procedures involved in the modification of behavior. Most of the *Stanford* participants felt that further efforts should be made to define a basic professional core.

The conferences and committees that have been concerned with the development of training programs in the various fields of psychology have all recognized the impossibility of *completing* special training prior to the Ph.D. The goal has been to train the student sufficiently to enable him to function at a beginning professional level. Since professional training must continue beyond attainment of the degree, increased efforts should be made to provide inservice and postgraduate training opportunities to assure the development of full professional competence.

VD. The *Miami* conferees did not pay particular attention to specialization.

VE. At *Princeton,* opinion was divided as to the advisability of having professional schools for psychologists. Almost all agreed, however, that experimentation was in order.

V. SUMMARY

At every conference there was agreement as to the need for specialization but differences as to its timing—pre- or post-doctoral. Recent sentiment seems to have swung to at least experimenting with professional schools and postdoctoral training.

VI. *Training for psychotherapy*

VIA. The *Shakow* Report recommended the following division for training in psychotherapy: 1) therapeutic theory and methods (lectures and discussion). Introductory course in therapy and counseling; methods and techniques; evaluation of results. There should be considerable emphasis on different points of view in therapy and on common factors in the various forms of therapy. 2) Remedial aspects of special disabilities (lectures and systematic supervised practice). 3) Techniques of guidance and counseling (lectures and systematic practice under supervision in individual personality guidance and counseling of minor problems). 4) Personality therapy (detailed consideration of case material in seminars; carefully supervised practice). 5) Techniques of group therapy (lectures, systematic participation, and supervised practice).

VIB. It was the consensus at *Boulder* that, "Really advance training in therapy is, with few exceptions, a problem of the postdoctoral period . . ." The conferees added, however, that all students in doctoral programs in clinical psychology should have training in the theory and practice of psychotherapy even though many might not become therapists. This training was viewed as only an introduction to psychotherapy; true competence depended upon supervised postdoctoral training. Except under unusual circumstances, it was expected that final competence in psychotherapy would be achieved at the postdoctoral level. There was a generally felt need for the development of better facilities for this more advanced kind of training. Integrated courses which reflect the basic principles of psychodynamics, supplemented by supervised experience in the practical clinical situations, were considered preferable to a series of discrete technical courses.

The *Boulder* Conference participants agreed that psychiatrists and psychiatric social workers of recognized competence should be included in supervisory programs wherever possible. The need for research in, and systematization of, psychotherapy was considered as important as the need for training for practice. There was considerable agreement, too, that the training period should be utilized continuously as a means of developing self-awareness and self-evaluation.

The consensus was: "We are opposed to the practice of psychotherapy (not to include remedial teaching or vocational and educational counseling) by psychologists that does not meet conditions of genuine collaboration with physicians most qualified to deal with the borderline problems which occur (e.g., differential diagnosis, intercurrent organic disease, psychosomatic problems)."

VIC. The *Stanford* participants made the point that most university departments had had little, if any, experience in providing psychotherapy training. The participants were substantially agreed on the following: 1) training in psychotherapy is essential for psychologists working in the mental health field. 2) It is a responsibility of the university to provide initial training in psychotherapy. 3) Training must be experimental and should preferably begin fairly early in the graduate program. 4) Postdoctoral training will be required for the development of professional competence in therapy.

Psychotherapy should encompass the range of techniques which the professional psychologist is expected to know: mental health education, preventive intervention to counteract potentially traumatic environmental influences, personal counseling, intensive individual therapy, group therapy, and the creation and utilization of a therapeutic environment. The student, although he might not be trained in all of these techniques, should have some appreciation of the importance and role of various approaches to the modification of behavior.

VID, E. At *Miami* and *Princeton*, the issue of training in psychotherapy was not gone into specifically. However, at both conferences the recommendation was made for experimentation with *professional degrees* or *professional schools* in psychology.

VI. SUMMARY

From the *Shakow* Report to the *Princeton* Conference, it was agreed that clinical psychologists should be introduced by the university to the principles and practice of psychotherapy. The latter function often is largely delegated to the field agency but competency in therapy comes as a result of supervised postdoctoral training.

VII. *Training for research*

VIIA. The *Shakow* Report recommended the following research preparation: 1) experimental psychology—conference and laboratory course of a basic kind in experimental techniques, devoted mainly to the more meaningful problems in general psychology, e.g., learning, reaction mechanisms, work activity, etc. Consideration should be given to variability of response— to significance of the extremes of the distribution as well as to the modal and typical response—and to the clinical implications of these general problems. 2) Advanced statistics and quantitative methods in psychology and psychopathology. 3) Research in dynamic psychology—conference and laboratory course, considering theory and design of experiments in personality characteristics and dynamics; application of experimental and other research methods to the problems in the clinical field. 4) Dissertation; preliminary work on the dissertation including the setting of the problem, preparatory reading, and the outlining of the project in detail during the second year. Actual experimental work on the dissertation carried out during the third (internship) year under joint supervision of university and field center. Final work on the dissertation during the fourth year. VIIB. It was resolved at *Boulder* that the dissertation may be in any field of psychology but that it would be desirable for such research to be in the field of personality, broadly conceived. Single case or technical exploration at the expense of *personality* exploration was thought less desirable.

The following research skills were stressed as important for development in the clinical psychologist: 1) relevant analysis of clinical phenomena in order that *fruitful* concepts and hypotheses may be developed. 2) Training in careful definitions of concepts as a check upon the "intuitive" judgments often required in such practical situations as staff meetings and clinical reports. 3) Training in the explicit formulation of research problems in the design of appropriate investigations in the field of personality and clinical problems. 4) Competence in the statistical analysis of data. 5) Ability to communicate effectively in writing both to psychologists and other professional writers.

VIIC. The *Stanford* participants recognized the multiplicity of cultural and social factors involved in behavior and so they urged broad research training. In addition to familiarity with the instruments, methodologies, experimental designs, and statistical techniques utilized in the psychology laboratory, it was recommended that the student develop skills in field and laboratory research. Interdisciplinary research was also stressed as invaluable experience. The implications for coursework have been discussed (*see* IIC).

VIID. The *Miami* Conference "insisted" on research training for all psychologists and approved a broad definition of research. It was agreed that the continuum of research methodologies included not only the most rigorous hypothesis testing but also the use of clinical and naturalistic devices for the formulation of communicable and testable generalizations. Influenced by the Estes Park Report[9], the following recommendations were made at *Miami*:

1. Statistics, theory, and scholarship are all important to research personnel but each of these can be overdone, and they should be thought of as means to an end, not an end in themselves.

2. There should be diversity among universities as regards the relative emphasis on statistics and other methodologies, theory, technical skills, content areas, etc.

3. Students trained for a research role shall include not just the top 10% in terms of ability but the 40-60% who may be spending a great deal of their time on research. These individuals may be thought of as having a strong orientation towards research regardless of the level of creativity at which they can function.

4. A close apprenticeship relation to a faculty member and the atmosphere of research in progress are important considerations. The feeling that research is rewarded is significant. Some research assistantships are not apprenticeships in the sense of the report; they are exploitative rather than instructional.

5. Ideally, research apprenticeships are at least preparation for minor roles. Individual research projects should start in the first year and should move rapidly to the point at which the student has the opportunity to make decisions about his research program.

It was agreed that early experience with research was very desirable, regardless of specialty. "Low level" research, such as data-gathering activities, was considered acceptable while participation in team research and replication studies were also suggested as methods for creating a research attitude.

Sentiment at *Miami* favored relaxation of traditional specifications for the doctoral dissertation: accept research yielding negative findings whether publishable or not; accept varying degrees of rigor as the requirements within the several areas of psychology allow to be feasible; accept research primarily exploratory in nature; accept research which is the product of teams; and accept these which are not empirical studies. It was suggested that doctoral work should be directed only by those who have had considerable research experience. "This implies that, for example, the dissertation advisor in a clinical study should be one who has had considerable practical experience in the clinic as well as experience in research relevant to the thesis problem."

Consensus was also expressed at *Miami* that, while a knowledge of statistics is a valuable adjunct of research training, it alone is a poor substitute for the intuitive skill of a good researcher—just as formal design of experiments is a poor substitute for contact with ongoing research in the graduate department.

VIIE. The reference to research training most reiterated at *Princeton* was the suggestion that research training in clinical psychology ought to be a collaborative endeavor between the university-based orientation in method and design and the field-based context of live clinical material and problems.

VII. SUMMARY

Every conference stressed the need for research training and its relevance to clinical problems or exploration of personality. The last two meetings, *Miami* and *Princeton*, emphasized the importance of field experience and of the need for supervisors in research training.

VIII. *Staff training*

VIIIB. The only meeting at which staff training was intensively discussed was *Boulder*. There seemed to be no opposition at the Conference to the proposition that "teachers of clinical psychology should maintain their clinical skills by continuing some clinical practice." Since the *Boulder* Conference set a double goal of research and practice for the training of clinical psychologists, they understandably recommended that those persons engaged in the teaching of clinical skills should also be constantly engaged in work of this sort. It was reported by many that using "live" case material not only was stimulating to the students, but also provided the instructor with frequent new problems and insights. At least one department had striven to formalize this necessary part of inservice training by providing for each full-time teacher in the graduate program a course load that routinely included one large lecture course on basic subject matter, one seminar or other course with small enrollment, and one practicum course that provided continuous experience in actual clinical work. Variations of this arrangement could, of course, be worked out. General approval was voiced regarding the suggestion that university staff members should also consider accepting full-time clinical positions for a limited period of time, possibly exchanging duties with the staff members whom they replace. It was also stated that the use of large classes might militate against the development of the attitudes and skills that mark the finished scholar and the accomplished clinician. Both the amount of time required for supervision of clinical work and the desirability of close personal contact between teacher and student would seem to argue for maintaining small classes in the greater part of graduate instruction. It was suggested that undergraduate courses in abnormal psychology or psychopathology might well be taught by experienced clinicians.

IX. *Relations with other professions*

IXB. This issue was discussed particularly at *Boulder* and *Miami*. The *Boulder* Conference participants resolved that the training of the clinical psychologist *must include* supervised experience in a psychiatric center but they did not imply that the practice of clinical psychology should always be in medical settings. In general, the conferees believed that collaboration of the professions on an equal footing was in the best interests of the patient. The necessary implication is: equality of status is recognized, but it is recognized in the context of differing fields of competence and responsibility.

The *Boulder* group agreed that clinical psychologists can gain from contact with concepts and procedures in the counseling field, and that all clinical psychology students should have some experience in educational and vocational counseling. More specific advantages to be found in closer contact would include: 1) a language of personality description that deals with the normal; 2) attention to reality adjustment as well as to "deeper" areas of personality; and 3) attention to the intellectual, cognitive processes which are often ignored because of our more recent emphasis on the conative and affective.

The following recommendations were suggested at the *Boulder* Conference for consideration by the APA's Committee on Relations with the Social Work Profession. As a basis for insuring more satisfactory contact between the two professions, training staffs at the local level should work toward common understanding in regard to the following items:

1. Selection of students.

2. Overlapping of clerkship and internship assignments with the field training of psychiatric social work students. Definite efforts should be made to assist the students of both groups to work together at times other than formal staff conferences.

3. Possible routine assignment of clinical psychology students to social work departments in clinics or hospitals during periods of indoctrination into agency functions.

4. Interdisciplinary seminars held at field stations.

5. Overlapping courses and seminars, which could provide information and mutual training in interviewing, case work methods, community organizations, and community resources. (The excellence of present methods of supervision of social work students in interviewing was frequently mentioned during the discussion.)

IXD. Since school teaching, pastoral counseling, social work, and personnel management, among other disciplines, all involve the application of psychological principles, the *Miami* Conference recommended that psychologists contribute to the training of these groups, and affirmed the desirability of psychology being taught to other specialities by psychologists. The concern was expressed that there was insufficient application of psychology to education, and the need existed for a joint approach to theoretical and practical problems of mutual interest.

X. *Selection of students*

XA. The *Shakow* Report presented a long list of desirable characteristics for clinical psychology students. The list was so encompassing and "good" that any and all self-interested occupations might well lay claim to the same list. In addition to the ordinary selective devices, such as are provided by the credentials of the candidate and the Graduate Record Exam, hope was expressed for devices then being developed in a research project at Michigan University.[2] Desire was expressed that the candidate's undergraduate program would supply a broad cultural and scientific base for specialized graduate study.

XB. It was stated at *Boulder* that the ratio of applicants to available openings in graduate programs of clinical psychology was encouraging from the standpoint of the future of the profession, but there were problems for the applicant and the university alike. One informal survey at *Boulder* disclosed that graduate schools were admitting from 1 in 10 to 1 in 30 of the students applying for graduate training in clinical psychology.

It was recommended that a systematic effort be made to inform undergraduate students of opportunities in the field of clinical psychology and of the requirements necessary to enter the field. Some undergraduates have viewed clinical psychology as a means of gratifying their interest in humanitarian activities. The science and research requirements of the graduate schools led to their disillusionment. Other students have persevered in their hopes of entering the field of clinical psychology despite undergraduate records that are mediocre in quality. For a number of years to come, it appeared that admission to an accredited graduate school in clinical psychology would require a distinctly superior undergraduate record. (*See* discussion of *Princeton* Conference, the editors' paper "Crisis in Clinical Psychology," 1963, and Chapter 13.) Excellence in undergraduate psychology courses without corresponding quality in other courses had been found to be a relatively poor recommendation for obtaining the Ph.D. degree.

On the basis of the data available at *Boulder* it appeared that most of the clinical procedures in use for the selection of graduate students had little value in predicting academic achievement and clinical skills as judged by supervisors at the university and in the clinic, once an initial selection is made that eliminates students who do not possess a capacity for graduate work. It appeared that the appraisal of objective tests and records of students predicted success in graduate school work in clinical psychology as well as, if not better than, selection procedures involving projective techniques and interviews. There was strong sentiment in favor of encouraging the university departments of psychology to agree upon a common date for announcing acceptances to graduate work in clinical psychology. The problem of selecting students who will later develop into good diagnosticians and psychotherapists continued to be a vexing problem requiring research.

The *1947 Report of the Committee on Training in Clinical Psychology* lists a number of logically defensible personality requirements in clinical candidates. Various participants at the *Boulder* Conference listed a number of others, but the consensus seemed to be that the necessary qualities may not be discernible under ordinary conditions of observation. On the negative side, participants reported certain traits that they found from personal experience to be undesirable. Among these were rigidity and pronounced social prejudice. Also persons who frequently switched from one course of study to another and those who seemed *excessively* concerned with helping people seemed to make poor clinicians.[3,4]

Most department staffs hold quarterly or semi-annual meetings to which members of the field training staff are invited for the purpose of discussing each student. Formal reports from field agencies were also considered desirable and sentiment at *Boulder* seemed to be in favor of developing a semi-annual reporting form for this purpose. The chief causes for separation, reported at *Boulder,* were scholastic failure, lack of clinical aptitude, and personality deficiencies. The rate of separation, if VA trainee data could be taken as representative, seemed to be in the neighborhood of 12% of admissions, a figure closely approaching that of American medical schools. Discussion of the mechanics of separation resulted in suggestion of two generally desirable procedures. First, it was felt that when separation becomes essential the necessary decision and subsequent action should be taken by a responsible committee rather than an individual faculty member. Such group action not only protects one staff member from bearing the brunt of student dissatisfaction, but also, by making it clear to the student that the action taken was a departmental rather than individual decision, increases the likelihood of his accepting it in the proper spirit. The second suggestion was that students, upon separation, should be given, whenever possible, guidance relative to their future vocational careers.

XI. *Accreditation and licensing*

XIB. The *Boulder* conferees resolved that two lists should be published: an alphabetical list of accredited departments without differentiation or classification; and a similar list of departments visited and regarded as in a promising stage of development. The conferees also suggested that the Committee on Training should routinely adopt two further procedures that might be difficult to administer, but that would help to insure objectivity in the rating process. The first procedure would make it incumbent upon the Committee to publish as explicitly as possible the criteria used in evaluating training departments. While no one suggested that matters pertaining to individual schools should be made public, the general policies upon which the Committee acts should be made available. The second procedure suggested was that any discussion of the results of the evaluation made by visitors should be made at the time of the visit. The *Boulder* conferees recommended that the APA consider the possible advantages of separating the two functions: 1) establishing objectives and standards for training in psychology, and 2) accreditation.

With respect to licensing and certification of psychologists, the *Boulder* Conferees held: "We counsel a policy of watchful and critical delay, which is not to be conceived as a desire to interfere with or impede legislation in states which feel ready and have satisfactorily worked out the complex relationships with other groups. While following this policy of evaluative waiting, we should be willing to take an active stand both against unethical behavior of members of our own group and against legislative proposals which would circumvent or prevent psychologists from functioning at the level of their greatest social usefulness."

XIC. While there was agreement at *Stanford,* in principle at least, with criteria for training developed by APA committees, there was a strong feeling that they should be reviewed. Opinion was expressed that the accreditation authorized by the ETB of the APA might be premature. Since the *Stanford* Conference, however, the Committee on Evaluation has published the first list of agencies in the American Psychologist of 1956.

XID. At *Miami,* the consensus was for accreditation and there was agreement that the APA was the most appropriate agency. There were repeated cautions against pressures for conformity. There was also strong support for accreditation of postdoctoral centers for training in various specialities as well as of nondoctoral centers. Although no criteria were suggested, it was recommended that the APA develop some mechanism, independent of accreditation, for providing advice to departments for improving their programs in psychology to follow at any level.

SUMMARY

The salient features of the *Shakow* Report and the training conferences at *Boulder, Stanford, Miami,* and *Princeton* have been reviewed in this chapter. Focus has been placed on the following issues: Undergraduate Program, Graduate Program, Field Training and Internship, Subdoctoral Training, Specialization in Training, Training for Psychotherapy, Training for Research, Staff Training, Relationship with Other Professions, Selection of Students, and Accreditation and Licensing.

In Chapters 2-13 each of these issues are studied in detail or related to a discussion of clinical training resources.

References

1. David, Henry P., and Blank, Leonard, eds., *Manpower and psychology: Joint responsibilities of states and universities.* Washington, D. C.: Government Printing Office, 1963.
2. Kelly, E. L., Research on the selection of clinical psychologists. *J. Clin. Psychol.,* 1947, *3,* 39-42.
3. Kelly, E. L., and Fiske, D. W., *The prediction of performance in clinical psychology.* Ann Arbor, Michigan: Univ. of Michigan Press, 1951.

4. Kennelly, T. W., The selection of psychological interns. In *Training for clinical psychology*. M. H. P. Finn, and F. Brown, eds., New York: International Universities Press, 1959, 9-23.
5. Raimy, Victor C., ed., *Training in clinical psychology*. New York: Prentice-Hall, 1950.
6. Roe, Anne, et al., eds., *Graduate education in psychology*. Washington, D. C.: APA, 1958.
7. Shakow, David, Recommended graduate training program in clinical psychology. *Amer. Psychol.*, 1947, *2*, 539-558.
8. Strother, Chas. R., ed., *Psychology and mental health*. Washington, D.C.: APA, 1956.
9. Taylor, Donald, et al., Education for research in psychology. *Amer. Psychol.*, 1959, *14*, 167-179.
10. Tyler, F. B., Integrating scientific and professional training at the graduate level. *J. Clin. Psychol.*, 1963, *19*, 116-120.

Program Support for Training by the National Institute of Mental Health: 1947-1963

HAROLD BASOWITZ
JOSEPH C. SPEISMAN

The National Institute of Mental Health (NIMH) is one of nine organizational units which in the aggregate comprise the National Institutes of Health* and serve as the principal research arm of the United States Public Health Service (USPHS).

The NIMH was established as a consequence of Congressional action in 1946. Its mandate is to improve the mental health of the nation. Four basic functions are involved: 1) the conduct of reach into the etiology, diagnosis, treatment and prevention of mental illness; 2) assistance and support of such research activities by universities, medical schools and other public and private agencies; 3) consultation, technical services and grants to states and communities to aid in the development of comprehensive mental health programs; and 4) support of mental health manpower training for research and service.

The present chapter deals with the last of these four functions—training—as it bears particularly upon the field of psychology. As is well known to most workers in the mental health field, all of the NIMH activities have expanded remarkably in scope and diversity since funds were first allocated for their implementation 16 years ago. This is as true of training as it is of the other program objectives, a fact that will readily become apparent.

Support for training in the mental health disciplines has from

*The other institutes are: National Cancer Institute, National Heart Institute, National Institute of Allergy and Infectious Diseases, National Institute of Arthritis and Metabolic Diseases, National Institute of Child Health and Human Development, National Institute of Dental Research, National Institute of General Medical Sciences, and National Institute of Neurological Diseases and Blindness.

the very outset been the primary responsibility of the Training Branch. The Branch mission is viewed as a unified effort and the evolution of assistance for any single discipline is understandable only in the context of this totality. The story of grant support in psychology, therefore, must necessarily reflect much of the development of the entire Branch program. However, what follows should not be taken as a recapitulation of all of the Branch activities. This review is intended to cover only those activities which relate directly or indirectly to the training of psychologists.

At the same time, it would be incomplete were one not to note that aspects of NIMH support other than those of the Training Branch also contribute to the training of psychologists. Of these, the research fellowship and research grant programs are most significant in their impact. Their relevance to the subject at hand will receive comment as well, although more briefly.

Basic philosophy of support

The recent advent of large scale government support for research and training inevitably raises issues of federal relations to science and higher education. It is clear that both the government and education are engaged in a mutually dependent enterprise. The government is committed, in the national interest, to the development of science and of scientific and professional talent through the support of various kinds of educational endeavors. In making available large sums of money for these purposes, the government faces the question of how to avoid the specter of federal control while exercising its obligations with respect to the prudent use of public funds.

This is a general problem which has seriously concerned the NIMH from its inception. The approach taken in the training grants program mirrors the philosophy existing throughout the National Institutes of Health at large and resembles practices commonly found in other government agencies as well. The principle followed is one of inviting the participation of the different fields involved to help in determining policy and to make recommendations concerning the judicious deployment of available funds. This is accomplished by employing panels of experts in guiding various features of the program affecting their particular disciplines.

The Training Branch operates through a Mental Health Training Committee comprised of a series of subcommittees, each concerned with a particular area in which grant support is given. The field of psychology, therefore, has its own Subcommittee on Psychology. The members of all subcommittees are outside consultants selected on the basis of their prominence and knowledge of training in their respective specialities. It is their task, with the assistance of staff, to evolve and propose the policies governing grant awards. They deal with such specific issues as: what categories of support are most required to advance the area and the Branch mission? What priorities should be assigned these categories? What grant mechanisms and staff measures may be taken to fulfill these objectives? How should available funds be distributed? What are the criteria to be utilized in reviewing grant proposals? In addition, the subcommittees review each application within their area and recommend appropriate action.

The recommendations of the subcommittees are then scrutinized by the National Advisory Mental Health Council, a body of eminent representatives of the mental health disciplines and the lay public. The Council is charged by law with advising the Surgeon General of the USPHS on all matters relating to the NIMH programs. On review, the Council may accept or reverse the recommendations of the subcommittees. The action of the Council is final except for the rare possibility of a veto by the Surgeon General. The sequential actions of the subcommittees and the Council incorporate the basic principle of a double-review system both as regards policy and grant evaluation.

Apart from the grant procedures just described, the effort to maintain liaison with those responsible for training is seen in still another realm. The case of clinical psychology is a particularly apt example. When NIMH support in clinical psychology was initiated soon after the conclusion of World War II, the guidelines for training in this area were still being formulated. The field was then debating this problem with a great deal of zest and the Shakow Committee had just presented its recommendations to the American Psychological Association. At that

time the NIMH turned to the Association for advice. It also
sought to aid problem-solving by the field by providing funds
for meetings, institutes, and the like. This is a practice that has
regularly characterized NIMH support. The *Boulder* Conference[1]
and, subsequently, the *Stanford* and *Miami* Conferences[2,3] are
all instances in which training grants assisted the field in its
dialogues on graduate training. Dialogues of this type have provided a major framework for the emergence and elaboration of
training grant policy that could be responsive to the statements of
those actually engaged in training.

In this connection, it is also pertinent that the activities of
the Education and Training Board (E & T Board) of APA
throughout its entire history have been partially supported by a
training grant. In turn, the standards and accreditation procedures
of the Board are significant criteria in determining eligibility for
grant awards in clinical psychology. However, the operations of
each of these bodies—the E & T Board and the NIMH—remain
totally independent of one another.

Stability and flexibility of support are two additional principles
which reflect the deliberate policies and the philosophy of the
training grants program. It is recognized that support must not
be capricious if institutions are to make the long range commitments and plans required to nurture and sustain the training
endeavor. Stability in funding has never to this point been in
question. For example, 20 programs in clinical psychology have
been continuously supported for 15 or more years; an additional
26 have been so supported for 10 years or more.

In the utilization of grant monies considerable flexibility is
permitted the grantee. The purpose here is to allow the institution to retain control over its own program. Funds are awarded
in terms of broad categories such as personnel, equipment and
student traineeships. Specific allocation of these monies is the
responsibility of the institution so long as expenditures are consistent with the aims for which the grant is given. Thus the
grantee has considerable option in assigning its teaching funds
in a manner it considers would most advance the program. Similarly, the institution rather than the NIMH selects the students
who are to receive stipend assistance and, in the case of the university, decides whether stipends should be applied to incoming,

intermediate or advanced graduate students and how they may best be distributed.

The conscious effort within NIMH, therefore, is to preserve the autonomy of the field and the institutions in determining the character of training in a particular area or discipline. When, from the viewpoint of national policy, training needs are perceived, leaders and responsible agents from the field are enlisted to advise on the most appropriate course of action. The procedures and grants mechanisms alluded to in this section illustrate the efforts to give substance to this underlying philosophy.

Development of the program

Funds were first made available for the training grants program of NIMH in July 1947. When the program was inaugurated, there were enormous and urgent needs for competent clinical personnel to serve in the areas long identified as central to the mental health area—psychiatrists, clinical psychologists, psychiatric social workers and psychiatric nurses.

Clinical psychology. Within the discipline of psychology, therefore, initial emphasis was placed upon the clinical specialty. Although interest was high, the field was hardly equipped at that time to undertake training in this area on the scale required. The immediate task was to increase the level of capability existing for such training.

To this end, grants were provided for assistance in the establishment, improvement and/or expansion of programs in clinical psychology. Two types were involved: awards to university departments of psychology, and to internship centers which would afford a year of full-time field experience to students in the university programs. The grants, then as now, included monies to defray teaching costs and to provide trainee stipends for students enrolled in the programs. The category of teaching costs is especially significant in that the funds therein permit the augmentation of staff resources and other features relevant to instruction. All training grants containing student stipends continue to allow requests for teaching support as well.

The inception of any grants program brings with it the question of standards for support. Although the NIMH was acutely cognizant of the pressing manpower problem, it still decided to stress quality rather than mere quantity in training. The goal sought, in keeping with the values expressed within APA, was the creation of the scientist-practitioner model and the molding of a substantial professional base in clinical psychology which could guide its progress to greater maturity. In order to gear training support to the surer level of competence, only doctoral programs became eligible for awards. In addition, limited assistance was soon initiated for postdoctoral clinical training. The purpose was to help prepare a small number of highly selected Ph.D.s in clinical psychology for future leadership roles, especially in clinical teaching and supervision.

The paramount concern with quality still persists and is mirrored in the criteria employed in evaluating grant applications. Applications are judged primarily on the basis of the merit of the program proposed. The factors weighed are the excellence and potentiality of the program and the adequacy of the leadership, staff and facilities. In university programs strength in the non-clinical as well as clinical areas are considered. Correspondingly, in internship centers the strength of other disciplines (psychiatry, social work, etc.) and their impact on training in psychology are taken into account. A genuine commitment to training, within the area and as a general institutional endeavor, also must be evident.

A further element influencing the criteria is that of regional need since, in terms of national perspective, it is desirable to have training centers reasonably dispersed throughout the entire country. Apart from other considerations, it is known that more than half the psychologists tend to begin their careers in the same geographic region where they take their training. The proper distribution of available manpower is enhanced, therefore, to the extent that active training efforts are represented in all geographic regions.

Broadened support. While the demand for trained clinical specialists commanded first priority in early years, the need for greatly increased numbers of research personnel, always evident, swiftly became more apparent. Thus in 1957, development of research training support at the graduate level in psychiatry, psychology, social work and nursing was undertaken. Psychology, by virtue of its long tradition as a basic research discipline, was affected differently from the other areas. In psychology, grants were initiated to include research training in such specialities as personality, child, physiological, social and experimental psychology. In addition, support was offered to train psychologists for research as well as service roles in particular problem areas where there are acute shortages of personnel. Examples are mental retardation, geriatrics, alcoholism, community mental health and school psychology, although for special reasons described later only limited funding was intended for the last-named area.

The broadened training support in psychology was of enormous significance both philosophically and pragmatically. A step towards generic support of the field was taken which affirms that other areas of concentration besides clinical psychology can and do make important contributions to the solution of mental health problems. Moreover, extended support was seen as having the virtue of helping to correct the imbalance that was created within the discipline when grants were restricted to clinical psychology.

The phenomena surrounding an understanding of the behavior disorders, however, are so complex as to require the investigative talents of individuals trained not only in the conventional mental health disciplines but in the biological and social sciences also. Since, at this time, the original core programs were deemed to be on solid ground, an expanded approach to training was taken which included these fields. At first, grants were awarded on a pilot basis to a few medical schools and universities for the training of biological and social scientists in the field of mental illness. Two years later these pilot awards were incorporated into regular and stable areas of research training in the biological sciences and the social sciences.

These program categories are independent but operate in a similar fashion. They provide support for: 1) programs oriented towards the training of biological and social scientists for careers as investigators in the mental health field, and 2) programs directed to the instruction of psychiatrists, psychologists, psychiatric social workers and psychiatric nurses in the research techniques and methods of the biological and social sciences.

By definition, training under these circumstances is interdisciplinary and psychologists, particularly at the postdoctoral level, have availed themselves of these opportunities to extend their horizons. In the first instance, they receive intensive exposure to the data and techniques of anatomy, biochemistry, pharmacology and physiology, and, in the second, they ordinarily enrich their backgrounds in anthropology and sociology.

Other developments. Both before and after the commencement of broadened support, a variety of other developments occurred which served to lend versatility and scope to the programs of the Training Branch. Not only psychology, but all of the areas supported are affected by the activities to be reviewed.

As soon as the graduate programs were announced, various groups, such as professional associations, training institutions and voluntary organizations, began to inquire about support for institutes, workshops, conferences, demonstrations and surveys. In 1948 support was initiated for these types of undertakings in a category that has come to be termed *special grants*. In the field of psychology, the *Boulder, Stanford* and *Miami* Conferences referred to earlier were funded as a consequence of this action. Other conferences receiving support of this kind at one time or other throughout the years have been directed to counseling psychology, school psychology, aging, and such topical issues as motivation and computer simulation of personality.

The year 1950 witnessed the start of support in the area of *public health* as related to mental health. As one element in this program trainee stipends are offered to psychologists, psychiatrists, social scientists, social workers, and psychiatric and public health nurses who are enrolled for the master's degree in schools of public health. The value of such training as preparation for work on problems of community mental health scarcely requires further comment.

In 1953 a novel type of support was inaugurated in the form of *pilot projects*. These grants are designed to assist in 1) the development of new and experimental methods of training, and 2) the evaluation of teaching and training methods in any of the mental health disciplines. In addition, they seek to stimulate the development of training programs—1) for new types of mental health personnel, 2) for persons whose roles or functions may be related to mental health (e.g., educators, lawyers and the clergy), and 3) of an interdisciplinary nature in the significant problem areas characterized by serious needs for personnel (e.g., delinquency, penology, alcoholism, mental retardation and aging). Pilot projects are essentially a formal mechanism for giving expression to innovation and new ideas at a variety of levels.

Another category of support—the *career teacher program*—was undertaken for the four core disciplines in 1955. Its purpose was to encourage persons with exceptional potentiality to choose careers in teaching and to provide support for them while they are prepared for faculty positions in university and medical training centers. This support was discontinued in psychology in 1959 since this discipline has a long academic tradition and the program was viewed as less urgent than other areas to which funds could be allocated.

In 1956, the *senior stipend program* was begun. It is aimed at providing opportunities for advanced training for individuals of outstanding competence or potential who seek to improve or extend their skills within their own or related fields. The candidates sought are persons with significant training responsibility who, through appropriate additions to their backgrounds, may enhance their own capacity to train others.

Finally, the picture of training activities within psychology is rounded out by taking note of a small "experimental" program of *undergraduate research stipends*. This is an exploratory effort in training whose goal is the recruiting of more promising students into the field of psychology. Selected undergraduates in this program are given a modest stipend for supervised research activity in psychology after completing their junior year in college. The effects of this program have yet to be evaluated.

Some illustrative problems. The business of making grants hardly follows a perfectly smooth or predictable course. Although Congressional allocations have been generous from year to year, funds have simply not been available in sufficient abundance to handle the many worthwhile activities emerging in the ever-widening realm of mental health. New opportunities arise, new needs appear, and old needs are alleviated or seem less compelling in the light of experience. In the weighing of program alternatives, many of which may be highly desirable in their own right, decisions must involve a heavy dose of pragmatism while, hopefully, still clinging to principle.

In the interest of providing further insight into the functioning of the training grants program in psychology, it may be useful to identify a few of the problems faced recently and to describe briefly the approaches taken towards meeting them. For purposes of illustration we shall refer to certain issues in expanded research training, school psychology and internship training. The questions confronted in these instances are typical though obviously not exhaustive.

When broadened support for research training in the various areas of psychology was undertaken, its immediate implementation posed sizeable problems in funding. The number of applications that could have been submitted in such specialty fields as personality, social, child, physiological and experimental psychology was potentially staggering. Program support, as has already been indicated, is long-range in nature and the launching of any new programs requires a budget over and above that necessary to maintain existing commitments. And existing commitments are increasingly expensive to maintain in this inflationary era. Salaries of personnel paid through grants spiral upwards; the general level of student stipends must periodically be raised to keep pace with the cost of living; and tuition and fees for the trainees mount regularly. In addition, there is an obligation to provide increased support for training programs just begun so as to ensure their normal growth and development.

Since monies for new programming are limited, it was necessary to find some means to restrict the number of incoming applications, and yet to do so according to some cogent rationale. Thus, as a strong criterion for support, the immediate relevance of the proposed research training for problems of mental health was adopted. This policy was one of expediency only and did not reflect a basic orientation. The fundamental view held was that psychology as a science is generic to an understanding of mental health and illness, and that every variety of research training effort of sufficient excellence should find a possibility for support. Yet, the criterion of mental health relevance served a useful function. It was reasonable in terms of the central mission of the NIMH, and it was sufficiently clear so as to avoid large numbers of disappointed applicants. Fortunately, increasing annual appropriations have made realization of the ideal of generic support more possible since the program was undertaken.

School psychology presented a different type of problem. When grants were first made in this area, it was recognized that school psychology was a gradually unfolding specialty whose direction and training requirements were in the process of formulation. Thus only a restricted number of awards were given— and these to institutions not only highly motivated but fully prepared to undertake such training. This venture in grant support was frankly experimental in character. Its purpose was the creation of a variety of program models which could be instructive and provide stimulation for the definition of goals and criteria for training. Whether and how full-scale grant support for this or any developing field occurs must follow from such prior clarification.

Internship training has recently introduced still a different order of vexing issues. Support of internship programs in clinical psychology began in 1947 with the aim of aiding in the development of high caliber field training centers since few— outside of the VA—existed at that time. By 1960, 84 clinical centers had received awards for one or more years; 12 had been supported continuously for 10 or more years. By then, considerable evidence had accumulated to indicate that, taking the nation as a whole, the total number of internship training opportunities was adequate to meet the requirements of graduate school enrollment in clinical psychology. Surveys conducted by the NIMH Training Branch and the E & T Board of APA suggested that there were roughly twice as many trainee openings available as there were students to fill them. Educational campaigns at state and community levels evidently had effected an enlarged pool of clinical facilities capable of providing training.

Thus, at first view, supply appeared sufficient to cope with demand. However, other matters complicated the picture. Among these was the fact that internship centers had not developed at comparable rates in various sections of the country. Certain regions, particularly those in dire need of trained personnel, had matured more slowly in this respect. In addition, a growing tendency had occurred for students to take their internship near their home universities. It was also observed that about half the students were completing their internship requirements through the accrual of part-time experiences rather than the continuous full year of immersion in a clinical installation. Clearly, the simple proliferation of further internship support did not seem justified. Yet the problems of geographic imbalance and changing patterns of training in the field suggested that solutions other than mere reduction in support were required.

These are but the highlights of the considerations calling for attention. Policies were revised to minimize unneeded proliferation while continuing support that would be consistent with the requirements of the field. At the same time, now that the number of training opportunities was no longer a critical matter, it was decided to focus on invigorating the training offered by stimulating experimentation and innovation. In general, therefore, criteria for the approval of an internship application were elevated. Yet, within the framework of the new criteria, the guiding orientation adopted was that continued grant awards in this area should: 1) serve to maintain stable support for strong and well-established internship centers; 2) meet regional needs; 3) encourage new patterns of training; and 4) encourage further improvement in the quality of training.

A decrease in the absolute level of funds for this area was not contemplated. However, it was judged that, as the total budget for training increased, less relative support could be provided for internships and greater support for programs minimally assisted to that point in time, e.g., research training and special areas. The notion embodied was that of a slow-down of grants for internship assistance and a speed-up of grants for other worthwhile endeavors. These operations permitted the necessary shift in emphasis of support without dislocating the field.

The practice of awarding grants for full-time, full-year internships only was reviewed and reaffirmed as making sense in terms of existing circumstances. Implicit in this action was the recognition that other sources of internship stipends throughout the country were ample enough to sustain variants of this pattern, and that NIMH funds could usefully be concentrated on strengthening the most predictably substantial model. Finally, the variety of experiences deemed acceptable for internship training was broadened. It was decided to encourage, whenever possible, the utilization of field settings that are not necessarily in the psychiatric mold, e.g., those dealing with the physically handicapped, juvenile offenders, mentally deficient, etc.

Policy reviews of this sort are expected in the life of any granting agency. With changing conditions in the field, corresponding changes must occur in grant policies. The task is to ensure that the changes are both rational and constructively directed towards long-range as well as immediate goals.

Present status of support

With the background of information just offered, it is now appropriate to turn to some details of actual training program support in psychology. How are the program developments cited earlier represented in current budget allocations? These data appear in Table 1 which presents the year grants were first given in each of the program areas and the distribution of awards among each in 1962-63. But, before reviewing these data, it may be useful to introduce some selected statistics for previous years of funding in order to provide an impression of trends in support over time.

In 1947-48 grants in psychology totaled $209,600. The entire budget permitted the support of 19 programs in clinical psychology, 16 of which were anchored in university departments of psychology and 3 in field training centers. Funds were supplied for 40 student stipends, 33 for departmental and 7 for internship programs. In 1952-53 the budget in psychology was $684,122. With the exception of a special project costing $9,796, all of the monies still were assigned to clinical psychology. The numbers of departmental programs and student stipends accommodated were 43 and 89, respectively; for field training centers they were 20 and 35.

By 1958-59 the budget had grown to $3,141,585. The program areas supported had, by then, expanded considerably. Grants were made for 53 departmental and 46 internship training programs in clinical psychology, for 10 in applied psychology other than clinical, 18 in graduate research training,

4 in special areas, and for 2 pilot projects. In addition, 5 career teacher awards and 1 special project were funded. Support sufficient for 590 stipends was offered.

As indicated in Table 1, allocations for the year 1962-63 increased to $5,666,517. Of this amount, about 53%, ($3,032,289) was awarded for 58 departmental programs in clinical psychology, and 20% ($1,141,589) for 65 programs in field training centers. The next largest category—graduate research training—commanded 15% of the budget ($854,597)

TABLE 1   NIMH TRAINING PROGRAM SUPPORT IN PSYCHOLOGY: 1962-63

Area of training and year support began	Awards active in 1962-63		
	No. of awards	Trainee stipends	Total funds
Clinical psychology (1947)			
University departments	58	523	$3,032,289
Field training centers	65	179	1,141,589
Applied psychology other than clinical (1957)	9	55	262,474
Counseling psychology	1		
School psychology	8		
Research training—graduate (1958)	32	164	854,597
Biometrics	1		
Child & developmental	8		
Experimental	8		
Physiological	7		
Social & personality-social	8		
Special areas (1955)	7	39	248,847
Aging	2		
Community mental health	1		
Mental retardation	3		
Rehabilitation	1		
Pilot projects (1954)	1	4	10,788
Senior stipends (1957)	1		10,908
Special projects (1949)	3		82,428
Undergraduate research training (1959)	17	28	22,597
TOTALS:	193	992	$5,666,517

for 32 programs. These programs included 8 each in the child and developmental, experimental-general, and social and personality-social areas, 7 in physiological psychology, and 1 in biometrics. The remaining funds are distributed, in order of amounts allotted, among the various other categories supported: applied psychology other than clinical, special areas, special projects, undergraduate research training, senior stipends and pilot projects. The number of awards made in this fiscal year was 193. Trainee stipends totaled 992.

The general picture, therefore, is that of burgeoning support for the field of psychology as a whole. The budgets sampled in successive 5-6 year intervals reflect fairly faithfully year to year changes as well, although the curve is by no means a smooth one. Overall, growing support is evident for more diverse areas in psychology in addition to the core clinical specialty.

Since the focus of the present volume is clinical psychology, the current status of support in this area warrants perhaps closer scrutiny. There were 60 APA-approved university programs in clinical psychology in 1962-63. Of these, 55 received NIMH training grants. In addition, 3 non-approved programs were also given short-term developmental grants whose purpose was to enhance the capability of the institutions concernen in obtaining APA approval. Developmental grants of this type are offered selectively to universities which demonstrate readiness and promise for the establishment of programs that will meet the standards of the field. Under these circumstances, the awards provide support for personnel only. Their aim is to buttress staff resources. Until APA approval is secured, these universities are not eligible for student stipends.

The 65 field training centers supported in 1962-63 display a wide range of functions, populations served and types of problems handled. Included among the grantees were such varied settings as state hospitals, child guidance clinics, medical schools, residential treatment centers for children, community mental health centers, a school for the retarded and disturbed, a county probation department, a city department of public health, and a physical rehabilitation center. Of the entire group, 13 are devoted primarily or exclusively to work with children. The rest almost in all instances provide services both for adults and children. Fifteen of the institutions had grants permitting them to offer postdoctoral stipends in clinical psychology. Among the total of 179 stipends awarded, 32 were designated for trainees at the postdoctoral level.

When the nation-wide graduate enrollment in doctoral programs in clinical psychology is examined, the extent of NIMH support for students is even more impressive. It is estimated that roughly 2500 students were registered in this area in 1962-63.* Excepting the 32 postdoctoral traineeships at field training centers, the total number of stipends awarded by the NIMH in clinical psychology for this year was 670. In other words, funds were provided for the support of a little more than 1 of every 4 students in this program area.

Research fellowships and research grants. Early in this chapter it was pointed out that other aspects of NIMH support, apart from the activities of the Training Branch, also contribute to the training of psychologists. Notable among these are the research fellowship and research grant programs.

The research fellowship program, the second of the NIMH's first two training programs, was also initiated in 1947. It is part of the overall fellowship program of the National Institutes of Health. Its primary objective is to increase the number of scientists qualified to conduct independent research by providing opportunities for research training in any field of science which bears upon the problems of mental health and illness.

Support is given on an individual basis to persons in the biological, medical, psychological and social science disciplines each of whose applications compete for available funds. Three levels of research fellowships are offered: predoctoral, postdoctoral and special. Postdoctoral fellowships are intended for individuals of demonstrated promise who are beginning their research careers. Special fellowships are designed for the mature, experienced scientist seeking to obtain advanced specialized training either in his own field of research or in a related field.

The NIMH has steadily expanded its program of research fellowships as the research facilities of the country have grown. Starting with an initial appropriation of $70,000 in 1947-48,

*This approximation was kindly provided by Dr. Sherman Ross, Executive Secretary, E & T Board of APA.

the amount of funds allocated for the program rose to $4,097,336 in 1962-63. Psychologists have made extensive use of these training opportunities throughout the years. The year 1962-63 is as good an indication as any. Of a total of 717 research fellowships awarded in this period, 481 went to psychologists. These figures break down as follows among the three fellowship levels: predoctoral—clinical psychology (72), other areas of psychology (207), other disciplines (174); postdoctoral—clinical psychology (7), other areas of psychology (78), other disciplines (26); special—clinical psychology (5), other areas of psychology (32), other disciplines (36).

As distinguished from research fellowships, the NIMH research grant program, of course, has as its primary goal the support of investigative activities pertinent to mental health. Yet, it is certainly valid to recognize that a significant amount of research training is also provided, albeit indirectly, through the research grant program. In 1962-63, for example, the Institute supported 1884 research projects for a total of $51,497,248. Of these, 889 grants amounting to $20,468,993 had psychologists as principal investigators. It is estimated that approximately 50-60% of the funds in the research grant program are utilized for personnel; of this amount at least 40% is used to hire student research assistants at the graduate and postdoctoral levels. Although such experience is only a part of that needed for a full program of research training, the work which these students perform often serves as a most valuable training device, affording, as it does, an occasion to learn specific research techniques under the direct supervision of a senior investigator. In addition, the number of doctoral theses carried out in conjuction with a research grant surely must be sizeable.

Conclusion

An effort has been made to present within these pages the underlying philosophy and an overview of NIMH support for training in psychology. By most standards its history has proven the program viable. From modest beginnings in 1947, training support has enlarged considerably over the past 16 years. Increased funds have been provided, not only for student stipends, but for the augmentation of teaching and staff wherewithal. The areas in which grants have been made available, limited originally to clinical psychology, have been broadened so as to approach generic support of the field. A matrix of additional support programs also have developed all of which afford psychologists enriched opportunity to obtain further advanced training—in related fields within the biological sciences, social sciences and public health, as well as within psychology itself.

What of the future? No one at this juncture can claim omniscience. It seems evident that the present programs of support will be strengthened and imagination and experimentation encouraged. Yet the entire mental health movement is on the threshold of drastic changes both in the conception of and approach to emotional disorder. These changes are most clearly forecast in the vast federal programs of assistance planned for the establishment of community mental health centers. They portend a much greater concern with diverse forms of treatment, with early detection and prevention of disturbance, and with early return of patients to the community and to work. As in the past, success in meeting the many problems inherent in these developments will require the continued cooperative efforts of the field and the NIMH.

References

1. Raimy, V. C., ed., *Training in clinical psychology*. New York: Prentice-Hall, 1950.
2. Roe, Anne, et al., eds., *Graduate education in psychology*. Washington, D.C.: American Psychological Association, 1959.
3. Strother, C. R., ed., *Psychology and mental health*. Washington, D.C.: American Psychological Association, 1956.

Training in the Veterans Administration

CECIL P. PECK
ELTON ASH

Development of the program

Clinical psychology was introduced into the VA in 1946 as a direct outgrowth of World War II and coincided with a reorganization and expansion of the VA.

The official mission of the Department of Medicine and Surgery of the VA is to provide hospital, outpatient and domiciliary care to eligible veterans, to conduct a research program to improve methods of diagnosis and treatment, and to carry on an education and training program to improve the professional competence of its staff. This mission is carried out in a system of 170 hospitals, 18 domiciliaries, and 93 outpatient clinics. To provide the veteran patient with a high standard of medical care, the VA medical system uses an integrated team approach in carrying out its comprehensive treatment program. The skills of many specialists—physician, dentist, nurse, pharmacist, laboratory technician, psychologist, dietitian, social worker, therapist, librarian, chaplain, and so forth—are combined to achieve an effective program for diagnosis, treatment, rehabilitation, training and research. This mission is carried out in close collaboration with the nation's medical schools and universities and many members of university faculties serve in advisory, consultant, and training capacities.

The VA medical program is of significant importance to veterans. On June 30, 1962, there were 183.7 million American civilians of whom 80.9 million were veterans, members of veterans' families, or dependent survivors of deceased veterans. About 44% of the total population of the United States were men, women, and children who were potentially eligible to receive VA services and benefits. At the present time almost 40 out of every 100 males, 18 or more years old in the United States, are war veterans. For every 100 veterans, about 70 served in World War II, 20 were in the Korean conflict, and 10 saw service in earlier wars.

The VA is also of great importance to the general population because of its wide scope and geographical coverage—the VA hospital system contains more than 7% of the nation's hospital beds. It provides the clinical training for a significant portion of the nation's physicians (50%) and other specialists who work in health settings. Its vast resources have made possible and have resulted in major contributions to the general advancement of medical science. Professional personnel from foreign countries frequently visit VA hospitals and clinics to study medical advances and VA research findings. Such research findings are solicited and distributed on a world-wide basis.

The VA hospitals are designated by type as follows: 123 general medical and surgical hospitals, 39 psychiatric hospitals, and 8 tuberculosis hospitals. During a year there are approximately 600,000 admissions and discharges from VA hospitals. Post-hospital observation and follow-up care is provided to somewhat more than 200,000 patients. In the VA outpatient clinic program, approximately 2.4 million visits are made by patients annually. In 67 of the 93 outpatient clinics, mental hygiene programs are provided for patients by one or more teams consisting of a psychiatrist, psychologist, and social worker.

Within this background and structure, the Clinical Psychology Program in the Department of Medicine and Surgery was instituted and continues to function. Its inauguration, development, and achievements have been influenced by the setting in which they took place, and many of the major agency changes have also been reflected in the psychology program.

Expansion of the program

There was no formal Clinical Psychology Program in the VA before World War II. A few psychologists at various times had previously been employed by individual hospitals, the earliest known was George Van Ness Dearborn, M.D., Ph.D., who established a psychological laboratory at the VA Hospital, Bronx, N.Y., in the 1920's. In the fall of 1945, a number of psychologists on duty in Washington were consulted on the new Clinical Psychology Program. In December 1945, Dr. George A. Kelly, presently at Ohio State University, came to the VA in a consultant capacity to initiate the new Clinical Psychology Program. It was during this period that initial standards for clinical psychologists were developed. In the spring of 1946, the first full time head of the new Clinical Psychology Program was appointed, Dr. James G. Miller. One of the most significant steps of this early development period was the establishment of the Clinical Psychology Training Program. At that time the number of qualified clinical psychologists in the nation was extremely small, and with widespread demand for their post-war services in many agencies, it was clear that there would be a shortage for years to come. In 1946, the Chief Medical Director met with representatives of leading universities to ask them to undertake the training of clinical psychologists at the doctorate level for the VA. This they agreed to do, and with the cooperation of an initial group of 22 universities the first 200 clinical psychology trainees went on duty in the fall of 1946. Since then the number of collaborating universities has tripled, and presently the departments of psychology in 61 universities, approved by the APA, are participating. Sixty of the universities are approved for training in clinical psychology and 36 are approved for training in counseling psychology. Since 1950, approximately 700 psychology trainees per year have been on duty in a training capacity with the VA.

Figure 1 indicates, from 1946 through 1963, the number of doctorate level psychologists and graduate students in psychology on duty in the Department of Medicine and Surgery. The relationship of the Psychology Training Program to meeting staffing needs with fully trained clinical and counseling psychologists is obvious. On January 1, 1963, there were 820 Ph.D. psychologists employed by the Department of Medicine and Surgery.

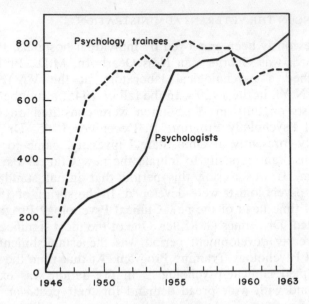

Figure 1   Doctoral level psychologists and graduate
students in psychology on duty.

Soon after the initiation of the Clinical Psychology Training
Program in 1946, the VA, with the support of the USPHS,
requested the APA to undertake evaluation and accreditation
of universities for doctoral training in clinical psychology.
This was to provide a guide for all federal agencies involved in
training activities. This development eventually led to the
APA establishing an Education and Training Board which has
been of inestimable value to the psychology program of the VA
as well as other federal agencies. It placed the responsibility for
basic educational decisions in the hands of a professional and
scientific organization and has provided a solid foundation for
the free and cooperative relationships which have existed between the VA and the training universities.

The Vocational Counseling Psychology Service was established
in the Department of Medicine and Surgery in July 1952.
The purpose of this program was to provide specialized skills
and knowledge in assisting patients in re-establishing their
occupational potential for gainful employment, and thereby
decrease the likelihood of their remaining in hospitals unneces-

sarily as well as forestalling their rehospitalization. In anticipation of a shortage of fully trained counseling psychologists, the VA initiated during this same year the Counseling Psychology Training Program. This program followed the earlier model established for training in clinical psychology.

As psychology continued to grow and diversify in hospitals and clinics, some stations began to initiate special programs in physiological and social psychology. These programs were predominantly of a research nature and frequently the need for specialized laboratory facilities and equipment developed. In 1956, some trainees in physiological psychology, social psychology, and experimental psychology were incorporated into the Psychology Training Program but the number of students in these specialty areas has remained relatively small. With the reorganization of the Psychology Training Program in 1957, all psychology training was consolidated into one unified psy-

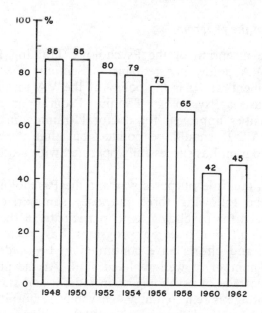

Figure 2 Percentage of VA psychology trainees who completed doctorate degree and took first positions with the VA.

chology training program. Since then, approximately 73% of the psychology trainees have been in clinical psychology, 17% in counseling psychology, and 10% in social, physiological, or experimental psychology.

Figure 2 shows the percentage of VA Psychology Trainees who completed the doctorate degree and took their first positions as psychologists with the VA. The changes are due to the expanding opportunities for psychologists in attractive academic faculty positions in universities and colleges, challenging opportunities for teaching and research in medical schools, salary competition and excellent career opportunities in a wide variety of research and training situations. Practically no graduating psychology trainees enter private practice and it is of interest to note that during the past three years, 1960-1962, a total of only 29 VA staff psychologists terminated employment for private practice.

Objectives of the program

Since the inception of the Psychology Training Program in 1946, the VA policy has remained essentially the same. The policy statement is: "It is the policy of the VA to conduct on a VA-wide basis a Psychology Training Program in cooperation with universities approved for doctoral training in psychology by the APA." It should be pointed out that the Psychology Training Program has successfully operated with a non-indenture philosophy.

Although multiple purposes warrant the Psychology Training Program, the following three purposes summarize the need:

1. The need for psychologists to participate in the VA treatment, training, and research programs has been recognized since 1946, and efforts have continued to be made to recruit a sufficient number of well-qualified staff. At the present time, there is a shortage of psychologists in federal and state agencies, and this shortage is reflected in VA psychiatric hospitals, general medical and surgical hospitals, mental hygiene clinics, and domiciliaries. The most pressing need in psychology service in the VA continues to be for clinical psychologists and counseling psychologists. There has developed a limited, but significant

demand for the selective assignment of social psychologists, physiological psychologists, and psychologists with other specialties.

2. The VA Psychology Training Program is the primary source of recruitment of fully trained psychologists for work in VA hospitals, clinics, and domiciliaries. As of February 1, 1962, 68% of the present clinical psychology staff had been VA trainees, 59% of the counseling psychologists had been VA trainees, and 73% of those psychologists in the VA working predominantly in research had been VA trainees.

3. The VA Psychology Training Program provides continuity in the assignment of graduate psychology students for supervised experiences in medical settings. The psychology students acquire an equivalent of two years of supervised professional experience with a wide variety of patients in hospitals, clinic, and domiciliary settings. This experience is an integral part of training and development leading to the acquisition of broader knowledge, skills, and insights pertinent to and essential for eventual work in a health setting.

The training universities and the VA share certain common objectives in the Psychology Training Program as well as gain certain unique and complementary advantages for training, service, and research. For the VA, these are: 1) to participate with educational institutions in efforts to improve the quality of professional personnel for service. 2) To help provide in VA hospitals, clinics, and domiciliaries an environment which stimulates and challenges regular staff to strive for improved performance. 3) To provide a greater comprehensiveness and effectiveness in training as well as broader assistance to patients and staff. 4) To provide a continuing source of recruitment of well-qualified, full-time staff psychologists who are familiar with VA patients, operations and structure.

For the affiliating universities the objectives can be summarized as follows: 1) to provide psychology trainees with superior training in a practicum setting which gives them an opportunity to combine theory with practice and secure supervised training. 2) To provide a financially supported opportunity for students to secure training in VA hospitals, clinics, and domiciliaries. 3) To secure additional stimulation, knowledge, and skills by associating with VA hospitals, clinics, and domiciliary staffs in diagnosis, treatment, training, and research.

Revised training appointments

From 1946 through 1962, the Psychology Training Program has been functioning with psychology trainees being appointed as part-time employees. During the tenure of appointment they were expected to accumulate approximately 4,000 hours of supervised experience which in turn was qualifying experience for a staff appointment upon completion of the doctorate degree. In May 1963, the Psychology Training Program was revised to meet changing needs, but the basic structure which emphasizes close cooperation and collaboration with training universities has been maintained. Changes in the program provide for two types of psychology trainee appointments, namely, a stipend program and a psychological assistantship program. In both programs a psychology trainee is defined as a graduate student enrolled in an approved university as a candidate for the doctorate degree in psychology or sponsored for postdoctoral qualification in a specialty area of psychology.

The stipend program for psychology graduate students is designed to provide stipends while working for the doctorate at approved universities. It requires that a specified minimum number of hours of training experience be acquired in a VA station each stipend year. The minimum number of hours of supervised training experience required for first year trainees is 500 hours. The second, third, and fourth year stipend trainees must acquire a minimum of 1,100 hours each year. Stipend trainees may, if they so desire or if it is requested by the Station Psychology Training Committee or Regional Psychology Training Committee, secure additional hours of training experience at any given stipend level over and above the required minimum number of hours. The stipend trainee will not receive additional stipend funds for any additional number of training hours. He will receive regular stipend payments on a prorated basis for a defined stipend year of nine months or twelve months. progress of the graduate student.
The length of the stipend year is determined by the academic

The psychological assistantship program provides for an opportunity to acquire more intensive and continuous experiences which could not be acquired if the trainees were to be assigned to a VA installation for a shorter period of time. In addition, he has the opportunity to identify more closely with the professional environment and staff and to learn more intimately the structure and organization of health settings as well as the functions of the psychology service. Opportunity is available, as part of this service and training assignment, to carry out or participate in more comprehensive research. This frequently gives the psychological assistant time to gather data or complete his doctoral dissertation.

The psychological assistantship program is designed to offer second, third, and fourth year graduate students an intensive and continuous service and training experience at VA stations at which they will be compensated on an hourly basis. Psychological assistants must have scheduled assignments of a minimum of 24 hours per week with a maximum of 39 hours per week. Graduate students who participate in this program agree in advance to accept a station assignment for a specified period of from six months to one year. While at the VA installation they are not eligible for a VA stipend. Assignments of less than six months cannot be used in the psychological assistantship type of appointment.

A limited number of postdoctoral psychologists are also assigned to the training program as psychological assistants. They remain at VA installations for a sufficient period of time to qualify for staff positions.

Variety of psychological services

In the VA, psychological services are planned to meet comprehensive needs in hospitals or outpatient clinics. The psychologists are responsible for the providing of psychological services in the patient service unit or area of a hospital to which they are assigned. In outpatient programs, the majority of psychological services provided are in the mental hygiene clinics. Psychology trainees are systematically assigned to staff psychologists from whom they receive supervised experience in all psychological functions and activities in their areas of functioning and competence. Several experiential settings are utilized during training in the VA, not only within a hospital but also by combining outpatient clinic assignments with hospital and domiciliary assignments. All training provides a graduated opportunity for development of essential professional skills as well as the development of sense of responsibility for work inherent in the context of a hospital or outpatient clinic.

The descriptions of psychological services, functions, and responsibilities which follow are roughly grouped according to specified and general categories of patients. It should be pointed out that these categories are somewhat artificial and that considerable overlap does occur in actual practice. As the psychology trainees are assigned to the staff psychologist for supervised experience, the functional descriptions frequently vary from rather clearly identified training experience to an intermixing of training and staff functions. In the latter, however, experiential learning is provided by the nature of the training assignment as the trainees participate as fully as possible in the functional activities and responsibilities of the staff psychologist.

Psychiatric patients

Usually the earliest training experience is in assessment, evaluation, and diagnostic activities utilizing both individual and group methods with psychiatric patients. The diagnoses of the majority of these patients are the various types of neuroses, psychoses (acute, incipient, chronic or in some degree of remission), character disorders, psychosomatic conditions, and acute or chronic brain syndromes. Psychological tests, interview methods, rating techniques, and case history evaluations are generally utilized for this process, although a variety of special or unique procedures may be used. Depending on the problems presented, the interests of the staff psychologist supervising the trainee, and the needs of the trainee, the assignment of functions is determined. Cases of increasing complexity are assigned to trainees as they demonstrate greater and greater proficiency. Professional case conferences and training seminars are regularly held, focusing on the cases under study, the relationship of the case material to personality, psychopathology, intellectual functioning, therapeutic goals, vocational counseling, research, etc. The psychological assessment of each patient is reported orally and in official written reports which become a part of the patient's medical records. Emphasis is placed on clarity, conciseness, and comprehensiveness since the psychological reports are one of the principal mechanisms by which other staff are made aware of the pertinent findings of the psychology service.

Individual psychotherapy and group psychotherapy are regularly utilized in the hospitals and clinics. Specialized forms of these therapeutic processes are many and varied, but they are generally patterned around the qualifications and interests of the professional staff. For example, some hospitals may have an intensive milieu therapy program in which psychotherapy processes are the major element of treatment, whereas another hospital may regularly use psychotherapy along with a specialized psychodrama treatment program. At times the psychotherapy process and various therapeutic interventions are reality-oriented at the ego-level, making use of personality dynamics implicitly rather than explicitly.

Opportunities to learn and to engage in both individual and group psychotherapy are afforded psychology trainees under supervision of psychologists and psychiatrists. Psychology trainees will frequently begin participation in group therapy as an observer-recorder, later as assistant therapist, then co-therapist, and then under supervision be responsible for independent groups. Ample opportunity is provided in the supervisory and learning process for conferences, seminars, and meetings with staff or consultants to discuss the therapeutic process, theories of psychotherapy, and the therapeutic interaction process which the trainee is experiencing.

Success in rehabilitation and maintaining the patient out of the hospital or mental hygiene clinic is related to the patient's ability to adapt to the stresses of social living and to work productively. Therapeutic work assignments and educational and transitional therapies are a regular part of the rehabilitation process. Counseling psychologists and trainees assume major responsibility for many phases of these programs. In addition to hospital or clinic resources being utilized in therapeutic work programs, actual work in local industry, contracts for industrial work done while hospitalized, and interaction with federal, state, and local rehabilitation and employment agencies are utilized in which the trainees acquire essential experience. As a part of these rehabilitation functions, opportunity for job placement and follow-up is provided.

Social psychology trainees have received training in hospitals having special therapeutic milieu programs. As yet there are no service functions in social psychology comparable to those in clinical psychology or counseling psychology. However, in these newer therapeutic programs in which research is under way, social psychology trainees have made valuable contributions in the study of social-behavioral components of treatment, the utilization of the ward's social environment as a therapeutic modality, and the understanding of social-behavioral aspects of group processes in rehabilitation. With more experience, it is anticipated that service aspects of their functions will crystallize. This program is generally operating in close harmony with university consultants and supervision by social psychologists employed by the VA.

Physiological psychology trainees are generally assigned to a research laboratory, but as an enriching experience also become acquainted with and participate in the patient's service programs. Depending on their interest and motivation they acquire knowledge and limited experience with a wide range of patient problems. This experience provides for greater appreciation of numerous research problems and materially assists identification and definition of research problems. These trainees, however, obtain their greatest amount of experience in laboratories devoted to physiological psychology, neurophysiology, neuropsychology, and electrophysiology. Interaction with neurologists, biochemists, physicists, neurosurgeons, etc. enriches the experience for physiological psychology trainees who learn under the supervision of a physiological psychologist.

Neurological and sensory processes

With neurological patients, the psychology trainee is introduced to the intensive application of psychological procedures to the diagnosis and treatment of central nervous system disorders. He is involved in the total program of rehabilitation of the neurologically handicapped, which also requires extensive use of vocational counseling methods. He may receive training in the diagnosis and treatment of organically determined language disorders, both on an individual and on a group basis. In general, the psychology program designed to serve the neurological patients encompasses five major functions which are as follows: 1) psychological assessment, evaluation, and diagnosis; 2) psychotherapy; 3) education; 4) coordination; and 5) aphasia therapy (at hospitals).

The assessment, evaluation, and diagnostic function encompasses all of the techniques used by the psychologist to appraise a patient's mental and emotional status. The majority of the diagnostic referrals call for differential diagnoses and evaluations of mental status after brain injury. There are also requests for personality evaluations, especially when the main consideration is the patient's ability to profit from psychotherapy. Besides the more or less classical forms of diagnostic procedures, there are requests for speech and language evaluations, and for the type of evaluation necessary for vocational counseling. Since the rehabilitation program is an important one for this service, most diagnostic reports are slanted towards planning a rehabilitation program for the patient. For this reason the diagnostic function is a dynamic, continuous process which is closely related to the active total treatment program. The therapeutic function performed by the psychologist is based on the general principles of psychotherapy. Usually, the therapy is supportive in nature rather than intensive.

The educational function for staff and trainees is conducted both formally and informally. The formal part of the program frequently uses the seminar approach which is predominantly patient oriented. Frequently the topics covered are suggested by the various therapists. Part of the seminar periods are also used to discuss patient problems that are affecting the therapist group as a whole. The informal educational function is predominantly between the medical staff and the psychologist, and consists of an exchange of ideas and knowledge which serves to bring the two disciplines into closer cooperation and to increase the understanding both groups have about patients.

Since treatment of the neurological patient requires the coordinated effort of many experts, these must be as well coordinated as possible to insure the continuity which is so essential in a rehabilitation program. The psychologist is uniquely qualified to assist the neurologist in coordination of therapeutic rehabilitation because he has usually seen the patient at the initial evaluation and, in most instances, follows the patient through his hospitalization. The mutual exchanges of information between the neurologist, the psychologist, and the physical medicine and rehabilitation therapists form the basis of the program's coordination. Modification of activities, and progress towards more complicated skills are planned on this basis, and more effective treatment is thus provided for the patient.

Pulmonary and communicable diseases

Staff psychologists and psychology trainees have provided psychological service and performed research on units devoted to the treatment and rehabilitation of patients with pulmonary diseases and communicative diseases. For illustrative purposes, the psychological functions and responsibilities are discussed within the framework of patients with tuberculosis. The problems which the psychologist faces are multifaceted and challenging. Psychology trainees learn by participation in all activities performed by the psychologist on these units.

Psychologists serve as members of the tuberculosis rehabilitation team and cooperate in the total treatment and rehabilitation of the patient. It should be noted that it is not the primary purpose of the psychologist in the tuberculosis setting to work with people who are mentally ill. Psychology is mainly interested in helping people who face the pressures and emotional stresses associated with having a communicable disease which requires a long hospitalization, which results in prolonged separation from family and friends, and means loss of income. The psychologist assists the patient in adjusting to these problems through individual and group contacts, both on a formal and informal basis.

Through a variety of services and activities involving contact with patients or with other hospital personnel, the staff psychologist seeks to create a psychological atmosphere conducive to achieving and maintaining a healthy emotional adjustment. The goal is to help the patients to accept not only their long hospitalization but also to participate actively in the medical and rehabilitation programs directed towards post-hospital adjustment.

Trainees regularly render services involving direct patient contact. These are personality assessment, vocational counseling and rehabilitation, and psychotherapy. Personality assessment frequently differs from the traditional methods used in a psychiatric setting. Patients are often too physically incapacitated to participate in extensive diagnostic procedures. In addition, aseptic techniques create difficulties in test administration. For these reasons, the diagnostic interview as an assessment technique is often used extensively.

Psychotherapeutic techniques often must be modified to meet the requirements of the patient's physical limitations and the special problems and emotional difficulties. Intensive individual psychotherapy is done, but most of the "psychotherapy" is accomplished through short supportive contacts with patients. These contacts may be of about 15 minutes duration and vary in frequency from daily to bi-weekly. These frequent supportive contacts are ideal for working out the situational conflicts which are characteristic for a tuberculous setting. The contacts can be varied in frequency, length, and intensity as the changing situation dictates, and they can be terminated without upset to the patient after the critical period has passed.

Vocational counseling and vocational rehabilitation is an important function of psychology. With tuberculosis, the possibility of relapse often makes it inadvisable for the patient to return to his former occupation. In this case, the patient is aided in the selection of new vocational objectives, and is referred to other members of the rehabilitation team for vocational exploration and training. Staff psychologists may also be active in the direct placement and follow-up of patients or, if appropriate, refer them to other agencies for post-hospital training or placement.

In the tuberculosis setting, much of the work of the psychologist with other hospital personnel is related to the rehabilitation program. This includes regular meetings of the Tuberculosis

Planning Committee which considers the more difficult rehabilitation cases. Also there are weekly meetings of the entire rehabilitation team.

Another important service by psychology is in the area of training. The principal duty is that of supervision of psychology trainees assigned to the tuberculosis service. This involves instruction and guidance towards the development of clinical skills in a non-psychiatric setting as well as development of an awareness of the administrative aspects of the psychological services. Formal and informal meetings are also scheduled with other disciplines working in the tuberculosis service for training purposes. Regularly scheduled formal lectures and seminars are conducted with affiliate nurse groups, and meetings with staff nurses and nursing assistants are scheduled when needed (e.g., when new members join the staff or when a particular problem arises). The psychology service is available to any group for consultation when there is a need to consider psychological factors.

Serious physical diseases and handicaps

A wide range of serious physical disease, with resultant handicaps, is found in patients for whom the VA provides services. Perhaps one of the most challenging assignments is with patients who have spinal cord injury, and this type of patient is utilized for illustrative purposes. In a training assignment, the psychology trainee is a full participant with the staff psychologist.

Spinal cord injury problems are the result of physical injuries (such as falls, automobile or diving accidents, and bullet wounds) and various disease processes involving the spinal cord. Most of these patients require at least 10 months hospitalization after their injury, and may have to have numerous readmissions. Total rehabilitation is usually the ultimate goal.

A paraplegic is a person with partial or complete paralysis of both legs. A quadriplegic has paralysis of the arms as well. Approximately 50% of the patients with spinal cord injury are quadriplegics. In the past, quadriplegia was considered a hopeless disability. Today, with the team approach in rehabilitation, this is no longer true. Although attendant care may always be needed, a majority of quadriplegic patients can, with motivation, live productive lives. Many have been able to do gainful work at home, such as providing a telephone answering service and telephone soliciting; a few are transported to schools to become prepared in professions such as law and literary or technical writing; and a few others are transported to their places of employment where, with the aid of self-help devices and clerical assistance, they operate satisfactorily. In addition to the traditional clinical and counseling functions, the psychologist works towards developing a milieu which will enhance the morale and rehabilitation striving of these patients.

The staff psychologist works very closely with other professional specialists in this service. He may be a member of special boards, such as the Spinal Cord Injury Board, which holds case conferences and conducts rounds every week. The Board may include representatives from orthopedics, urology, neurology, physical medicine and rehabilitation, nursing, and social service. The psychologist familiarizes himself with the case histories of all the patients on this service and prepares evaluation reports for the Board. He performs diagnostic, psychotherapeutic, and consultative functions as requested by the ward physician or as he may find necessary to achieve rehabilitation goals. Short supportive contacts in the wards and clinics are an important service to patients and personnel. The staff psychologist is involved in teaching selected aspects of psychology to physical medicine and rehabilitation therapists, nurses, and nursing assistants.

Medical and surgical patients

Medical and surgical patients constitute a large patient load in the VA. In many VA hospitals staff psychologists are assigned full time to these services, whereas in other hospitals the psychological services are provided by a part-time assignment or on a consulting basis. The techniques and methods used in providing psychological services on these units are similar to those discussed above under *Psychiatric patients*. Much of the psychotherapy, however, is modified to a short term process. Considerable opportunity exists for psychology research with medical and surgical problems as well as for the development of more discriminating psychological techniques in work with this patient population.

Psychological services and training opportunities are available with the medical patients and the surgical patients. As earlier described, the psychologist may use a wide variety of the traditional psychological techniques or may devise special approaches which contribute to assessment, treatment and ultimate rehabilitation. In a general hospital, about 12% of the patient load for psychological services originate with medical and surgical patients. Experiences for the student may include intellectual evaluation as an aid in differential diagnosis, determination of the degree of intellectual deterioration subsequent to illness, post-hospital planning, personality resources as related to major surgery, self-concept and body image as related to major surgery, emotional reactivity to illness, etc. Occasionally a patient may pose an in-hospital rehabilitation or ward management problem, and the psychologist is requested to determine what personality factors are contributing to the patient's difficulties in utilizing effectively the available rehabilitation resources.

Research

The opportunities for psychology trainees to learn, conduct, and participate in research are practically unlimited in the VA. Psychologists bring a background of knowledge in research methodology, research design, and statistics to the medical setting as a significant complement to the knowledge of the physicians. The multiplicity of unknown psychological factors in disease and health creates a rare opportunity for psychology to investigate, analyze, and synthesize information derived from scientific research in hospital, clinic, or domiciliary settings.

The psychology staff in the VA have been and will continue to be effective in carrying out a wide range of basic and applied research projects on an individual investigator basis. They have also carried out and participated in a large number of studies in collaboration with the psychiatric, medical, and surgical staff. During the last two fiscal years between 750 to 800 research studies have been underway each year. In Table 1 the research

TABLE 1   VA PSYCHOLOGY RESEARCH

	Research		Staff		Total	
	1962	1963	1962	1963	1962	1963
Projects completed:	90	65	125	124	215	189
Papers published:	89	134	115	138	213	272
Papers presented:	145	142	118	119	263	261

projects for the fiscal years 1962 and 1963 are presented. The "research" psychologists in this table are the 80 psychologists devoting their time predominantly to research activities. Those identified as "staff" are the 90% of the psychologists who are employed on service funds and who are given an opportunity to devote a portion of their time to research.

(Description of ongoing research in the VA is effectively communicated in the *Newsletter for Research in Psychology*, published quarterly at the VA Center, Kecoughtan, Virginia.— Eds.)

Research by psychology trainees is encouraged. Support of research activities is provided and, with the availability of space and equipment, trainees are expected to be alert for possible ways in which a scientific investigation might add to new knowledge or a modification in psychological techniques and processes. Research opportunities include informal discussions, seminars, participation in the continuing research programs, and the conducting of a trainee's own research. Practically all hospitals and most clinics have a library which contains current professional journals. Other books and periodicals can be obtained through the inter-library loan service. Many trainees complete their doctoral dissertation during their last year of training in the VA hospitals or clinics.

Trends

1. In cooperation with universities and guidelines provided by the APA it is expected that the VA will continue to be a training resource for professionally qualified psychologists.

2. With changing concepts of hospital and clinic operation and with the incorporation of new knowledge in solving health

and illness problems, the VA psychology program will change in harmony with improved rehabilitation concepts. Psychology staffs and trainees will develop new roles. Current examples of changing approaches to treatment are the unit system of operation in psychiatric hospitals, day care treatment centers in the outpatient mental hygiene clinics and the concepts inherent in the new type general hospital being developed.

3. Psychologists will continue to participate and develop therapeutic programs. Intensive efforts will be made to continue to encourage development of therapeutic programs related to extending the hospital into the community. Research approaches to problems encountered in these programs will be utilized and will offer many challenging opportunities for psychology staff and psychology trainees.

4. The organizational structure for psychology services in the VA will continue to be modified on a flexible basis in order to provide more effective psychological services in hospitals and outpatient clinics in harmony with the latest scientific and professional knowledge. Both staff and trainees will contribute to this change.

5. Psychology staff and trainees will continue to work creatively and devise methods and procedures to help meet the growing demands for vocational counseling services in hospitals, clinics, and domiciliaries. Focus will be placed not only upon counseling of patients in clinical settings but, to an even greater extent, efforts will be directed to working out better procedures, methods, and services regarding post-hospital vocational planning and job placement programs for patients and/or members and appropriate follow-up.

6. Psychology staff and trainees who have special talents and interest in the field of psychological aspects of aging will be given an opportunity to stimulate VA installations to plan and participate in research programs regarding relevant behavioral and social correlates of aging.

7. The treatment of hospitalized veterans will be improved through encouragement and stimulation of psychology staff and trainees to devote a balanced amount of time in research efforts related to the causes of maladjustment and illness.

8. Psychology staff and trainees will continue to develop and

utilize new concepts of motivation and learning in well-designed and evaluated therapeutic milieu programs which place emphasis on personal growth and adaptability of the patient as well as social and economic restoration. They will also plan therapeutic rehabilitative programs utilizing unique and creative approaches for that group of veterans having neuropsychiatric disorders which continue to prove resistant to modern treatment procedures.

9. Research opportunities on psychological problems in health and disease are unlimited in scope. Psychology as a body of knowledge and as a professional discipline in the health field has unlimited potentials in contributions that can be made to an adaptive and satisfying life. The basic human psychological processes of learning, motivation, perception, etc. are little understood in relation to health and disease but are widely acknowledged as crucial factors. Research, training, and services as interwoven characteristics of psychology in health settings, will continue to evolve new knowledge.

Supplement: An Example of
Training in the Armed Services

JAMES L. HEDLUND

Clinical psychology training in the United States Army

The Army Medical Service began a training program for both clinical and experimental psychologists in about 1948 and with the exception of a few years in the mid-fifties, this program has continued to function as a primary source of staffing for psychologists in the U. S. Army.

In general, the Graduate Psychology Student Program in Clinical Psychology operates as follows: graduate students who have been accepted as doctoral candidates in APA-approved universities are eligible when they are clearly within two years of completing their Ph.D. (including a calendar-year of internship). If accepted into the program, a student is commissioned as a Second Lieutenant and brought on active duty with full pay and allowances. He may take his clinical internship either during his third or fourth year of graduate work, and the other year is spent at his university completing other requirements for his doctorate. When the Ph.D. has been completed, including internship, or at the end of twenty-four months, whichever comes first, the student is promoted to First Lieutenant and is then obligated for a minimum of three additional years' service as a Staff psychologist.

Characteristically, the clinical internship is taken either at Walter Reed General Hospital in Washington, D. C., or at Letterman General Hospital in San Francisco, California. Both of these hospitals have large neuropsychiatric training centers and APA-approved clinical psychology internships. There is no provision, however, for internships for civilian students or those not accepted into the Graduate Psychology Student Program.

82

Clinical psychology staff assignments following the two-year training program include predominantly Army general hospitals, both within the United States and Europe, and Army Mental Hygiene Consultation Services, located throughout the United States, usually at large training posts. There are also some clinical assignments at various research installations, at the Medical Field Service School (teaching psychology), and at the U. S. Army Disciplinary Barracks.

For further information about the Graduate Psychology Student Program, including specific questions of eligibility, interested students should write to The Surgeon General, Attention: Chief, Personnel and Training Division, Department of the Army, Washington, D. C. 20315.

Summary of intern training program at Walter Reed General Hospital, Washington, D.C.

The Clinical Psychology Service is one of the six services which make up the department of neuropsychiatry. It functions within the setting of a large neuropsychiatric training program that involves approximately 25 neurology and psychiatry residents, rotating medical interns, and from 2 to 5 clinical psychology interns. With an authorization for a staff of 6 psychologists (all Ph.D.'s.), the clinical psychology service is engaged in psychodiagnosis, psychotherapy (both individual and group), professional training, and research throughout the Department. Neuropsychiatric admissions average approximately 150 per month, including military personnel and their dependents. The neuropsychiatric consultation service averages 500-600 adult outpatient treatments per month, and the child psychiatry service approximately 120 treatments.

Outline of the twelve-month program (about 2200 hours)

1. *Orientation* (approximately 200 hours) includes orientation from the Commanding General, Chief of the Clinical Psychology Service, and other key personnel. It also includes military indoctrination lectures and discussions; basic orientations to the several services with the department of neuropsychiatry, including an extensive introduction to closed-ward psychiatry

with on-the-ward observations of patients and staff procedures; field trips to correctional and mental health institutions; one week at nearby Mental Health Consultation Service.

2. *Psychodiagnostic evaluation of patients* (approximately 700 hours) involves development of experience and competence in administering, scoring, and interpreting a wide range of psychological tests given to a wide range of patients. Such training includes a) the selecting of psychological techniques appropriate to the individual patient and to the referral problem; b) administration, scoring, and interpretation; c) writing of psychological reports that integrate the test results; d) oral presentations and discussions in staff conferences; e) informal reports and discussions of examination findings to referring personnel; and f) supervision and utilization of clinical psychology specialists in the psychodiagnostic evaluation of patients.

3. *Development of psychotherapeutic skills* (approximately 400 hours) is an essential aspect of the training program. Interns are encouraged to begin seeing patients in therapy early in their internship. It is hoped that they will carry two adult outpatients in individual therapy throughout their internship, at least one child in play therapy, and gain some experience in group psychotherapy. All psychotherapy is under the close supervision of a competent therapist.

4. *Research* is viewed as an integral part of professional-scientific services. Interns are, therefore, expected to engage in research activities (approximately 400 hours). Although the intern is encouraged to spend some of this time on research associated with his dissertation, the thesis is felt to be primarily between the intern and his university. Whether or not he is working on his thesis, he is generally expected to formulate and carry out a clinical research project during his internship.

5. *Seminars and conferences* (approximately 450 hours) include attendance and participation in weekly seminars and conferences, such as: neuropsychiatric intake conferences and problem clinics; clinical psychology case presentation conferences, both psychodiagnostic and psychotherapeutic; clinical psychology seminars, wherein interns, staff members or outside consultants present and discuss research problems, review professional literature, or examine other professional topics.

6. *Teaching* (approximately 50 hours) includes the planning and oral presentation of psychological subjects to professional and non-professional groups.

Rotation of assignments. During his training program, the intern will rotate through each of the major units of Clinical Psychology Service. The general plan calls for a minimum of three months' experience in each the inpatient, outpatient (consultation service), and child psychiatry service.

Supervision. Throughout his internship, the intern is assigned to specific clinical psychology staff supervisors. A staff supervisor for research works with the intern through the duration of any research project. Psychodiagnostic and psychotherapy supervision rotates among the clinical psychology staff members. In psychodiagnosis, the intern's supervisor is one of the staff psychologists assigned to the section where the intern is working. Although supervision in psychotherapy rotates primarily among the clinical psychology staff members, it may involve social workers or psychiatrists. However, a single supervisor usually follows an intern throughout any given case.

Each supervisor is responsible for continual *evaluation* of interns assigned to him, for regularly scheduled, frank, constructive meetings with interns, and for informally discussing the progress of each intern at clinical psychology staff meetings. Formal evaluations of interns, in each area of supervision, are written at the end of each supervisory period and forwarded to the Director of Clinical Psychology Intern Training. At mid-year and again at the completion of the internship year, the Director of Intern Training and the Chief, Clinical Psychology Service, send comprehensive evaluations to the intern's home university. These latter reports are discussed with the intern.

Standards for Clinical Psychology: Origins and Evaluation

WILLIAM SCHOFIELD

The problem of standards for clinical psychology exists, as it does for other fields of professional service, at two levels: training and practice. Standards may be specified for the content, phasing, and duration of formal graduate instruction and for eligibility for professional practice. The established standards for each of these aspects of the process of professionalization permit of examination with respect to general dimensions of adequacy and quality. This chapter will review the origins and applications of procedures for the evaluation of both training and practice against the background of the evolution of standards as presented in Chapters 1, 3 and 5.

1. *The nature of standards and the purposes of accreditation*

If there can be some clear and standard explication of the individual units of instruction and practice, and of a program for integration of these units, it should then be possible to devise a single, unified process of evaluation whereby the end-product (and the social goal) of professional preparation, e.g., the clinical psychologist, could be tested and certified. But it is in the nature of preparation for careers of professional service that there are two very different, although related, phases: the phase of academic education (didactic and laboratory instruction) and the phase of clinical training (supervised apprenticeship practice). The appraisal of these two phases entails different points of focus, but the mechanisms of evaluation are comparable for the two inasmuch as *programs, personnel,* and *facilities* are under scrutiny.

The evaluation of both the academic instruction and the closely associated clinical apprenticeship is founded on the assumption that if either of these phases is inadequate, no subsequent post-training maturation or experience will qualify the professional aspirant to offer unrestricted clinical service to the public. However, it is recognized that there will be a wide range of educational achievement and development of basic skills among those who complete fully accredited programs of education and training, and that full seasoning of a mature professional requires field experiences beyond those of the formally specified years of training. For this reason, it is common to have a final evaluation of the *individual* as a practitioner.

Both the evaluation of educational and training programs and the certification of the individual's professional competence are generally carried out by the national society of the profession. These processes have the relevant and practical goal of maintaining standards that, in the eyes of the profession, are in the best interests of both society and the profession. But protection of the public against the abuses that may arise from the activities of unqualified practitioners is a legal matter; it is for this purpose that state laws may license or certify for practice. These laws generally stipulate requirements of training and experience that are in accord with the criteria used by the profession. Table 1 presents a summary of professional evaluation processes.

TABLE 1   GENERAL LEVELS, AGENCIES, AND METHODS OF EVALUATION OF
PROFESSIONAL COMPETENCE

Level of preparation	Object of evaluation	Agency of evaluation	Method
Academic graduate instruction	University in general, department of study in particular	National professional society, or regional accrediting body	Site visits, documents
Apprenticeship training	Field agency for apprenticeship	National professional society	Site visits, documents, interviews
Post-training experience	The individual	Professional: National board of examiners Legal: State board of examiners	Examinations: written and practical

The levels and general procedures of maintaining standards of training and practice by methods of regular, periodic evaluation are well exemplified in the field of medicine. Up to the present, it has proven expeditious to apply rather parallel procedures for evaluation in the profession of clinical psychology. Thus, special committees of the APA are responsible for evaluation and accreditation of university graduate programs leading to the doctorate and for clinical agencies offering internship training. The ABEPP provides a mechanism for certification of the full professional competence of the clinician. In a number of states, statutory legislation provides for the licensing or certification of psychologists who wish to offer service to the public. In some states without statutory legislation, the state psychological associations have developed procedures for voluntary certification of clinical psychologists. These processes of evaluation and accreditation are summarized in Table 2.

TABLE 2 GENERAL LEVELS, AGENCIES, AND METHODS OF
EVALUATION IN CLINICAL PSYCHOLOGY

Level of preparation	Object of evaluation	Agency of evaluation	Method
Doctoral (Ph.D.) program	University in general; psychology department; and graduate school	APA, Education and Training Board, Committee on Evaluation	Site visit, interview, questionn
Clinical internship	Internship agency (hospital, clinic, etc.)	as above	as abov
Post-doctoral experience	Graduate (Ph.D.) psychologist	Professional: ABEPP Legal: State board of examiners Voluntary: State professional society	Examinatio written ar practical

The following review of evaluation procedures in the field of clinical psychology should be examined against the general purposes of the accreditation process, holding in mind that the prescription of standards for professional education has public welfare as its basic goal. Assuming proper standards, good accreditation procedures serve to 1) provide an identification of those schools to which a professional aspirant may turn for sound basic education; 2) provide to clinical agencies equipped to offer apprenticeship training a means of identifying students who will be ready for supervised field work and able optimally to profit from their internship; 3) provide the student with an identification of those clinical settings adequately staffed and equipped to provide him with intensive, supervised clinical experience; 4) identify to the professional board of examiners those applicants whose basic education and training have met the standards of the profession; 5) identify to the public those practitioners whose education, training, experience, and skills have been examined and who are certified by their peers as competent to render professional service.

In the opening address at a conference on training in clinical psychology held in the spring of 1947, the keynoter made the point. ". . . we have, at the present time, *no discipline of clinical psychology* in the same sense that we have medicine, law, dentistry, or teaching. And . . . there *are*, in consequence, *no uniformly trained clinical psychologists in the sense* that there are doctors, lawyers, dentists, or educators."[1] In 1962, there were 60 departments of psychology with officially approved graduate programs for the doctorate in clinical psychology.[2] (*See* Appendix B for a list of these departments.) In the same year, the Division of Clinical Psychology, the largest of the 23 divisions of the APA, had a total of 2,577 fellows and members.[3] The annual report of ABEPP for 1962 indicated that a total of 1,240 psychologists had been awarded the diploma in the specialty of clinical psychology.[4] In recent years, a number of state psychological associations have vigorously supported legislation to establish legal certification or licensing of professional psychologists; it is primarily clinical psychologists whose qualifications and practices have been defined *and limited by such laws*. As of April, 1963, 25 states have passed laws to govern the practice of psychology or the public use of the title "psychologist."[5]

2. *Evolution of current standards*

The discipline of clinical psychology is now firmly established and socially visible, and there are meaningful uniformities in the professional preparation of the clinical psychologist. The initial standards necessarily had to be those specified and accepted by the university departments of psychology. Responsibility for these standards was undertaken by the APA in response to the recognized social needs following World War II, and in specific response to the requests of the USPHS and the VA, national agencies that wished to support sound programs for the recruitment and training of the greatly needed clinicians.

The earliest suggestions for standards are found in the report of the Committee on Training in Clinical (Applied) Psychology (Bruce V. Moore, Chairman) of the American Association for Applied Psychology (AAAP)[6]* and the report of the subcommittee on graduate internship training in psychology (David Shakow, Chairman) of the AAAP and the APA.[7] These reports of 1943 and 1945, respectively, were precursors of the formal statement of standards to be found in the now historical *Shakow* Report of 1947.[8] (Other members of this standard setting committee were Ernest R. Hilgard, E. Lowell Kelly, Bertha Luckey, R. Nevitt Sanford, and Laurance F. Shaffer.)

The CTCP had received three basic charges from the Board of Directors of APA in March, 1947: 1) to "formulate a recommended program for training in clinical psychology"; 2) to "formulate standards for institutions giving training in clinical psychology, including *both* universities and internship and other practicum facilities" (italics ours); and 3) to "study and visit institutions giving instruction in clinical psychology and make a detailed report on each institution."[8] Note that this committee was assigned a dual responsibility: to specify standards and to evaluate existing training facilities. The latter charge reflected the APA's continuing response to a specific request from the VA in 1945, and from the USPHS in 1946, for a list of universities with satisfactory programs in clinical psychology. The committee's formal recommendations did not include any such listing. Both the breadth and specificity of the recommendations can be briefly suggested. Major topics included: personal qualifications

---

*This association was founded in 1937 and dissolved in 1944, when the programs and interests of applied psychologists were incorporated in the reorganized American Psychological Association.

(intellectual and characterological) of student aspirants; undergraduate education; general emphases of the graduate program; didactic curriculum, internship, and dissertation. Specific recommendations included: approximately 20 semester hours of undergraduate psychology courses; reading knowledge of French and German; "conferences and laboratory work" in "experimental dynamic psychology"; courses in remedial techniques for special disabilities; a "third year" full time internship. (*See* Chapter 1 for a more detailed discussion of these recommendations.)

After the rapid formalization and expansion of training in clinical psychology in the immediate post-war years, it was appropriate to provide a means for review and analysis of basic issues on a scale broader than that afforded by the APA committees. Accordingly, the *Boulder* Conference in Graduate Education in Clinical Psychology was convened in August, 1949, under the auspices of the NIMH of the USPHS (*see* Chapter 1). In addition to representatives of the VA, USPHS, state hospitals, clinics, and medical schools, the academic community was represented by directors of clinical training and chairmen of psychology departments. The *Boulder* Conference essentially confirmed the major recommendations of the *Shakow* Report and deemed it desirable to include that report, in full, as an appendix of its published proceedings.[9] The most recent summary of the criteria currently used for evaluating training programs in clinical psychology was published in 1958.[12] (*See* Appendix B.) It is this statement which provides guidelines both for university departments and for psychologists who conduct the evaluation studies.

3. *University accreditation: origins and present procedures*

The history of accreditation in the area of clinical psychology begins with the referral of the VA request for a list of satisfactory doctoral programs in clinical psychology to the APA Committee on Graduate and Professional Training. On the basis of a questionnaire submitted to 102 psychology departments, this committee published, in 1946, a summary of the data on the staffs, curricula, and training stipends available for doctoral level graduate study in clinical psychology at each of 32 institutions, and for master's level training at 15 schools.[10] These lists did not constitute an official approval but simply summarized data on the presence of specialized clinical staff, special course offerings (e.g., projective techniques, therapy) and supervised practicum facilities.

In 1947, the same committee published a list of 29 schools with doctoral programs which "adequately" measured up to 113 criteria, as evaluated from extensive questionnaire data. (Members of this committee were: John G. Darley, E. Lowell Kelly, Elaine Kinder, Jean Walker Macfarlane, Donald G. Marquis, Bruce V. Moore, Marion W. Richardson, Robert R. Sears (chairman) and Carroll L. Shartle.)[11] This listing represented the first accrediting function of the APA in the area of clinical psychology. In February and March 1948, the CTCP, with the assistance of a number of other psychologists, made visits to all of the graduate departments of the 1947 list and to seven other departments. With the *Shakow* Report as a guide, these visits constituted the first site evaluations and led to a committee recommendation that approved programs should receive such visits every three or four years. At the annual APA meeting in 1948, it was voted to employ a full-time Executive Officer for this committee. For these earliest evaluation activities, the APA received financial assistance from the USPHS which has continued to make annual grants; these grants are supplemented by APA funds to cover the costs of the evaluation program. The growth in the number of approved doctoral programs in clinical psychology is charted in Figure 1.

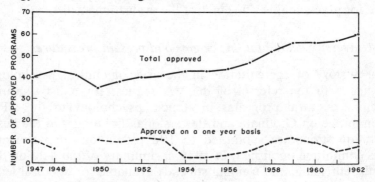

Figure 1   Number of approved doctoral programs.

As part of an extensive reorganization[13] of the APA in 1951, the Education and Training Board (ETB) was established to which five basic committees were responsible; one of these was the Committee on Doctoral Education and Training, and responsible to this committee was a sub-committee on Clinical Psychology. This sub-committee was specifically charged to carry on the evaluation activities of the CTCP which was dissolved with the reorganization. Also discontinued at this time was the Committee on Standards of Training Psychologists. Bruce V. Moore served as first chairman of the core committee on doctoral education and was subsequently appointed as the first Executive Officer of the ETB. In 1953, a Committee on Evaluation was established, replacing the sub-committee on clinical psychology, and it is this nine-member committeee which now is responsible for all evaluation and accreditation activities in the fields of clinical and counseling psychology, including evaluation of internship agencies. (*See* Appendix C.) In 1952, at the request of the VA the APA accepted responsibility for developing a list of approved training programs in counseling psychology.

The following statements, which summarize the philosophy, principles, and general practices of APA's evaluation activities, are drawn from a guidebook that is provided to each member of the evaluation committee.

"Principles and practices in the evaluation of doctoral programs in clinical psychology and counseling psychology by the American Psychological Association"

"Recommended standards for doctoral education in clinical psychology were accepted by the association and published in the *American Psychologist*, 1947, Vol. 2, pp. 539-558. In 1952 the Association's Council of Representatives voted to extend the evaluations to include doctoral programs in psychological counseling and tentatively to use standards published in the *American Psychologist*, 1952, Vol. 2, pp. 175-181. On the basis of experience since evaluations have been made, the following general principles of evaluation have emerged:

"1. *General philosophy of evaluation.* Since any program of evaluation carries with it the potential hazards of forcing too much standardization of training and of infringing on the independence of the universities concerned, the Association has sought to ascertain only that training programs meet standards of adequacy agreed upon by the profession. Beyond these standards, each department is encouraged to develop its programs of training in accordance with its own objectives and in a manner best suited to its staff and other resources. Such flexibility and experimentation with training programs is believed essential to the continued improvement of training.

"2. *Evaluation is limited to training programs in clinical and in couseling psychology.* Evaluation of training programs is limited to those in clinical psychology and in psychological counseling leading to a doctoral degree. Evaluation of training in other fields of psychology, e.g., experimental, physiological, or industrial, are made only insofar as these bear on the adequacy of training in clinical or counseling psychology. Similarly, training in related fields of graduate work, e.g., physiology and anthropology, is evaluated only to the degree that it is relevant to training in clinical psychology. In other words, the evaluation made applies only to the doctoral training programs in clinical or counseling psychology, not to the department as a whole nor to the university as a whole.

"3. *Evaluation is voluntary.* No training program is evaluated except with the approval and cooperation of the department. Each department provides the Committee information (on forms filled out in advance) regarding staff, courses, practicum facilities and other details of the training program. The actual evaluation is based on an intensive study of these forms and on a two-day visit to the institution made by the Executive Officer of the E & T Board and a member of the Committee on Evaluation.

"4. *Details of evaluations are confidential.* Each training program is reviewed annually at a meeting of the Committee on Evaluation and is assigned a rating. A rating of approval without any differentiating marks is assigned to a program which fully meets the standards accepted by the Association and published in the *American Psychologist* (*ibid*).

"A second category of programs shall be indicated by an asterisk. Schools marked with an asterisk have recently (as indicated by appended date of approval) developed programs which meet minimum standards for interim approval. Their programs are improving and appear likely to merit full approval after a few additional years of experience. These new programs are given this probationary period not to exceed five years.

"A third category is designated as marginal. Schools in this category will be informed of their rating but their marginal status will not be published. When a school which has been previously approved falls into this marginal category for five consecutive years, approval must be withdrawn; but this principle should not be interpreted to preclude dropping a school in less than five years.

"These ratings must be approved by the Education and Training Board with the concurrence of the Board of Directors before they are reported. They are then reported to: a) The chairman of the department, along with a detailed letter stating the Committee's impressions of the strengths and weaknesses of the program. b) The appropriate officials of the VA, the USPHS, and the Surgeon General's Office of the Army for the guidance of these agencies in their support of training in clinical and counseling psychology.

"5. *Right of appeal.* Any department which regards the rating assigned as unfair may appeal to the Committee for a revision of the rating. In the event of dissatisfaction with the action taken on the appeal, the department may further appeal to the Association's Board of Directors, whose decision is final.

"6. *Re-evaluation.* Approved programs are to be re-evaluated routinely every five years;* however, a department may submit evidence of a change of status and request re-evaluation any year; and the Committee may initiate a re-evaluation if it has reason to believe the status of the program has changed. A rating of a program will not be lowered without a year of warning and a re-visit.

"7. *Publication of lists of approved programs.* An alphabetical list of approved programs for training in clinical psychology, and an approved list for training in counseling psychology shall be published annually, usually in the spring, in the *American Psychologist.*

"8. *Costs of evaluation.* Evaluations, so far, have been made without cost to the department or institution concerned. The actual cost of evaluation has been covered by an annual grant from the U. S. Public Health Service, supplemented by an appropriation from the American Psychological Association.

"9. *Obligation of departments requesting evaluation.* Although no department is under obligation to have its program of training in clinical or in counseling psychology evaluated by the Association, after evaluation it is expected to honor the evaluation received. If the program is evaluated as 'not acceptable', the department should elect: a) to take immediate steps to improve its program, or b) to

---

*The five-year interval holds for *site* visits, at which time two representatives of the evaluation committee return to the university to make a direct appraisal of facilities, general academic atmosphere, conduct interviews with administrative officers, faculty, and students, and otherwise appraise directly the vitality of the program. Every approved program receives an annual audit based upon replies submitted by the department to a detailed questionnaire.

terminate training at the doctoral level in the program not approved, in which case, this fact rather than the department's rating will be reported to the federal agencies."

Since the establishment of the ETB, and its Committee on Evaluation, it has been an established principle that these agencies of the APA would provide not only for the appraisal and formal accrediting of university programs, but would also provide advisory services to any psychology department that requested a review of its current programs and facilities and recommendations as to desirable directions for further development. The committee has consistently viewed its advisory functions as one of its most appropriate and important ones. It has been a general principle to urge all departments that contemplate seeking accreditation to arrange initially for an advisory visit. Such advisory visits are not mandatory, but they provide an excellent means for the department to achieve an objective survey of its strengths and weaknesses and to have its developmental needs presented effectively to the university administration. As a standing rule, a department that has received an advisory visit will not be given a formal evaluation for possible approval of its training program until at least one year after the advisory visit. Likewise, in the case of a department that has not been approved following an evaluation visit, a second such visit will not be made in less than one year.

In 1961, the APA council voted that "a fee for advisory visits be instituted, and that a policy be instituted for a two-year period starting September 1, 1961, providing for a fee to be paid at the rate of $200 per man-day for advisory visits carried out by the Committee on Evaluation; however, the fee can be waived by the Committee on the recommendation of the Executive Officer."[22]

Careful attention should be given to the first principle quoted above. From the beginning, pressures of social need and resources of public agencies were joined to afford American psychologists an opportunity to draft at one time the basic educational and training criteria of a new service profession, rather than allowing for the gradual evolution of standards as occurred in older professions. Being forced to design these criteria without the advantage of long experience with a distinctly professional training program, the responsible officers and committees of the APA explicitly recognized the dangers of a too early rigidification and a too detailed specification of a mold that might prove subsequently to be seriously inadequate. Accordingly, individual departments have been encouraged to design programs which, within the broadly stipulated standards, permitted maximum realization of particular local strengths and facilites. Interpretation of standards and evaluation of programs by the APA committees have been liberal rather than strict. Consonant with this general principle have been the series of national conferences designed to provide intensive review of practices, problems, and potentials by representatives of the teaching, research, and clinical domains. (*See* Chapter 1.)*

Universities are naturally jealous of their academic prerogatives. Psychology departments are generally imbued with the philosophy of a research-oriented, scholastic Ph.D. program. There have been understandable anxieties aroused (but only rarely panic or hostility) when it has appeared that extra-university bodies were in the process of significantly altering the basic atmosphere of graduate instruction in psychology, or when it has seemed that special interest groups within applied psychology were gradually transforming academic departments of graduate education into professional training schools.

Total freedom of the educational institution is naturally antithetical to the operation of any extra-institutional standards. Yet it is the history of educational progress that the recruitment and education of students, the quality of faculty, and the attainment of adequate facilities have all been enhanced with the gradual, *voluntary,* and conscientious invention and acceptance of standards. In a concise review of the history and current status of accreditation in higher education, Selden observes that this process serves four major purposes: 1) to achieve necessary controls over admissions; 2) to establish and maintain minimum academic standards; 3) to stimulate institutional self-improvement; and 4) to provide a "countervailing force to the many external and some internal pressures that are continually being exerted on our educational institutions."[14]

*Such a "second look" conference to provide analysis and appraisal of the post-*Boulder* developments in the field of clinical psychology is now being planned by APA's Division of Clinical Psychology for 1965.

For the non-applied, academically identified member of a psychology faculty there has been added to any general antipathy to evaluation of externally imposed standards a particular skepticism that such evaluation should be the responsibility of his scientific society (APA). The psychological community has been clearly divided not simply on the question of what standards should be established, by whom, and how measured, but has been also without unity of opinion that the national scientific society should provide the machinery of accreditation. Nonetheless, the report of the *Miami Beach* Conference on Graduate Education in Psychology (1958), indicates that there "was a strong consensus that some form of accreditation is necessary as part of the social price that must be paid for development of the professional aspects of psychology," and that it "was fully agreed that if accreditation had to be done, it had better be the APA that did it."[15]

While many of the specific items of the published standards for doctoral clinical psychology programs have been subject to criticism at one time or another, from one quarter or another, perhaps the most frequently and vigorously attacked specification has been that of the predoctoral internship. (Cogent arguments for and against such intern arrangements are in the letter section of the *Newsl., Div. Clin. Psychol.*, 1963, *16*, May Issue.— Eds.) This is a period of 9 to 12 months of full-time (or equivalent at not less that half-time) supervised apprenticeship in a medically staffed clinic or hospital, occurring usually in the third year of a four-year program. From the point of view of the academic department, the internship slows the student's progress toward his degree (as contrasted with other, non-clinical students), takes him away from campus at a time when he should begin to formulate dissertation research plans with his major advisor, involves him intensively in professional apprenticeship training in a service setting and atmosphere that contrasts with the academic emphasis on scholarship and research. For these and other reasons, there have been repeated efforts to achieve an official revision of this requirement and to make the internship a postdoctoral experience. There has been essential unanimity on the revelance of an intensive internship as part of the total preparation of the clinical psychologist; the point at issue has been simply that of timing. When this question has confronted the ETB, there has been consistent reaffirmation of the values of the predoctoral internship as originally enunciated in the 1947 *Shakow* Report. The last formal statement on this requirement was given by the ETB and affirmed by the Council of Representatives in 1954.[16] It reads:

"It is the responsibility of any university offering a doctoral program designed to prepare students to assume professional psychological duties to arrange that each doctoral candidate in clinical or counseling will receive adequate supervised practical experience as an integral part of that program. At the present time the E & T Board adopts the following accreditation standards as desirable for the implementation of this principle. a) A supervised predoctoral internship of not less than one academic year preceded by one or more clerkships. b) A continuing contact between the university and the internship agency during the doctoral candidate's intern period."

Apart from objection to requiring the student to take his internship predoctorally, some psychologists are opposed to the principle that the academic department must take responsibility for arranging for an internship, for establishing liaison with the internship agency, and for evaluating the student's internship experience. (Field training is discussed in Chapter 1.—Eds.) These persons argue that the internship is an extra-academic experience which should be achieved post-degree and evaluated by an extra-academic agency. While the ETB has revealed recent tendencies to encourage departments to experiment with essentially postdoctoral internship arrangements, it has steadfastly insisted that the university must be responsible for seeing to it that the clinical graduate actually completes a satisfactory internship. Although assignment of such a responsibility to the academic center represents a clear deviation from the current pattern of qualification for medical practice, this position is responsive to the fact that there are no sufficiently established and widely recognized mechanisms for certification of the individual clinician that would preclude the hiring for clinical work of psychologists whose apprenticeship training was either inadequate or absent. Until such accrediting apparatus, as are represented by ABEPP and by the several state certifying or licensing boards, are more widely and regularly referred to in establishing the minimum qualifications for professional practice (a condition likely to be delayed so long as demand for psychological services greatly exceeds the supply of personnel) the basic training institution, i.e., the department of psychology, must be responsible for this aspect of the total preparation of the clinical psychologist, and it can exercise this responsibility most readily and reliably by requiring the internship as part of the program leading to conferral of the degree.*

4. Accreditation of practicum agencies

In the original charge of the APA Board of Directors to the Committee on Training in Clinical Psychology (1947),[8] the committee was assigned responsibility to formulate standards for practicum and internship agencies. After giving necessary initial and extended attention to the criteria for academic doctoral training in clinical psychology, the committee was able to turn its attention to practicum training. In 1950, it published a detailed report of tentative standards.[17] This report included definitions of various levels of practical training, a statement of objectives and methods of practicum training, a general review of a variety of potential practicum agencies, and concluded with a checklist for the evaluation of practicum training and agencies. Table 3 below is taken from this report. In the following year a survey of the practicum agencies used by the students of 41 evaluated psychology departments revealed a total of 296 such agencies, representing some 15 different clinical settings. Exploratory visits were made to 10 practicum centers for the purpose of developing suggestions and criteria for the ultimate evaluation of practicum training.

In 1952, Foster, Benton, and Rabin, in collaboration with the CTCP, published an account of three alternative plans for the internship.[18] Foster proposed that the first two years of a five-year doctoral program should be composed exclusively of a rigor-

*Reactions to the proposal for a postdoctoral internship were strong. Typical was the objection to the view of the internship as compatmentalized and an appendage rather than "reconciliation of theory and psychopathology on the hoof." (Bennett, C.C. Comment in Div. 12 Newsl., No. 2, 16, 1963, p. 10 and Pottharst, K., ibid.)—Eds.

ous program of entirely academic study of general, theoretical, and experimental psychology, to be followed by a "drastically remodeled" *two-year* internship. The first year of internship would consist of tutorial practice in psychodiagnostics and intensive *personal* therapy; in the second year, the intern would have extensive and intensive experience in closely supervised psychotherapy. The fifth year, on campus, would be devoted to completion of the dissertation.

Benton reviewed the rationale of the decision by the Iowa

TABLE 3   LEVELS OF NON-ACADEMIC TRAINING IN
CLINICAL PSYCHOLOGY WITH THEIR DISTINGUISHING ASPECTS *

Levels ts	Pre-practicum Laboratory	Practicum Clerkship	Internship
:ts	Normal persons, classmates, etc.	Patients or clients	Patients or clients
·ry ·tions	Learning administration of various techniques	Using techniques in studies of patients	Integrating the results of various techniques
·ial ·rvision	Instructor	Agency psychologist	Agency personnel representative of different professions
·on	Sufficient to learn administration of methods	Variable, but not less than equivalent of 3 months in at least 4 different agencies or settings	Variable, but no less than the equivalent of 11 months. Not necessarily but preferably in one agency
·ution ·ne	Scheduled hours	At least the equivalent of one day per week	Full or half time
·teristics ·rk	Drill and observation	Extensive use of many methods with many patients	Intensive use of many methods with follow-up with relatively few patients
·eration	None	None	Scholarship or stipend

* Reproduced with the permission of the APA, from Kelly, E. Lowell, Standards for practicum training in clinical psychology: tentative recommendations. *American Psychologist*, 1950, 5, 394-595.

department to shift the internship to the fourth year, and the entailed "explicit acceptance of the idea that the internship would *not* be a requirement for the Ph.D. degree." (It was this decision, in part, that led to the formal APA reaffirmation in 1954, that the university must be "responsible" for the completion of an internship by its clinical graduates.) Rabin reviewed and argued in favor of the "conventional" plan for the internship as specified by the *Boulder* Conference.

With the organization of the ETB in 1951, a Committee on Practicum Training was established to develop standards, provide services, and conduct evaluations of internship agencies. In its first year, this committee collected data from 105 intern training centers and visited 18 agencies. With this fund of information at hand, the committee recommended that qualified agencies should be required to provide intensive, supervised experience in two of the following areas: psychodiagnosis, psychotherapy, and research, rather than in all three as had been recommended in the CTCP standards of 1950. By 1954, this practicum committee had visited 40 agencies and analyzed questionnaire data from 176 centers.[19] At this time, it recommended that its activities be transferred to the Committee on Evaluation. Since 1954, this latter committee has been responsible for the appraisal and accrediting of both university and clinical agency programs.

The first list of approved internship agencies was published in 1956.[20] This list included only *independent* agencies, i.e., agencies that accepted interns from more than one university. (Captive agencies, which offer supervised experience to students of only a particular university, are evaluated as part of the review of the total university program and have not been included in any lists of approved independent agencies.) The initial list identified 27 approved internship centers. In 1958, the APA, upon recommendation of ETB, completed a contract with the VA for evaluation visits to the internship training programs of VA clinics and hospitals.

Within the next year, the Committee on Evaluation became overwhelmed by the burden imposed by dual responsibility for the accrediting not only of university programs but also of the burgeoning number of internship agencies seeking accreditation. The necessary schedule of site visits greatly exceeded both the financial and personnel resources of the committee. Furthermore, it appeared desirable to appraise carefully the meaning of the accreditation of independent practicum centers apart from the academic clinical programs of the universities from which their interns were drawn. Accordingly, at the recommendation of ETB, the APA council in 1959 declared a moratorium on further evaluation of independent practicum agencies and established an *ad hoc* Committee on Problems of Internship Evaluation. (Consonant with this action, the contract to provide evaluation of VA agencies was terminated in 1960.) This *ad hoc* committee had representatives from intern training centers, state mental health programs, and university training programs. It received the thoughtful recommendations of representatives of NIMH, the VA, and the Conference of Chief Psychologists in State Mental Health Programs. The report of this *ad hoc* committee and a position paper by ETB were presented in 1961 to the APA council which voted favorably on the *ad hoc* committee's recommendation for a lifting of the moratorium. In anticipation of a renewed program of internship accreditation, the *ad hoc* committee prepared a revised specification of classes of predoctoral internship in clinical and counseling psychology. (Copies of this report are available from the APA.) Accreditation is now provided for three types of internship programs:[21]

Type G (general)—an internship providing "relatively broad experience with a wide variety of patients."

Type S (special)—an internship providing "intensive and varied experience, but with relatively restricted clinical material," e.g., a children's clinic.

Type U (university)—a captive agency restricting its training program to students from a single university, or a group of agencies providing "an organized pattern of rotations coordinated with a university training program."

In the first list of approved agencies under the new standards, there are 34 Type G centers, and 11 Type S agencies. (*See* Appendix C for list.) These are considered to satisfy the minimal basic standards for internship programs as published in 1958.[12]

During the period of the moratorium on internship accreditation, the Committee on Evaluation took advantage of the opportunity to review the rapid evolution of the APA's role in monitoring graduate education in the clinical and counseling fields. Responding to the sheer magnitude of its dual responsibility, and questioning the propriety of having the appraisal of both academic preparation and professional field experience fall to the same committee of a scientific association, the Committee on Evaluation urged: 1) that its function should be changed to one of providing only advisory services; and 2) that accreditation of internship agencies should be assumed by some other, extra-APA organization. If it were to continue actively in an accrediting function the committee argued that it might best take a "single focus" approach in evaluating combined 'academic-practicum" programs.

The suggestion of an independent organization to be responsible for the approval of internship centers had some promise of accomplishment with the founding of the American Board for Psychological Services. ABPS was incorporated in Missouri in 1954. It was a direct outgrowth of an APA Committee on a Directory of Psychological Service Centers. The purposes of ABPS were stated to be: "a) to serve the public welfare by providing lists of agencies and *individuals* who are qualified to give competent psychological services; b) to determine the qualifications of agencies and individuals who apply for professional listing as established by the Board; c) to maintain a register of holders of such listings; and d) to *issue certificates* in witness thereof." [23] (Italics ours.) Those who wished listing in the directory had to be APA members with the Ph.D. and a minimum of five years of appropriate postdoctoral experience. They did not have to be diplomats of ABEPP, nor was this required of the "ranking psychologist" of an agency.[24] In brief, through provision for the certification of *individuals,* ABPS was directly competitive with ABEPP, and by virtue of offering a cheaper diploma threatened to seriously retard the growth of the earlier and sounder program for certification of the individual psychological specialist. This overlapping function plus the fact that ABPS's operations had to be underwritten by the members of APA who were already providing financial support to ABEPP brought criticism to bear on the former board. ABPS published one report[25] and one directory; it dissolved, at the recommendation of APA's Board of

Professional Affairs, in 1961.[22] Had this separately incorporated accrediting apparatus had a more thoughtful charter and a more restrictive function, i.e., to provide a registry of competent *agencies,* it could very well have assumed the responsibility for evaluating internship centers. Possibly a separate board, fashioned in part along the lines of ABPS, may appear one day and become responsible for this heavy burden of evaluation.

5. *The American Board of Examiners in Professional Psychology* (*ABEPP*)

At nearly the same time as it responded to the requests of federal agencies for lists of graduate psychology departments equipped to offer satisfactory doctoral programs in clinical psychology, the APA recognized the desirability of some procedure for examining the individual professional competence of the graduates of such programs. The procedure for examination and certification of individual practitioners is now provided by the ABEPP. A succinct history of the ABEPP is provided in an article that examines its philosophy, reports on its procedures, and evaluates the success of its function.[26]

In 1946, the Policy and Planning Board of the APA recommended that the association's bylaws be amended to establish an examining board; the proposed amendment was approved by an overwhelming majority of APA members. Further consideration of the functions of such an examination board led to the recommendation that it should be established as an independent corporation; this would legally protect the APA and its financial responsibilities; also, it was believed that "a separate corporate body composed of competent and sincere persons with freedom and responsibility for independent action could best perform the tasks assigned."[26] This required repeal of the new amendment; again the APA membership showed nearly unanimous accord in supporting the recommendation of an independent agency.

ABEPP was incorporated in the District of Columbia in April, 1947, with a first Board of Examiners elected by APA's Council of Representatives. (Members of the first board were: Carlyle Jacobsen, President; George A. Kelly, Vice-President; John G. Darley, Secretary-Treasurer; Marion A. Bills, John G.

Jenkins, David Shakow, Carroll Q. Shartle, David Wechsler, and
Frederick L. Wells.) The bylaws of the corporation provide that
one-third of the ten-member Board of Trustees shall be elected
to four-year terms at the annual meeting of the corporation, from
a slate of nominees provided by the Council of Representatives.
Five of the trustees represent clinical psychology, two represent
counseling psychology, and two industrial. These nine are diplomates. The tenth trustee, a non-diplomate, is a representative at
large and "is carefully selected to provide leadership by serving
as President of the board."[26]

There are 1,116 "grandfather" diplomates for whom the
Ph.D. requirement, the examination procedures, or both, were
waived on the basis of seniority (baccalaureate degree conferred
on or before December 31, 1935), training, professional history,
and positive endorsement of colleagues. Applications were received under the "grandfather" clause until December 31, 1949.

The first written examinations were offered in the fall of 1949,
and the first orals were conducted in November, 1950. Over the
ensuing 13-year period a total of nearly 600 psychologists have
successfully completed the board examinations; these constitute
nearly two-thirds of all applicants for examination. Table 4
summarizes the distribution of diplomates by specialty.

TABLE 4   DISTRIBUTION OF ABEPP DIPLOMATES
BY SPECIALTY AND SOURCE *

Via "Grandfather" Provision			
Clinical	719	(64%)	
Counseling	237	(21%)	
Industrial	160	(15%)	
	1,116		(65%)
By Examination			
Clinical	521	(87%)	
Counseling	37	(6%)	
Industrial	40	(7%)	
	598		(35%)
Grand Total	1,714		

* Reproduced with the permission of the APA, from 1962 Annual Reports, ABEPP.
American Psychologist, 1962, *17*, 924-926.

Applicants for ABEPP examinations must meet the following requirements: 1) be a member of the APA or Canadian Psychological Association; 2) hold a Ph.D. in psychology from a university that was on the APA's approved list for training in the applicant's specialty at the time his degree was conferred; 3) have had five years of "acceptable qualifying professional experience" (e.g., for the clinical applicant a medical setting is specified), at least four years of which must have been postdoctoral; 4) be engaged in professional work in *the specialty field.*

The Board has gained increasing experience in the conduct of examinations and been responsive to changes in each of the professional specialties; the examination procedures are under constant evaluation and have been changed to achieve enhanced validities. At present, the one day of written examinations covers "psychological knowledge and principles basic to each of the . . . specialities." Both objective (e.g., multiple choice) items and essay questions are utilized. The oral examination has three parts: 1) diagnosis or appraisal (identification of the problem confronting the psychologist); 2) therapy, counseling, or consultative action; 3) organizational, administrative, and ethical problems.

The existence of ABEPP and its provision of a medium for certification of the professional competence of the individual psychological practitioner has met with no greater degree of general acceptance, or unanimity of opinion, than has been true for the accreditation of university or internship programs. In 1959 a questionnaire survey was made of the 315 most recent diploma recipients; 85% of this sample responded. Only 27% of these diplomates indicated that they had received direct and immediate material benefit as a result of their status; over two-thirds, however, indicated a positive effect on professional status and prestige; 90% felt that the time, energy, and money required in taking the examinations was well worth the personal satisfaction they achieved.

Despite the generally positive attitude of recipients toward the ABEPP diploma, it is apparent that sizeable numbers of "board eligible" psychologists have not applied for examinations. There are undoubtedly many reasons for this, most notable of which has been the general failure thus far of employers of psychologists to recognize the meaning of an ABEPP diploma with the immediate rewards of salary increases and promotions (as is true, for example, in the VA for physicians who pass their specialty boards). ABEPP provides a vital criterion of individual proficiency which is important not only to the profession of psychology but to the public in need of certain types of psychological expertness.

In the evaluation of university faculty and internship supervisors the Committee on Evaluation is attentive to the number of eligible psychologists who do and who do not hold the ABEPP diploma.

6. *Legislation and non-statutory regulation*

The establishment of criteria for the accreditation of individual psychologists and their practices by statutory legislation constitutes one of the most complex and one of the most controversial areas of standardization. It is complex not only because of the complexity of existing laws governing the "healing arts," "diagnosis," and "therapy," but because of the great state-by-state variation in these laws. It is controversial because it has served most pointedly to bring to open and frequently extreme statement the fears of some psychiatrists, and of the national and state medical associations, concerning the activities of the clinical psychologist—especially in the realm of the private practice of psychotherapy.

It is neither possible nor appropriate to review here in detail the many facets of law, social control, and professional philosophy that relate to legislation designed to govern the offering of professional services to the public. There are several excellent review articles available. The *Columbia Law Review* of 1951 contains an excellent survey of the laws existing at that time for the "regulation of psychological counseling and psychotherapy."[27] The American Medical Association in 1951 received the report of a special committee appointed to "establish a medical viewpoint" ... "as to whether psychologists should or should not be registered under state laws." This committee recommended for certification and against licensure of clinical psychologists, and recommended that state statutes be carefully reviewed, and amended if necessary, in order to bring psychotherapy clearly under medical jurisdiction.[28] Professor David Louisell has provided extensive, case-oriented reviews of the psychologist's legal status as an expert witness and in relation to confidential communications. [29,30]

In 1954, the APA Council ordered a comprehensive review of its existing policy on legislation. This review was accomplished jointly by a special APA committee and the Committee on Legislation of the former Conference of State Psychological Associations and resulted in a joint report published in 1955.[31] This is a thoughtful and comprehensive analysis of the general problems of social control of professional work as well as of existing and ideal patterns of legislation. It points out that the rationale for any program for social control of psychology must provide: 1) protection of the welfare of the recipient of psychological services; 2) protection of "the profession as a whole from irresponsible behavior by a small number of persons called psychologists," and 3) facilitation of the "highest standards of scientific and professional performance by all psychologists." In analyzing existing state laws governing psychological practice and in laying a foundation for ideal statutory controls, the committee raised a total of 31 highly penetrating questions under such rubrics as: effect on the public, effect on the profession, effect on relations with allied professions. A few of the specific questions were: "Should the legislation prevent practice by unqualified practitioners in the area in which psychologists practice, regardless of whether such persons identify themselves as psychologists?" "Will the legislation tend to freeze professional standards or will it encourage growth and development by raising professional standards?" "Should the legislation provide for a periodic re-evaluation of the psychologist's qualifications for practice?"

The report identified three basic types of legislation then governing psychological practice: 1) laws restricting the use of a particular title (e.g., *certified* psychologist); 2) laws restricting a general title (e.g., psychologist) and/or specified functions (e.g., psychodiagnostic testing); and 3) laws restricting practice of certain functions to duly licensed psychologists. It was recognized by the committee that some uniformity of legislation was desirable in order to clarify "the public image of psychology," to provide a basis for interstate reciprocity, and to define "in a general way the conditions of practice of psychology."

The history of state laws governing the title or functions of psychologists begins in 1945 with legislation passed in Connecticut and extends most recently to Nevada (1963).[5] Of the 25 states that presently provide statutory regulation, 16 have laws that restrict both the title and function of the psychologist, 5 have licensing laws (restricting the practice of psychological services to licensed psychologists), and 4 have laws which simply restrict a particular professional title. The New York state bill, passed in 1956, has been sanctioned as "model" legislation by the APA Committee on Relations with Psychiatry and by the American Psychiatric Association's Committee on Relations with Psychology. (Copies of the New York bill may be obtained from the APA Central Office.)

In addition to the 25 states with statutory regulation, there are 20 states that have established non-statutory regulation of psychological practice. In these states there is a program of voluntary certification (frequently restricting only the title of *clinical* psychologist or *consulting* psychologist), usually under the auspices of the state psychological association which reviews credentials and supervises special examinations. Table 5 summarizes the status of state regulatory mechanisms as of April, 1963.

There has been wide variation in the amount and form of resistance encountered by psychologists when they have sought state legislation to control professional practice. As each new state joins the list of those with such legal controls, the weight of precedent is increased. It is reasonable to anticipate that within the next ten years a sizeable majority of states will have passed laws regulating the public practice of professional psychology. An agency to assist in the desired goal of general uniformity, particularly with respect to reciprocity between the states, is the American Association of State Psychology Boards, founded in 1962.

7. *Summary*

To paraphrase the psychologist who was quoted in the introduction to this chapter,[1] we now have a *discipline* of clinical psy-

TABLE 5 PROVISION OF STATUTORY AND NON-STATUTORY REGULATION OF THE TITLES AND/OR FUNCTIONS OF PSYCHOLOGISTS (APRIL, 1963)*

Year	Statutory	Non-Statutory**
1945	Connecticut	
1946	Virginia	
1947		
1948	Kentucky	
1949		Ohio
1950		
1951	Georgia, Minnesota	
1952		
1953	Maine, Tennessee	West Virginia
1954		
1955	Arkansas, Washington	Oregon
1956	New York	New Jersey
1957	California, (Florida), Maryland, New Hampshire	Arizona, Illinois, Louisiana Massachusetts, Nebraska Rhode Island***
1958		Missouri
1959	Michigan, Utah	Alabama, North Dakota, Montana***
1960	Alberta, Ontario	Pennsylvania, South Carolina, New Mexico***
1961	Colorado, Florida	South Dakota
1962	Delaware, Quebec, Saskatchewan	Texas
1963	Idaho, Nevada, New Mexico	

* Information provided by Jane Hildreth, Legislative Consultant, APA.
** An approximate chronological order
*** Year of establishment not confirmed.

chology just as we have medicine, law, dentistry, and teaching, and there are a large number of *uniformly trained* clinical psychologists "in the same sense" that there are doctors, lawyers, dentists, and teachers. A visible and viable profession, responsive to social need, has been created and stabilized in the last 15 years. This has been possible because the prototypes of the present clinician invented a program of education and training and criteria of evaluation that have proven generally sound and practical, and because the officers and committees of the APA have provided wise counsel and firm leadership in encouraging the staging and maintenance of these programs.

The specification of standards has covered a great range of particulars, from qualifications of faculty to physical provisions (e.g., office space) for the intern. As is necessarily the case when standards are prescribed for multiple and complex aspects of a program of graduate education and training, certain of the specifications are more readily achievable, and hence acceptable, to a majority of schools or agencies, and others appear objectionable to many persons who must subscribe to them or forego accreditation. The APA and ABEPP, as the chief sources of evaluation to date, have both enunciated and manifested the principle of flexibility. The standards have not been interpreted legalistically, evaluation procedures have not been applied rigidly, and requirements have not been frozen. Experimentation has been and should continue to be encouraged. But the very concept of experimentation, even in education, implies some controls.

Every profession, at all times, stands in need of bold pioneers who will break from the current mold and try out innovations. But, true to the spirit of innovation, and with respect for the welfare of their profession, the pioneers should not attempt to achieve or maintain accreditation, the sign of standardization and of a certain established level of quality, during the period of experimentation.

Some of the potential defects of accreditation have been catalogued. For the sake of accreditation, a weak institution may be tempted to actions that are of questionable academic value for that institution (e.g., gross overemphasis of one program at the cost of others). Approval may encourage mediocrity—the institution which has once achieved accreditation may drift and lack impetus to further growth and strengthening. These are possible but not inevitable weaknesses. "One of the more perplexing philosophical problems is that of insuring quality of performance while permitting and even encouraging diversity . . ."[32]

It may be that the present standards of evaluation do not provide sufficiently for the inherent differences between the academic department's goals for graduate education in research and scholarship and the average clinical student's goals of preparation for a practitioner's career. If this be so, and much evidence suggests this incompatibility, the best solution would appear to be not in alteration of the existing standards for the Ph.D. degree in clinical psychology, but rather in the development of a new and different program of training, leading to a different degree— such a program to have its own, and different, standards of evaluation. It must be understood that the need for new training programs is not simply a function of the inappropriateness or inflexibility of the standards under which our current graduate curricula and professional criteria evolved and are evaluated. If experimental programs yield good results and are deemed worthy of extension as established curricula, they must and will have their own standards and mechanisms of evaluation. In final analysis, standards and accreditation are in the interest of quality and will be formulated and applied whenever it is desired to duplicate a quality product.

References

1. Harrower, Molly R., The Evolution of a clinical psychologist. In Transactions of the First Conference on Training in Clinical Psychology, New York City, March 27-28, 1947. *J. Clin. Psychol. Monog. Suppl. No. 3*, July, 1948, 11-15.
2. Ross, Sherman, APA Approved Programs in Clinical and in Counseling Psychology, 1962. *Amer. Psychol.*, 1962, *17*, 501-502.
3. *1962 Directory*. APA, Washington, D.C.
4. American Board of Examiners in Professional Psychology, Inc. *1962 Annual Report, Amer. Psychol.*, 1962, *17*, 924-926.
5. Hildreth, Jane D., Legislative Consultant, APA, Washington, D.C., April 10, 1963. Personal communication.
6. Moore, Bruce V., Proposed program of professional training in clinical psychology, *J. Consult. Psychol.*, 1943, *7*, 23-26.
7. Shakow, David, Subcommittee report on graduate internship training in psychology. *J. Consult. Psychol.*, 1945, *9*, 243-266.
8. Shakow, David, Recommended graduate training program in clinical psychology. *Amer. Psychol.*, 1947, *2*, 539-558.
9. Raimy, Victor C., ed., *Training in clinical psychology*. New York: Prentice-Hall, Inc., 1950.
10. Sears, Robert R., Graduate training facilities: I. General information, II. Clinical psychology. *Amer. Psychol.*, 1946, *1*, 135-150.
11. Sears, Robert R., Clinical training facilities: 1947. *Amer. Psychol.*, 1947, *2*, 199-205.
12. Moore, Bruce V., Criteria for evaluating training programs in clinical or in counseling psychology. *Amer. Psychol.*, 1958, *13*, 59-60.
13. Stanford, Fillmore H., Summary report on the 1951 annual meeting. *Amer. Psychol.*, 1951, *6*, 583-584.

14. Selden, William K., *Accreditation—A Struggle Over Standards in Higher Education.* New York: Harper, 1960.
15. Roe, Anne, et al., eds., *Graduate education in psychology.* APA, Washington D.C.: 1959.
16. Hobbs, Nicholas, Proceedings of the Sixty-second Annual Business Meeting of the APA, New York, September 4 and 7, 1954. *Amer. Psychol.,* 1954, *9,* 723.
17. Kelly, E. Lowell, Standards for practicum training in clinical psychology: tentative recommendations. *Amer. Psychol.,* 1950, *5,* 594-595.
18. Foster, Austin, Benton, Arthur L., and Rabin, A.I., The internship in clinical psychology: three alternative plans. *Amer. Psychol.,* 1952, *7,* 7-13.
19. Thompson, Clare W., Internship training in clinical psychology. *Amer. Psychol.,* 1954, *9,* 760-764.
20. Internships for Doctoral Training in Clinical Psychology Approved by the APA. *Amer. Psychol.,* 1956, *11,* 710-711.
21. Ross, Sherman, Internships for doctoral training in clinical psychology approved by the APA. *Amer. Psychol.,* 1962, *17,* 571-572.
22. Carter, Launor F., Proceedings of the Sixty-ninth Annual Business Meeting of the APA. *Amer. Psychol.,* 1961, *16,* 768.
23. Kohn, Jr., Nathan, Organization and operation of the American Board for Psychological Services. *Amer. Psychol.,* 1954, *9,* 771-772.
24. Kohn, Jr., Nathan, Report by the American Board for Psychological Services: Purposes, Standards, and Procedures. *Amer. Psychol.,* 1956, *11,* 21-23.
25. Kohn, Jr., Nathan, American Board for Psychological Services, 1955 Annual Report. *Amer. Psychol.,* 1956, *11,* 24.
26. Kelly, Noble H., Sanford, Fillmore H., and Clark, Kenneth E., The meaning of the ABEPP diploma. *Amer. Psychol.,* 1961, *16,* 132-141.
27. Notes: Regulation of psychological counseling and psychotherapy. *Columbia Law Review,* 1951, *51,* 474-495.
28. Gerty, Francis J., Holloway, Jr., J. W., and Mackay, R.P.; Licensure or certification for clinical psychologists. *J.A.M.A.,* 1952, *148,* 271-273.
29. Louisell, David W., The psychologist in today's legal world. *Minnesota Law Review,* 1955, *39,* 235-272.
30. Louisell, David W., The psychologist in today's legal world. *Minnesota Law Review,* 1957, *41,* 731-750.
31. Cook, Stuart W., and Hales, William M., Joint report of the APA and CSPA committees on legislation. *Amer. Psychol.,* 1955, *10,* 727-756.
32. Stuit, Dewey B., Accreditation—its problems and its future. *Teachers College Record,* 1961, *62,* 1-13.

Clinical Psychology Training in the University

GEORGE J. WISCHNER

The graduate training programs in clinical psychology are the primary ones which produce our future generations of clinical psychologists. It is difficult, however, to discuss university training programs in clinical psychology without considering the larger picture of graduate training in psychology. On the one hand the general pattern and setting of graduate education in psychology affects the atmosphere and certain of the specifics of the clinical training program; on the other hand the acceptance by departments of psychology has influenced the broader pattern of graduate education in psychology.

At the *Miami* Conference,[7] which focused not on clinical psychology but on the wider problems of graduate education in the field, Bobbitt, in his opening remarks, stated: "There are several reasons of course why this conference should be held, but the really pressing one is the need to resolve as best we can the difficulties growing out of our dual development as both a science and a profession." It is this development, accelerated particularly since World War II, which led to the adoption of the current scientist-professional training model—a model which attempts to train "the compleat psychologist," scientist, scholar, and professional, within the one traditional Ph.D. degree framework. It is this training model, functioning in its present degree context, which has influenced existing patterns of graduate training and created problems not only in clinical psychology training but in psychology training programs generally.

The ensuing discussion is not based on an analysis of any sampling of university programs. To obtain material other than that available in institution bulletins and catalogues is suprisingly difficult, and these sources, it will be readily agreed, do not capture or communicate the flavor of a departmental training program.

This chapter will depict those general and specific features of graduate training programs in clinical psychology which it is hoped will highlight the typical nature of such programs, the idiosyncratic characteristics of particular programs, and the problems and difficulties encountered and the issues raised by the current trends in training programs. Thus we shall consider not only curriculum characteristics, but also working assumptions and objectives, and even the implications of the general setting in which most programs operate. In this endeavor I can draw directly on only my own experience and vicariously on the experience of others obtained through individual and group discussions, formal conferences, and published proceedings of such conferences.

The setting

The only training avenue available to the student interested in clinical psychology is, for all practical purposes, graduate training, usually in a department of psychology (there are a very few exceptions), leading to the Ph.D. degree. And since the Ph.D. degree is traditionally and properly defined as a scholarly, research degree, departments are located, broadly speaking, within the framework of a graduate school or its equivalent. These facts alone are highly significant for the potential student having strong interests in professional aspects of psychology. The Ph.D. is not a professional degree; it is a scholarly degree with all the rights, privileges, and *requirements* pertaining thereto. These requirements contain certain general features applicable to Ph.D. training anywhere in a particular university and usually include: a) demonstration of some degree of competence in foreign languages, typically French and German, b) a comprehensive examination of some kind which the student may take perhaps at the end of his second or third year of full-time study, c) perhaps the garnering of a Master's degree which may or may not involve a thesis, and d) the Ph.D. dissertation and its defense before a committee. In most instances students are also required to achieve in course work some minimum level of performance, and the comprehensive examination for degree candidacy may be preceded by some preliminary or core screening examination early in graduate study.

The above general statement is not the whole story. In different institutions, psychology programs offering clinical training may be located in, or at least be closely allied with, divisions or programs of social sciences, biological sciences, natural sciences, and schools of education. It is reasonable to assume that such location or association may provide some basis for inferences about the training atmosphere of the department and the intra-university forces to which it is responsive.

In addition to what we may call the primary setting, there may be secondary settings within the university framework which may affect the character of clinical psychology training programs. These may include personality research centers and institutes, child development institutes, university counseling centers, speech pathology and audiology programs, and medical psychology programs. The latter are typically located in departments of psychiatry in medical schools and usually do not grant degrees, although they may cooperate in the clinical psychology training program. The relationships between departments of psychology and these secondary settings can, of course, affect the overall character of a clinical psychology training program.

University psychology training programs are also subject to the influences of external forces which have arisen largely as a result of the development of clinical psychology. These include the outcomes of the several conferences described in Chapter 1, the various evaluation and accreditation agencies which have evolved within the structure of the APA, and state certification and licensure programs. Departments of psychology offering clinical training submit annual reports to the Education and Training Board (E & T Board) of the APA, are visited periodically by the Board's representatives, and are accredited for training in clinical psychology on the basis of such evaluation procedures. It should be observed that the expressed attitude of the Board is not to impose rigid programs on universities. (*See* Chapter 4.)

Training programs cannot help but be influenced in varying degree by such external forces. But at this stage of our development it seems that although departments must take cognizance of those external forces which tend to influence education and training policies, they should not succumb to them or be unduly controlled by them.

Philosophy and objectives of training

The training objectives of the greater number of departments of psychology and the thinking underlying them may be gleaned most appropriately from the *Miami* Conference. This meeting, it will be recalled, was concerned with the overall problems of graduate education in psychology and not with clinical psychology *per se*. Moreover the representation was constituted primarily of heads of departments of psychology. Significantly, when specialty training was considered, it was usually with reference to clinical psychology.

It would appear that most departments emphasize the broadest possible training with heavy stress on training in the research function. Training is oriented almost exclusively toward the doctoral level. Some departments have eliminated the Master's degree as a requirement for the Ph.D. Other departments, which do not admit students interested primarily in a Master's degree, may require attainment of such a degree, requirements for which usually include an experimental thesis as part of doctoral level training.

This general view of graduate education in psychology is in keeping with the recognition, by psychologists in all specialties, of the Ph.D. as one of the important criteria defining the competent psychologist. The *Miami* Conference reaffirmed this and there was virtual unanimity that the Ph.D. is a research degree and is to be retained as such. At the same time, however, the *Miami* group clearly recognized that there are specialties in psychology, and that specialty training had to be carried out within the Ph.D. frame of reference. And so it is that the stated objective of many departments of psychology which offer clinical training is to produce Ph.D.'s prepared for scientific activity (research and teaching) and for professional clinical work. Following are (to some extent paraphrased) excerpts from published statements appearing in university catalogues:

The graduate program in psychology is planned primarily for training at the Ph.D. level. It is designed to prepare psychologists to function effectively as scientific investigators, as college and university teachers, and as professional workers in some areas of psychology.

The graduate program prepares students to engage in the teaching of psychology and in psychological research.

The primary objective of graduate education in the Department of Psychology is to develop doctoral psychologists who are creative scholars; a primary purpose of graduate teaching is to guide students in self-instruction and self-development of scholarly characteristics . . . Every major program of study is designed to develop a purely scientific psychologist or a scientific and professional psychologist.

The Doctoral Courses and program of the Department are planned to prepare students primarily for research and training, and for whatever professional work is necessary as an adjunct to these activities.

Somewhat in contrast to the above, which I believe characterizes by far the greater proportion of graduate psychology programs offering clinical training, is the following which appears to accept more openly the professional training objective within the Ph.D. degree framework:

The clinical psychology program offers a unique approach to education in this field. . . . The curriculum is organized as in a professional school with emphases on the four-fold function of the clinical psychologist: prevention, diagnosis, therapy, and research.

The training objective, then, of most departments of psychology offering clinical training is to produce the Ph.D. scientist-professional. Difficulty arises, I believe, concerning a) the relative weight to be given to these two aspects of training and b) the timing of specialty training, which the *Miami* Conference reported is still essentially unresolved.

Patterns and emphases in training

In so far as graduate training programs in clinical· psychology follow the broad outlines of training developed and recommended by the various conferences (discussed in Chapter 1) they would appear to be highly similar. Yet there are differences in the patterns of training that have emerged which are related to factors previously suggested and which tend to create the atmosphere of a particular department. The deliberate cultivation of such differences presumably would be in accord with the philosophy of flexibility and breadth of training stressed at the earlier conferences and again at *Miami* where there "was strong consensus for a conception of doctoral education in psychology which would make for maximum flexibility in adapting to new problems and opportunities."

Despite the general acceptance of both scholarly and professional graduate training objectives as required by the adoption of the Ph.D. scientist-professional model, many, if not most universities have put the greater weight to the left side of the hyphen. A very few would argue that even within this model the entire emphasis should be on the training of clinician-researchers. It is instructive to note in this connection the comment made by Dr. Robert H. Felix, Director, National Institute of Mental Health, at the *Stanford* Conference: "I want to reiterate the urgency of the adequate training of researchers for the mental health field. No other category of personnel is as desperately needed if we are to achieve a breakthrough in the mental health field."

We may also recall here the correspondence appearing in the *American Psychologist* a few years ago concerning the pros and cons of producing primarily research clinicians in experimental-clinical programs.

It is this emphasis on the production of research clinicians which has led those who would hope for a better training balance within the scientist-professional model to say (as I have heard them at various conferences) that for many departments, clinical training, although accepted as a responsibility, is viewed as something that interferes with traditional Ph.D. training and as something appended to the doctoral program. In far fewer settings has there been given at least equal weight to both sides of the hyphen and it is the rare department that goes on record as giving more emphasis to professional than scholarly training objectives. It should be noted perhaps that in an occasional setting there has been emphasis on a particular specialization phase within clinical psychology itself, for example, training for the psychotherapy function.

Correlated with these different patterns and emphases are other departmental behaviors which reflect the attitudes and create the atmosphere of a training program. The *Shakow*[2] Report stressed that throughout the training program both academic and clinical training should be combined, that both academic and field persons should be involved, and that students should have contact with clinical material throughout training, beginning with the first year. The degree to which departments pursue such a course varies widely. In some settings the student in the early part of his training may have little or no contact with substantive courses related to clinical psychology and even less opportunity for contact with case material. This sometimes is due to local conditions but often it would appear to be by design, and operationally reflects the prevailing atmosphere with respect to the clinical program. Some departments give token recognition to the implications of these recommendations by including in the first year a course or exposure to personality theories, an area, incidentally, which for some reason is to be found anyway in most listings of so-called core curricula. And again the rare department may follow literally the recommendations of the *Shakow* Report.

Some specifics of graduate training programs

Admission requirements and selection of students. There are typically more applicants for admission to a particular institution than will be accepted; and departmental requirements often exceed the minimum stated by the institution as a whole. Most departments specify at least a B average in undergraduate study, a record of performance on one or more tests such as the Miller Analogies Test or Graduate Record Examination, and letters of recommendation, preferably from psychology professors. Departments usually have an admissions committee with which the student can correspond directly concerning more specific requirements.

A few words might be said about the undergraduate preparation of the student planning to go on in psychology. As a rule departments give preference to a student with a broad background over one who has taken every psychology course in the catalogue at the expense of other areas. In my experience special weight is given to work in mathematics and the biological and physical sciences. This suggests that the student who has not majored in psychology as an undergraduate should not necessarily be discouraged from applying for graduate study in this field. Such students however should plan to have as a minimum in psychology the introductory course, statistics, experimental psychology, and perhaps a course in the psychology of learning.

What has been stated so far applies to all applicants. Are there additional criteria for admission for those who at the time of application indicate a specialization interest such as clinical psychology? (Most students who go on to specialize in clinical psychology do, in fact, indicate this specialization at the time of application. Such initial expression of interest becomes a determiner of both the kind of appointment the admitted student may be offered and the faculty advisor to whom he may be assigned. This, in turn, serves to reinforce the originally stated preference even though that preference be based on inadequate knowledge of an area of specialization.) In answer to our question, I would say that if there are additional criteria these are at best applied informally. In the case of students who initially profess an interest in clinical psychology, a personal interview would appear to be highly desirable. A few departments located in institutions in large metropolitan areas actually require a personal interview with students interested in clinical psychology. This procedure is obviously not feasible in all instances. Recent experience suggests that more and more applicants in all areas request personal interviews and arrange at their own expense to travel relatively long distances from their home to the institution for such a purpose. Observation would suggest the value of personal interviews for all graduate students and not only for those leaning toward clinical psychology.

We tend then to use the same broad criteria for selecting all students for graduate work in psychology despite the fact that they bring different attitudes, different general interest patterns, and from the very beginning in most cases different specialization orientations. This is in line with the prevailing general objectives and philosophy of training. We do train broad-based psychologists first, and specialists second. Moreover, most departments are interested primarily in the prospective clinical student who shows research potential and not merely an interest in, or even a history of, successful application of clinical skills.

The curriculum in general. In contrast to both the *Shakow* and *Boulder* reports which attempted to spell out in some detail the fields of study that should be covered to produce the broadly trained psychologist, the *Stanford* and *Miami* reports avoided specificity. At *Miami* it was agreed that there is a common core, but it was also agreed, somewhat paradoxically, that this core should not be specified lest we discourage departmental ingenuity and creativity in setting up training programs; at *Stanford,* it was felt that each department should be free to organize its curriculum in terms of its own program needs and capabilities.

Most programs incorporate the concept of a core curriculum either by way of requiring a set of specific courses or a pro-seminar of some kind of all students, typically during the first calendar year of graduate study. Although there is variation from program to program, the topics or courses comprising the so-called core include some combination of the following: measurement, statistics and research design, experimental psychology (most often with emphasis on learning), personality theory, history, and physiological psychology. The variations that appear in core curricula probably reflect at least in part a particular emphasis in a department. For example, a department may place stress on physiological psychology, or on mathematical models, or on social psychology. It is customary to administer a core comprehensive examination at the end of the first year primarily for initial screening purposes.

It is my impression that, beyond the core, the general trend is to minimize required courses. For the clinical psychology student, however, there are usually additional requirements including substantive courses and practicum training at various levels. These include courses or exposure to psychological evaluation sequences, behavior disorders, special research courses, and supervised practicum experience either within or outside of the departmental framework. Because of the structure of compre-

hensive examinations for doctoral candidacy, it is not atypical
for the clinical psychology student to take practically all the
courses taken by other students and in addition to have to complete the special clinical requirements.

Practicum training. We are concerned here, not with the
internship which generally occurs after admission to doctoral
candidacy, but with the prior practicum training required by
and under the more direct control of a department. The nature
and extensiveness of such a requirement probably varies over a
wide range from one department to another and reflects the
operation of such factors as training philosophies, staff capabilities, and availability of practicum facilities.

One level of such training usually occurs as part of the psychological evaluation or diagnostic testing courses which typically have a "lab" associated with them. This involves experience
with various test instruments under intensive supervision and
hopefully with a wide variety of subjects. Under optimal conditions the student may gain experience not only with his fellow
students but also with children in local school systems and even
with various adult and child clients in community hospitals and
clinics.

In addition to such courses, students may be required at
another level to enroll for practicum training for which they are
given credits and grades. Now, perhaps for the first time, the
student functions in a professional manner in a professional setting which provides psychological services to real clients. These
settings may include department clinics, other university clinics,
and non-university agencies.

In my experience a good way of providing this level of training is through a psychological clinic operating within the department of psychology as an integral part of the graduate training
program. The emphasis in such a clinic is on the training function, although it may be possible, depending upon the size of
the operation, the community, and the interests of individual
faculty members, to develop an appropriate research function
as well. Although the primary function of the clinic is to help
implement the training objectives of the clinical program, the
professional character and obligations of such a training clinic
must be recognized. It does provide a real service to real clients

and requires appropriate professional full-time and part-time staff, including a psychiatrist, who participates in didactic training, staff conferences, and even student supervision.

The professional staff of such a clinic usually includes regular faculty members identified with the clinical program who, in addition to all of their other duties and activities, supervise students enrolled for clinic practicum. In settings with which I am familiar, such faculty persons usually supervise not more than two trainees at any given time. There seems to be a reluctance in some academic quarters to recognize that practicum supervision is as important and as much a legitimate teaching-training function as is the teaching of more conventional courses. Problems often arise concerning the amount of teaching credit to be given to faculty who engage in practicum training. It can be readily demonstrated that intensive supervision of one or two students requires as much, if not more time, than teaching a course.

In our program clinical students are required to enroll for a minimum of 6 credits (two trimesters) in the Practicum in Psychological Clinic course associated with the department clinic. The requirement applies to all students including those who may have had previous clinical training or experience or those currently in some kind of training situation, such as the VA Psychology Training Program or other university or community agency programs. There is a tendency, I think, for some community settings to be less than eager to cooperate in training at this level. Their total program, preference, and financial resources for trainee support are geared more toward the advanced internship level of training.

In my view then, commitment to a clinical training objective should involve commitment to the development and support of a clinical facility which is under the control of the departmental training program and through which the clinical student may achieve some degree of professional as well as academic identification with faculty members.

The internship. This is included here since it is generally viewed as an integral part of the Ph.D. training of the clinical student. Early conferences had established, as a requirement for the Ph.D. with specialization in clinical psychology, the equivalent of a year of internship in an appropriate setting. This typically has occurred predoctorally and subsequent to the equivalent of admission to doctoral candidacy. The predoctorally completed internship has become one of the important criteria for APA accreditation of a departmental clinical training program. Most institutions have incorporated this requirement, albeit in some cases, grudgingly. It is on the issue of the timing of the internship that problems of training and accreditation have resulted. At the *Miami* Conference the proposition that the internship should be only predoctoral was indecisive; that it be only postdoctoral was rejected. It is significant that there is at present a strong move to make the postdoctoral internship the acceptable pattern. At the *Miami* Conference discussion led to an *ad hoc* committee proposal of a two year postdoctoral internship. The clinically oriented student would graduate with a Ph.D. with an emphasis, perhaps, in the personality and behavior disorders areas, but would not fulfill the requirements for clinical psychologist until the internship has been completed postdoctorally. The pros and cons of such an important change in pattern of training are discussed in Chapter 4. With regard to the problem of how to control the student's (and society's) behavior once he has the Ph.D., the departments of psychology certainly would have a far easier time if the internship occurred after the completion of the Ph.D. degree.

Currently, most clinical students complete their internship predoctorally in an agency approved by their departments. These agencies are most often outside the department framework and may be geographically distant from the university. It may be noted that the APA has developed a program for accrediting internship agencies and the accreditation status of an agency may be a factor in its selection for internship training. (*See* Appendix C.)

It is fortunate when a university and suitable internship settings are located in close proximity. This enhances communication between the department and agency and enables better integration of the student's university and internship activities. A perennial problem in clinical training has been the lack of cooperation and interaction between the university and field agency. Although geographical factors should not be important determinants of the selection of an internship setting, it is our experience that they do play a role. Most students, particularly those who are married and have children, prefer if possible to remain in the university area and to take their internship in acceptable community settings. It is not always easy to spell out to the student the advantages of moving several hundred miles to an internship setting with which neither he nor his advisor is well acquainted. Obviously each of us has pet internship settings with which we are familiar and toward which we try to direct our pet students. But it is becoming increasingly difficult to know very much about many settings beyond what is contained in brochures that reach the departments in increasing numbers every year. There is a reluctance on the part of both the department and student to select a distant center particularly when the student is in the early stages of his dissertation. Many of my colleagues prefer that a student be well along with the dissertation before he embarks on an internship program, a view that is consistent with departmental objectives and with the move to push the internship to the postdoctoral level. But this view minimizes the possibility, thought to be highly desirable by some of us, that a problem important for the dissertation might be suggested by the internship experience.

Another factor influencing student preference for an internship center is the development of a special interest, for example, a desire to work with children rather than adults. Such students will then seek an internship at a children's hospital or child guidance center. In view of the widely held view that practicum training should be broad and involve exposure to a wide range of clinical material it is worth noting that the APA has recently adopted a classification of agencies which indicates the generality or specificity of the training offered and has seen fit to approve both kinds of settings.[7] At present there is no adequate basis for judging the relative effectiveness of the two kinds of internship experiences.

Research training. Specialized research training is considered in detail in Chapter 9. But some comment about research training as part of the total Ph.D. experience seems appropriate here.

Albee argues that only by training research personnel can we hope to achieve significant advances in the mental health area. He states: ". . . in view of both the manpower picture and pure logic I would underline the necessity of making the painful decision to concentrate on training research personnel rather than treatment personnel . . . only by research can we achieve our goal of reducing suffering. Attempts to solve the problem of mental disorder through approaches based on one-to-one, face-to-face relationships, however moral and admirable, are simply not sensible from our manpower point of view."[1]

This view is in accord with the research sentiments expressed at the *Miami* Conference. But Albee himself feels that "most winds seem to be blowing in the other direction!" He also cites evidence suggesting that only a very small fraction of clinical psychologists engage in research activity to any considerable degree. (This probably holds for other psychologists as well.) Can this be reconciled with the research emphasis in graduate training?

A department of psychology attempts to implement its research training objectives by various means, informal and formal. It strives to provide an appropriate model and atmosphere by developing a faculty in all areas which is actively engaged in research. It encourages or may even require that all students participate in some research from the moment of their arrival on the graduate scene. Recognition of the need for specialized research training for the clinical student beyond the common core is indicated in some programs by the inclusion of a laboratory course in the personality area. The Ph.D. dissertation and the Master's thesis (where the corresponding degree is offered) constitute the more formal research training experiences of the graduate student.

The appropriateness of various facets of departmental research training for the clinical student has been questioned. For example, Cook[5] questions some of our research training methods which often are centered around areas not closely related to the immediate interests and activities of the clinical student. Tryon[10] believes the Ph.D. dissertation ritual is an enterprise that defeats many graduate students. ". . . most graduate curricula and research are designed to fulfill the false image that all graduate students will in due course become 'pure' scientists and scholars." In his keynote address to the *Princeton* Conference, Schofield[8] evaluated the dissertation as "an experience which is least attractive, least stimulating, least productive, and least satisfying for a majority of students."

There is justification for this kind of criticism of our research training efforts and an awareness of the problem was evident at the *Miami* Conference which, it will be recalled, favored a broader definition of "research" and modification of the criteria defining an acceptable dissertation. We should more systematically evaluate our training programs and procedures in an endeavor to determine how we can make the research experiences of the clinical (and other) student more acceptable and meaningful, not because we need to cater to the student, but because we need to maximize the number of our graduates who may eventually make a research contribution.

Various conferences have stressed the need for university-field cooperation in research training, including research for the dissertation. As a working principle this is highly acceptable. Unfortunately many field-agency personnel are not interested in doing research, or feel that this is the university's job, or their research staff and facilities are not adequate. I venture to suggest: if some departments of psychology were more acceptant of the professional training objectives in the scientist-professional model and if more field agencies developed and implemented, as part of their practicum training programs, appropriate research objectives, the basis of some of the current discord would vanish.

Training for psychotherapy. Many clinical students come to graduate study with a strong interest in the practice of psychotherapy and with the assumption that the Ph.D. degree will qualify them for this function. The assumption is wrong. Most programs provide only minimal exposure to psychotherapy in any form and certainly not with the objective of producing psychotherapists. Even in departments where there may be relatively strong acceptance of such an objective it is recognized that the Ph.D. program does not permit adequate preparation for the psychotherapy function. Only through postdoctoral training can adequate competence be developed for the practice of therapy. This is the general view, expressed, too, at the various training conferences.

In our own program, for example, there are currently only two formal courses in psychotherapy, an introductory course and a seminar. The special interest of a clinical faculty member recently has led to the introduction of a practicum-type course in group play therapy for children. As part of the required Practicum in Psychological Clinic, referred to previously, the student carries one or two cases in therapy at any given time. But when and whether a therapy case should be assigned to a particular student is dependent upon the judgment of the clinic staff, including the consulting psychiatrist. Students may gain additional psychotherapy training by registering for additional practicum for this express purpose. As part of their internship training, students may obtain additional psychotherapy experience, but the amount and kind of such training undoubtedly varies with the setting. It is evident that students interested in psychotherapy must plan seriously for postdoctoral training in this area.

Thus far we have been commenting on training for the practice of psychotherapy. What about training for research in this very complex field? It might be argued that only the person with substantial psychotherapy experience is equipped to do research on the important aspects of the psychotherapeutic interaction. But there are all kinds of research problems which can be tackled by the predoctoral student and certainly by the student who has attained the Ph.D. degree. The point I wish to make is that the relatively limited training in psychotherapy provided in our Ph.D. programs is not necessarily incompatible with encouraging students to engage in research on problems related to psychotherapy or with the expectation that they can make a research contribution in this area.

Support for graduate clinical programs (and students)

Specific programs of support for university clinical psychology training programs are described in other chapters of this volume. I should like, however, to comment on certain aspects of such support which seem related to the purposes of this chapter. It is significant that the amount of support currently available insures some kind of assistance for practically all students. In our own program it is the exception for a student in the clinical program not to have some kind of appointment. These include VA and USPHS traineeships and also departmental graduate and research assistantships. The latter are usually associated with grant-supported research projects of individual faculty members. Most students consequently spend part of their time, typically half-time, in formal graduate study and half-time on some type of appointment. The exception is the USPHS trainee who is supported on a full-time basis—the only student who generally meets the older, literal definition of "full time." In most institutions and for various organizational record-keeping purposes, students who divide their time equally between an appointment and formal graduate study are tallied as full-time students. This situation has tended to some extent to confuse both departmental and student planning and thinking. I have the impression that curriculum planning, for example, often does not adequately take into account the half-time commitment of most students. There is a reluctance to realize that the half-time registrant literally should take double the time required by the full-time student to complete the Ph.D. degree. If it is assumed that a full-time clinical student normally should take three years plus one year for the internship, it seems reasonable that the half-time student should require seven years. Actually our clinical students (including the half-time-full-time student) complete the Ph.D. in substantially less time than this. Most program planning is oriented toward this student, and consequently there has been a tendency to omit certain items from his program or to revise and compress the calendar of critical events.

I should like to suggest that programs of assistance for clinical psychology training be designed to support graduate students on a full-time basis for at least the first year without any obligation on the part of the student. This does not mean of course that an appropriate training program should not be planned for him by the department. The USPHS training grant program in clinical psychology of course does exactly this and more. The VA psychology training program has recently moved a bit in this direction. The beginning VA trainee now can be appointed on a stipend basis which guarantees a fixed sum for a 12-month period and for which the student is required to log only a minimum number of trainee hours. I believe many current problems in clinical training could be alleviated if as many students as possible could have full-time support and thus be able to pursue a full curriculum for at least the first and preferably for the first two years of graduate study.

It seems clear that the various kinds of programs of assistance available for graduate training in clinical psychology are competitive in nature. As a consequence they differ in the amount of support for students and the obligations expected from them. In my judgment it would be highly desirable to centralize and standardize the amount of support for all graduate students at various levels regardless of the original source of support. This would increase the flexibility of graduate programs and tend to eliminate the intrusion of irrelevant considerations in assigning and re-assigning students to different programs at various stages of graduate study. The implementation of such a step involving different agencies with varying programs of support is not easy— and perhaps the whole idea is unrealistic. But serious thought should be given to the possibility of integrating and standardizing the programs of the different agencies currently supporting graduate training in clinical psychology.

The clinical faculty

I should like first to comment on the full-time academic clinical psychologist and then to consider the part-time utilization, in graduate clinical programs, of psychologists functioning primarily in professional community settings.

The full-time university clinical psychologist, just like the clinical graduate student, is selected primarily for his research potential or research history. He is not selected, typically, for his clinical experience or even for his teaching (including his clinical supervisory) capabilities. In view of this assertion, it is of interest to note the general character of descriptions of university clinical staff openings. These usually indicate the need for an individual whose responsibilities would include, among other things, teaching a formal course or two in the clinical area, participating in the practicum supervision of clinical graduate students, and supervising the research of such students. Occasionally, a particular kind of clinical experience, for example, experience in clinical child psychology, may be indicated. Although a person with clinical experience is preferred, a solid new Ph.D. will also be considered.

The level of a position often may result in the appointment of a new Ph.D., an occurrence which is of some interest in relation to the concern expressed at the *Miami* Conference about the utilization of new Ph.D.'s as intern supervisors in practicum agencies. It is not infrequent for the new clinical graduate, who often has little clinical experience beyond his internship, to have immediate responsibility for the practicum supervision of clinical students in the university setting. That the *Miami* participants were aware of this state of affairs is evident in the following statement:

". . . One of the reasons for the few points of contact between clinical and its so-called basic area of psychology is in the composition of our clinical faculties. Usually they are administrators who spend too little time in clinical activity themselves or we have on the clinical staff people who have recently received their Ph.D.'s after one year of internship and they become the imparters of clinical wisdom to this generation of students." [6] (*See* p. 58 of the report.)

There are instances, of course, when a department is fortunate in being able to add to its full-time clinical faculty persons with a good history of clinical field experience, persons who in fact may come directly from a professional clinical setting. For many departments, it is probably of greater significance that such individuals have a research bibliography as well. The new appointees initially may have a reasonable interest in pursuing clinical activities and clinical teaching within a departmental program. For a variety of reasons, they perceive an academic appointment as an opportunity not only to function as clinicians on a part-time basis in what is viewed as a preferred setting, but also to engage in teaching, either of a didactic or clinical nature. Assumed prestige factors and academic value systems acquired as graduate students probably play a role in such preference. It is likely that individuals with clinical interests who prefer academic environments for their expression and satisfaction are basically more like their non-clinical academic colleagues than they are like their non-academic clinical colleagues. In any event, the university clinical psychologist may soon find himself caught in a net of diverse activities and academic pressures, and be subjected to a system of reinforcements which tend increasingly to divert him from professional activities within the departmental program. It is ironical that this same person may pursue professional activities on a part-time private practice or consulting basis outside of and unrelated to the departmental framework.

I would like to suggest here, that sincere acceptance of a clinical training objective, even within the scientist-professional Ph.D. model, requires that clinical faculty be accorded recognition and rewards by their universities for departmental clinical teaching and clinical activities equal to the rewards accorded to other teaching and research activities engaged in by both clinical and non-clinical faculty.

I should like to consider now the integration within departmental programs of professional clinical psychologists functioning in community settings. But first let me emphasize my view that good graduate programs are those based primarily on the development of an active full-time faculty, and that they must be internally strong. Having achieved this stage of growth, a department may well consider the role of community persons who can contribute to the implementation of certain of its educational objectives.

At *Miami* it was proposed "that universities consider making fuller use of practitioners as additional faculty members under conditions which would insure the practitioner's genuine participation in the educational process." This proposal was offered in the context of a discussion of research training which emphasized an apprenticeship relation as representing the most fruitful kind of research training atmosphere. But it was also suggested that the addition of the practitioner faculty member "might also make possible his taking students into an apprenticeship relation in his own professional activity."

The extent to which a department may make use of professional psychologists in the community is a function of a number of factors, including its own level of development and strengths, community resources, and even the specific persons involved. For some departments it would be very difficult to obtain or even recommend academic rank for professional persons who have no research histories.

I should like to suggest that there may be a more basic consideration here, one that extends beyond the field of psychology; and that is the nature of the relationship between academic departments and professional agencies, the attitudes held toward each other by academic persons in various disciplines and their professional counterparts in the non-academic community. Intriguing in this connection is the following sentence quoted by Anne Roe in her review of the recent volume by Strauss and Rainwater, *The Professional Scientist: A Study of American Chemists*:

"As the post war history of psychology has demonstrated, tensions develop when academicians are reluctant to legitimize the work of colleagues outside the universities—unless they themselves can retain secure control over the training and work." *Contemporary Psychology*, 1963, *8*, 326.)

Is one to attach special significance to the fact that in a book about chemists it is deemed fitting to make this point by specific reference to psychology?

Our medical friends interestingly enough are also confronted with this issue despite the fact that their education occurs within the framework of a professional school. The following is taken from the recent presidential address by C. H. Hardin Branch to the American Psychiatric Association:

"As to the university centers, it has always been a problem to try to achieve an adequate relationship between the faculties of the colleges of medicine and the practitioners in the community. The goals of the two groups are not often the same . . . Instruction is often given by individuals who have not themselves had the experience of making a living in the practice of medicine and whose explicit interests even within their specialties may equip the student to deal at a high academic level with rather exotic conditions, but provide him with no practical experience in the management of the run-of-the-mill patients who come to his office." [4] (*See* p. 585-6.)

If there indeed exists a basic incompatibility between academic persons and their non-academic counterparts in the disciplines and even in the professions, is it at all surprising that a major unsolved problem, which has plagued all of our psychology conferences on graduate education, has been the coordination between universities and field agencies, the integration of theory and practice? When stated in these terms, I don't think we really come to grips with what may be the more fundamental problem— the role of professional education within the Ph.D. framework, the extent to which we are willing to accept, in psychology, the professionalization of the Ph.D. degree. That this problem is not unique to psychology is clear from Berelson's[3] discussion of the serious issues and impasses that are accompanying "the mutual infiltration of academic and professional fields within the university."

Many of us can point to quite excellent working relationships that have been developed between specific university psychology programs or specific university persons and particular field agencies or people. But focusing attention on such instances, or reiterating, as we have, that there is a need for more and better cooperation between university and field setting, does not strike at the foundation problem of professionalization in all of its aspects. Interactions between university and field can operate at various levels and in varying degree and do not necessarily suggest adequate integration of programs of graduate education developed independently by university departments and training programs developed independently by field agencies in which we place our students.

Returning now to more specific consideration of departmental utilization of professional persons, I perceive no necessary incompatibility between a strong research orientation in a graduate clinical program and the addition, as part-time faculty, of professional community persons. I find it increasingly difficult to see how we can accept the scientist-professional model and fail to consider the advantages of integrating, within an academic clinical program, the professional attitudes, skills, and knowledge of those who view as their primary function the professional practice of psychology.

I am not saying that graduate education in clinical psychology, or in any graduate area, can be based on the part-time utilization of community persons. I am saying that an already strong clinical program, purporting to operate within the current scientist-professional education model in psychology, may be enhanced by the integration of such individuals in the total education process.

Concluding commentary

For some fifteen years now, most of our academic clinical psychology programs, influenced in varying degree by the patterns of education suggested by the *Shakow* and *Boulder* reports, have attempted to select, educate, and train the scientist-professional, with the Ph.D. degree as the badge of competence. We have assumed that we can take students with diverse motivational and interest patterns, somehow judge which of them offer the greatest research promise, and cast them into the same mold, a mold which would produce them in our own image. We have clung to the objective of turning out clinician-researchers rather than clinical-professionals, despite the evidence that this objective, desirable as it may be, has not been adequately achieved, or at best has probably been achieved inefficiently. Its pursuit, I venture to say, may even have had the unfortunate effect of formalizing and strait-jacketing our non-clinical Ph.D. programs, a possibility which merits serious consideration.

It is difficult, of course, to evaluate the success of our approach thus far. Perhaps it may eventually turn out to be the best one we could have adopted. Nevertheless there are increasing signs of restlessness, uncertainty, and dissatisfaction with the present clinical training model on the part of both clinical and non-clinical faculty. Only recently has the latter group begun to feel more directly the potential impact on graduate education in psychology of some of the less predictable ramifications of our clinical training efforts.

There seems to be developing increased acceptance of the desirability of experimentation and innovation even to the point of considering new programs geared more frankly to the training of professional clinical psychologists. In short, there seems to be a growing awareness of the urgent need to face squarely the issue of professionalization in the field.

That professional education can be accomodated within a graduate school framework has become acceptable to some educators. Recently I had the opportunity to hear Dr. Bryce Crawford, Dean of the Graduate School, University of Minnesota, and Chairman, Council of Graduate Schools in the United States, address a group representing a field closely allied to psychology, on the matter of professionalization in graduate education. Dr. Crawford's paper is to be published, and since my comments are based on notes, I would not want to hold him responsible for them. To me, he seemed to be making the following significant points: a) professional education is a highly responsible and necessary part of many facets of graduate education, b) professional programs are acceptable within a graduate school framework and need not necessarily emphasize a research component, c) professional and scholarly components of graduate education are not mutually exclusive, yet they are sufficiently different and not necessarily preparatory to one another, d) there is a danger of freezing scholarly education conjoined with professional education (here Dr. Crawford made specific reference to a recent issue in psychology), e) professional education needs to be based on a knowledge of the relevant underlying disciplines.

In relation to the last point, it is significant to recall Berelson's[3] observation of the mutual infiltration of academic and professional programs. The latter are incorporating more academic material and academic personnel. There is increasing realization by many established professional schools that broad, discipline-based training is the most desirable. In psychology, this proposition has been fundamental in the graduate training of all psychologists. The assumption that frankly professional psychology programs must necessarily be diluted and oriented toward technology seems unwarranted.

There is no implication here that we water down the Ph.D. degree, that we reduce our research training efforts. If anything, the intent is that we decontaminate the present degree program that has resulted. The plea here is for a reappraisal of the academic and professional components in graduate education. There is a need for the open acceptance of training for the professional component in clinical psychology and experimenting with different kinds of programs, and different settings and atmospheres within which to accomplish such training.

With respect to the implementation of such innovation I tend to agree with Tryon and can do no better than to conclude with the statement of his position.

"Finally, it is unlikely that any particular department of psychology is likely, alone, to take a forward step in the directions indicated in this paper. The obvious solution is for the American Psychological Association as a body to face this issue of professionalization and, working with some of the leading universities, come up with a mature plan for professional training that everyone could be proud of. At the planning stage not only should the deliberations include psychologists, but also deans of leading graduate schools. If psychologists and university officials will work together in setting up standards for excellent graduate training in academic as well as in professional psychology, the result will be a masterful boon, not only for psychology but also for those other disciplines which confront the same problem of professionalization but have been just as reluctant to face it as has psychology."[10] (*See* p. 143.)

References

1. Albee, G. W., American psychology in the sixties. *Amer. Psychol.*, 1963, *18*, 90-95.
2. American Psychological Association, Committee on Training in Clinical Psychology, Recommended graduate training program in clinical psychology. *Amer. Psychol.*, 1947, *2*, 539-558.
3. Berelson, B., *Graduate education in the United States.* New York: McGraw-Hill, 1960.
4. Branch, C. H., Preparedness for progress. *Amer. Psychol.*, 1963, *18*, 581-588.
5. Cook, S. W., The psychologist of the future: scientist, professional or both. *Amer. Psychol.*, 1958, *13*, 635-644.
6. Roe Anne, et al. eds., *Graduate education in psychology.* Washington, D.C.: APA, 1959.
7. Ross, S., Internships for doctoral training in clinical psychology approved by the APA. *Amer. Psychol.*, 1963, *18*, 660-662.
8. Schofield, W., Logistics in professional psychology. *Manpower and psychology: joint responsibilities of states and universities.* H. P. David and L. Blank, eds. Washington, D.C.: Government Printing Office, 1963.
9. Strother, C. R., ed., *Psychology and mental health.* Washington, D.C.: APA, 1956.
10. Tryon, R. C., Psychology in flux: the academic-professional bipolarity. *Amer. Psychol.*, 1963, *18*, 134-143.

6

Postdoctoral Professional Training: How and Why?

MARTIN MAYMAN

Out of the ferment of recent discussions and publications, one fact which has emerged clearly is that postdoctoral training in some form is here to stay. It has been gaining ever wider attention as a desirable, perhaps even necessary phase in the development of the clinical psychologist. Consider, for example, some of these signs of the times.

1. Ten years ago formal postdoctoral clinical training (as distinct from on-the-job training) was available at only 3 clinical training centers; today there are 19 such programs in which post-doctoral clinical fellows are in training at all times, and 10 other programs which offer this training intermittently. In addition, as many as 40 universities offer postdoctoral training fellowships, almost all of these in research.

2. Although the total number of people trained in these programs has been small—no more than a hundred each year—this number represents only a fraction of large numbers of clinical psychologists interested in such advanced training opportunities. Take for example the interest shown in postdoctoral training opportunities at one of these training centers. Inquiries have averaged 50 a year, and applications were filed by an additional 15 a year, for the two to four fellowships available. Moreover, the applicants to these advanced programs are by no means limited to those psychologists who are likely to feel most in need of more training, those who are freshly out of graduate school or those from sub-standard graduate programs. More than half the applicants to this program had two or more years of clinical experience behind them; almost a fourth of them were two or

140

more years beyond their doctorate; and seven out of ten were graduates of APA-approved clinical programs. I might add that to complete one of the application forms for this program is sufficiently tedious and time consuming an undertaking as to eliminate people only casually interested in seeking further training.

3. The rapid spread of postdoctoral training is but one expression of the proliferating interest in problems of clinical training in general, an interest reflected in the growing number of papers concerned largely or exclusively with matters of training which have appeared in the journals and in our convention programs. A not-too-exhaustive survey of the literature from 1955 to the present yields the total of 81 published papers, 30 brief communications, 23 symposia, 7 books—in all, 223 titles concerned with graduate and postgraduate training in just nine years. And by far the largest part of these have appeared in the past five years. (A topical bibliography on clinical training concludes this chapter.)

4. Consider, too, such recent developments as the *Miami* Conference;[12] the concern of the recently organized Corresponding Committee of Fifty with problems of training; the plan for a national conference on training in clinical psychology presented to the Executive Committee of Division 12 by the Corresponding Committee of Fifty; and the recent appointment by Division 12 of a Committee on Training to guide university practicum programs and the E & T Board in their efforts to maintain and improve the quality of clinical training. We can say with assurance that "ferment" and "change" appropriately describe the state of clinical training today.

Inadequacy of predoctoral training

We have no accurate count available on how many psychologists seek and obtain for themselves some form of postdoctoral training, but the number must be far greater than one would at first suspect. Lubin[11] found, for example, that of the 72% of psychologists who responded to a random sampling survey by mail, over one-half stated that most of their training in adult psychotherapy occurred at the postdoctoral level, for many of them in formal training programs in psychotherapy. Postdoctoral training in diagnostic testing and clinical research may be less common, but again the figures would probably prove to be far greater than one would anticipate.

The reason for this thirst for more training is not hard to surmise. Large numbers of clinical psychologists simply do not feel that graduate school prepares one to take on the responsibilities of independent clinical practice. Consider, for example, the dissatisfaction with current clinical training reflected in the more than 1000 responses of Division 12 members to Kelly's survey on the practice of clinical psychology: 57% were in favor of creating a wholly new type of professional school for clinical psychologists, and 40% favored the development of a new course of graduate training leading to a degree other than the Ph.D.[9]

A number of criticisms of predoctoral clinical training figure in this general dissatisfaction. One is that not enough time is devoted to the more clinical aspects of training. Little,[5] after several years with the Standards and Training Branch of the NIMH, observed that, "The conception of clinical training appears to have changed somewhat in the universities . . . (The trend is) to reduce clinical field training to a minimum. The acquisition and exercise of clinical skills is more entrusted to the internship training centers, to be achieved in a very limited period of time." Moreover, the field training is too often fragmented and superficial. Garmezy,[5] who like Little had an excellent vantage point from which to observe trends in clinical training while he was with the Standards and Training Branch of NIMH, summarized his impressions of predoctoral internship training as follows: "Fifty percent of all clinical psychology Ph.D. graduates who hold NIMH traineeships did not take a full-time year of predoctoral internship. Many of these students had what I would term a 'pseudo'-year—compounded of bits and pieces of practicum training." This impression is emphatically supported by the parallel findings of Blank and David.[1] Perhaps it is to such deficiencies in training that we owe the disaffection which Kelly and Goldberg[10] found so widespread among clinicians ten years after they first went into graduate clinical training: 50% of them no longer believed in what they were doing and said they would choose some vocation other than clinical psychology if they had it to do over again.

Fine[3] points to a third deficiency in predoctoral clinical training, and speaks for many of his colleagues when he suggests that "This dissatisfaction reflects the kind of mediocre training clinicians underwent. Training programs at many universities are still largely inadequate, with poorly trained clinicians running them who, themselves, have had a bare minimum of clinical skills and experience. What right do we have to proclaim our maturity (as a profession) when our training, many times, is unrelated to the types of service or research positions that a clinician may seek or want?"

One could more easily reconcile himself to such criticisms of graduate training if it were really necessary to sacrifice good clinical training in the interest of sound research training. But many clinicians take an equally dim view of the preparation of clinical students to do meaningful clinical research. Too often in graduate training, rigorous methodology is vaunted at the expense of meaningful inquiry. 'What is detrimental to the best development of clinical psychology is the idea so widely held that once the student has an understanding of experimentation, research and theory construction, the clinical skills can be picked up anywhere. It is either unrecognized or denied that to be able to do meaningful clinical research one must also learn to be clinical." [15] Or: "We know all about theories . . . we know all about research methods, and are, by and large, decidedly rigorous research technicians. But we tend to utilize our methodological skill in attacking 'safe' and conventional problems. We appear to have a real fear of grappling with the new and unconventional. We are incisive critics, and are, I believe, much more adept than most professions in tearing a research report into shreds and tatters. So expert are we at this sport, that many a researcher shrinks in fear from committing his work to paper, where it will immediately be vulnerable to the kind of attack he has himself launched against others. It seems all too often true that we can analyze but not construct, criticize but not build, categorize but not create." [13]

It is little wonder, therefore, that we find many indications of a search for further training following the completion of a predoctoral clinical training program. Even a good internship of one or two years could hardly provide more than a beginning for the development of a sound, effectively implemented professional identity. It is all too soon that trainees are sent out on their own to provide for themselves whatever else they may need in the way of further professional training.

Reexamination of clinical training needed

A re-examination of clinical training at both predoctoral and postdoctoral levels seems vital for the future of the profession. Just such a re-examination is due to take place at the Conference on Clinical Training which will be convened in 1965 under Division 12 auspices. Further clarification of the pertinent issues may come from surveys such as that being carried out by the Committee on Standards of Training of the Illinois Psychological Association* which has set about determining "how relevant and useful clinical psychologists' training has been to their present-day professional functioning." Ideally, a reorganization of the clinical training program whether graduate or postgraduate or both, should rest upon a fact-finding study fed by several converging lines of inquiry. From *newly trained Ph.D.s* it would be useful to learn whether they feel that they are ready to undertake independent clinical practice, or that there remain areas in which they need further training. From *graduates of postdoctoral training programs* it would be useful to learn what benefits they derived from postdoctoral training, and whether they feel they could have done as well had they spent that year or two with routine staff responsibilities and catch-as-catch-can on-the-job training. From *clinical program directors* of APA-approved graduate programs, and from the *clinical supervisors* in these programs, it would be helpful to learn their views of their graduates' readiness to assume the duties of competent clinical practitioners, and what gaps in training they think need to be dealt with at the postgraduate level. From *employers of newly trained clinicians* we could learn how much, and what kind, of on-the-job training they feel called upon to provide young

*Private communication from Robert I. Yufit, Chairman of the Committee.

staff members fresh out of graduate training, and what their views are on the professional competence of these young staff members. Finally, from *clinical psychologists five years or more beyond their Ph.D.*, it would be useful to get a retrospective view of what would have constituted an ideal program of graduate and postgraduate training in clinical research, theory, and practice. Perhaps from such a comprehensive survey might come a clearer conception of currently neglected areas of clinical training and a clearer grasp of how to achieve a more effective implementation of training needs at the predoctoral and postdoctoral levels.

Postdoctoral models

A variety of postdoctoral programs aimed at supplementing predoctoral training, have emerged in this period of vigorous search for ways and means to advance the professional competence of clinical psychologists. The most intensive, though not the best known model for postdoctoral training is that represented by 19 programs (*see* the list) which share an ambitious concept of advanced training and have the support of NIMH in their efforts to provide this training. Candidates for postdoctoral fellowships in these programs must have obtained their Ph.D. in an approved clinical training program, must have had at least a year of supervised clinical experience, and should show the promise that they will eventually provide professional leadership in clinical practice, research, training, or administration.[14] Most of these training centers offer supervised experience in psychodiagnosis, psychotherapy, and research. Six emphasize psychotherapy (four of them, child psychotherapy), one stresses training for community mental health work, and one emphasizes training in clinical research. But, equally important, each gives its postdoctoral fellows a two-year professional moratorium in which to "re-examine their role as clinicians, experiment with changes in that role, and consolidate within that role the set of skills, concepts and values which best afford them both the conviction of an identity and the impetus to further growth."[2]

Postdoctoral Training Programs in Clinical Psychology

A person interested in obtaining information should write to the Director of the Postdoctoral Training Program in Clinical Psychology for each institution.

Albert Einstein College of Medicine
Department of Psychiatry
Yeshiva University
Eastchester Road and Morris Park Avenue
New York 61, New York

Austen Riggs Center
Department of Clinical Psychology
Stockbridge, Massachusetts

Clark University
Institute of Human Development
Department of Psychological Research
Worcester State Hospital
Worcester 1, Massachusetts

University of Colorado
Division of Clinical Psychology
4200 East Ninth Avenue
Denver, Colorado

The Devereux Foundation
Psychological Training
Institute for Research and Training
Devon, Pennsylvania

Judge Baker Guidance Center
295 Longwood Avenue
Boston 15, Massachusetts

Lafayette Clinic
Division of Psychology
951 East Lafayette
Detroit, Michigan

Massachusetts General Hospital
(Community Mental Health)
Department of Psychiatry
Boston 14, Massachusetts

The Menninger Foundation
Psychological Training
Department of Education
3617 West Sixth
Topeka, Kansas

Michael Reese Hospital
Institute for Psychosomatic and Psychiatric Research and Training
2945 South Ellis Avenue
Chicago 16, Illinois

Mount Sinai Hospital and Clinic
Psychiatric and Psychosomatic Research Institute
8720 Bevery Boulevard
Los Angeles 48, California

Mount Zion Hospital and Medical Center
Department of Psychiatry
2255 Post Street
San Francisco 14, California

New York University
(Training in Psychotherapy)
Department of Psychology
Graduate School of Arts and Science
100 Washington Square East
New York 3, New York

University of Oregon Medical School
Department of Medical Psychology
Portland 1, Oregon

Philadelphia Child Guidance Clinic
1700 Bainbridge Street
Philadelphia 46, Pennsylvania

Postgraduate Center for Psychotherapy
124 East 28th Street
New York 16, New York

Reiss-Davis Clinic for Child Guidance
Department of Clinical Psychology
715 North Fairfax Avenue
Los Angeles 46, California

University of Wisconsin Medical School
(Research in Psychotherapy)
Psychiatric Institute
1339 University Avenue
Madison 6, Wisconsin

Yale University School of Medicine
Department of Psychiatry
333 Cedar Street
New Haven, Connecticut

A superficially similar, but in principle quite different, model of training has been proposed recently. It would substitute two years of supervised postdoctoral experience for the one- or two-year predoctoral internship. This plan, formulated by a small group of clinicians at the *Miami* Conference, was summarized in the report of the Conference as follows: "The modification proposed by the *ad hoc* committee is to introduce a two-year internship following the Ph.D. The student would have a three-year (or four-year) program with a concentration in personality research or some related area. This would include practicum experience, especially in the areas of assessment and therapy, and ideally would attempt some integration between theory and practice. It would also provide research experience (hopefully, somehow integrated with the practicum) with an emphasis on direct participation in personality research and on acquisition of the skills necessary for such research (for example, naturalistic and systematic observation, interviewing, case study, as well as certain laboratory procedures). The graduate would have a Ph.D. but would not be designated a clinical psychologist. Following the Ph.D. he would enter a two-year residency program, given at an accredited postdoctoral training center, and including work in diagnostic evaluation, psychotherapy, and clinical research under the direct supervision of highly qualified staff members, and he would then be ready for 'minimal certification' as a clinical psychologist."[12]

The plan did not win any enthusiastic backing either at the Conference or afterward. A number of letters to the Division 12

Newsletter have discussed the plan. (A representative sample of these appears in the Spring, 1963, *Newsletter*.) Zimet[15] summarizes the pros and cons this way: "The advantages of such a procedure lie in the fact that the student could devote himself for two years to intensive clinical work . . . (in) a situation where identification figures or models would be readily available, where the intern would be able to move in a steady progression from apprenticeship to journeyman role with responsibilities at a level appropriate to the clinical skills mastered. (But), to delay a student's contact with clinical material for three years is detrimental, I believe, to his development as a clinical psychologist. The best program, potentially, still lies in clinical training programs within departments of psychology. . . . However, if these departments continue to disavow . . . their responsibilities for clinical training, the alternatives of postdoctoral training ought to be seriously considered."

It will be some years yet before this "four-two plan" is tried out on any extensive basis by the universities. In some essential respects it differs from the one-year postdoctoral internship which is currently being offered by the VA to psychologists who lack the prerequisites for a clinical staff position with the VA. The VA program will accept for training anyone who holds a doctoral degree in psychology (not necessarily clinical psychology) and has had two years of professional work comprising any combination of teaching assistantships, research assistantships, and practicum experience.

A quite different approach to postdoctoral training which has been widely employed, especially in the last five years, is the brief but intensive Postdoctoral Institute, usually limited to a one-week period of seminars on some particular area of clinical practice or theory. Such workshops have been offered privately for many years, but it is with the Division 12 Postdoctoral Institute program that this form of training came into its own. Each year, at least five workshops are scheduled for the week preceding the annual APA convention, with workshop leaders selected for their acknowledged expertness in a particular area of psychology. Some local societies—notably the Los Angeles Society of Clinical Psychologists—have taken it upon themselves to provide similar workshops on a local basis. Such postdoctoral workshops and institutes are probably highly effective as refresher courses, or to acquaint practicing psychologists with new developments in their field, but are of limited value for the newly trained clinical psychologist who needs more sustained training in basic skills.

Still a fifth model of postdoctoral training deserves mention, not because of its prevalence but because of its potential importance. This program would offer a one-year visiting fellowship based not on the apprenticeship model of more intensive programs, but on the sabbatical leave plan of the universities. Such a program would give staff members of one department a chance to visit and become better acquainted with the point of view and the practices of other departments. Such a fellowship would be particularly appropriate for psychologists who teach personality courses, courses in projective techniques, or are responsible for clinical training and supervision at a university, who need to come into closer touch with new developments in the field, or who feel the need to renew their clinical identities in a more intensively patient-oriented setting.

A radical departure from all these models of professional training is embodied in a plan recently advocated by Holt. He proposes that a new profession of psychotherapists be created, with a wholly new curriculum and set of training requirements.[6,7] It is too soon to know how viable this idea will prove to be, but it has already been given much careful thought, and has received some important backing.[8]

Despite this potpourri of choices open to someone seeking further training, we are still some distance from a solution to a number of crucial questions which are at the heart of the present-day unrest in clinical training. It would be important not to lose sight of these questions: to what extent should the university be asked to take the responsibility for the professional training of the clinical psychologist? To what extent should professional training be separated from academic doctoral studies? If the university does not want the full responsibility for clinical professional training, or is not equipped to accept it, who will assume that responsibility? Is there any cause for concern that clinical psychology, if it continues as the neglected (or only reluctantly cared for) child of graduate psychology departments, will eventually begin to show the developmental signs of such neglect? If so, where can clinical psychology find a suitable foster parent?

In the search for answers to such questions, it would be well for clinicians to bear in mind that any fault which they may find with present-day clinical training does not lie with the university. To blame the university is only to oversimplify the problem. Until a satisfactory program of clinical training is developed nationally, the many and varied experiments in postdoctoral training are sure to continue. It is to be hoped, however, that eventually these efforts will be integrated into an APA-endorsed plan of training in clinical psychology more comprehensive than the *Boulder* Conference plan which no longer fits the needs of our growing profession.

References

1. Blank, Leonard, and David, Henry P., The crisis in clinical psychology training. *Amer. Psychol.,* 1963, *4,* 216-219.
2. Ekstein, Rudolf, and Mayman, Martin, On the professional identity of the clinical psychologist. *Bull. Menninger Clin.,* 1957, *21,* 59-61.
3. Fine, Harold J.: The status of the clinical psychologist. *J. Clin. Psychol.,* 1961, *17,* 107-110.
4. Forer, Bertram, Psychologists: clinical and academic. Paper read at symposium: *The private practitioner and the psychologist,* APA, Division 12, New York, September 4, 1961.
5. Garmezy, Norman, Postdoctoral programs and their relation to graduate training. Presented at symposium: *Postdoctoral training programs in clinical psychology.* APA, Chicago, September, 1960.
6. Holt, Robert R., Would a special degree for psychotherapists be desirable? Presented at symposium: *Professional training for clinical psychologists,* APA, New York, September 2, 1961.
7. Holt, Robert R., *Proceedings of the Conference on an Ideal Training Program for Psychotherapists.* March, 1963, Gould House, Ardsley-on-Hudson, N.Y., unpublished; Report of Conference on an Ideal Training Program for Psychotherapists. *Amer. Psychol.,* 1963, *18,* 677-679.
8. Holt, Robert R., *Memo to participants in the Gould House Conference.* November, 1963, multilith.
9. Kelly, E. Lowell, Clinical psychology—1960: report of survey findings. APA, *Div. of Clin. Psychol. Newsletter,* 1961, *14,* 1-11.

10. Kelly, E. Lowell, and Goldberg, Lewis R., Correlates of later performance and specialization in psychology. *Psychol. Monogr.* 1959, #842, 32 pp.
11. Lubin, Bernard, Survey of psychotherapy training and activities of psychologists. *J. Clin. Psychol.*, 1962, *18*, 252-256.
12. Roe, Anne, et al., eds., *Graduate education in psychology*. (The Miami Conference Report), Washington, D.C.: APA, 1959.
13 Rogers, Carl, A personal view on some issues facing psychologists. *Amer. Psychol.*, 1955, *10*, 247-249.
14. Santostefano, Sebastian, Postdoctoral training in clinical psychology: a preliminary report by an interest group. *Amer. Psychol.*, 1960, *15*, 213-215.
15. Zimet, Carl N., Clinical training and university responsibility. *J. Clin. Psychol.*, 1961, *17*, 110-114.

Specialized Training and Innovations in Psychodiagnosis

LEONARD BLANK

LUCIANO L'ABATE

CONVENTIONAL TRAINING CONSIDERATIONS

LEONARD BLANK

There are three major steps in diagnostic preparation: course work, learning tools and techniques, and field experiences and supervision. All three are predicated on the ability of grasping the personality make-up or distortions of the diagnostic subject. Therefore, these steps will be considered in the context of understanding the dynamic functioning of the individual.

1. *Course preparation*

Suggested curricula pertinent to diagnosis have been cited in Chapter 1 and are further discussed later in this chapter. Despite the long-standing recommendations originating with the *Shakow* Report and *Boulder* Conference, complaints continue to be heard from the field with respect to the inadequate preparation of psychology trainees in psychopathology, abnormal and developmental psychology, tests and measurements, projective techniques, and introduction to psychotherapy.[4] (*See* also Chapter 12.) The internship was conceptualized by the *Boulder* conferees and is viewed by most *clinicians* in the field as an opportunity for the novice psychologist to gain experience and develop skills with information and methodology that he has *already* learned at the university. Many university training centers, however, apparently believe that such "applied" knowledge can and should be picked up by the student in a year's internship at which time he can also be trained to be a skilled diagnostician and therapist—if he cares for such things. What happens is that the field supervisors expend enormous energy in teaching the trainee to administer the Rorschach, score intelligence tests, etc., so that at the end of the year he might be sufficiently trained to gather clinical data for his thesis or really be ready to take on an internship.

2. Learning tools and techniques

Whatever the state of validity and reliability of current measures of personality assessment, we must employ the methodology available not only because there is a demand for service, but because the reasoned use of these techniques permits theoretical advancement, increased determination of validity and reliability, and ultimately substitution of better devices. I shall not take up here the cudgels for the "standard" personality battery, and I am aware that conviction is not always accompanied by high correlations. The second part of this chapter presents some of the limitations of such batteries and encourages a much broader spectrum of tests. Bass and Berg[2] suggest "objective" approaches to personality assessment while Brower and Abt[5] and Gurvitz,[10] among many others, suggest model test batteries. I, too, would like to suggest a model battery, but not with the implication that any one technique is irreplaceable or that many valuable others could not be added. The battery to be presented offers a comprehensive evaluation of the personality and provides a good *training* vehicle in that the use of these tests develops skills and appreciation of personality functioning that may be generalized to other techniques. Such questions as possibility of brain damage or degree of intellectual retardation will, of course, call for other tests.

Report. A report serves the function of communicating information—the evaluation of personality features. The reason for referral largely dictates its format; it must answer certain immediate questions. The report also serves as a record for future unspecified readers. The communicative function demands a meaningful interaction between the writer and any reader in terms of language as well as message.

A psychological report has value only if it contributes something additional, more comprehensive, with greater clarity, or quicker than would be the appraisal of professionals without test data.

Whatever battery of techniques is employed, the data gathering should be comprehensive, multidimensional, and multilevel. Each technique, indeed every test item, should generate as many hypothetical threads as possible. When an hypothesis is isolated, not corroborated by other evidence, it is a loose thread to be discarded, at least temporarily.

Hypotheses and speculations, however, are important. Whereas one contends with the peril of finding what one is looking for, the inability to tolerate ambiguity leads to a sterile report. The clinician must use himself as an instrument by responding to his reactions to the patient and test material as diagnostic cues. He must use his empirical knowledge to resolve contradictory evidence and postulate *new* behavior. Evidence converging from several sources suggests to the clinician substantiation of hypotheses, whereas conflicting data suggest either incorrect assumptions or the very reflection of the patient's conflicts.

So it is that any one test (or an entire battery) serves its function only to the degree that it generates hypotheses for a clinician. One clinician may favor the Rorschach, another the MMPI. Without doubt, the suggested "standard" battery will be altered, too.

As long as there is a clinician, however, rather than a diagnostic computer, the *techniques* of relating test data to a dynamic description of the testee's psychological processes will remain basically unchanged.

Rorschach. The student's work with this classic technique can teach him to appraise intellectual activity, inner psychological functioning, and fantasy life. He can gain an appreciation of unconscious and symbolic aspects of the personality as well as creative and imaginative functions. Emotional control, conceptual ability, and interpersonal percepts may be gauged as well. Rorschach users often stress pathology, but coping mechanisms and resistence of mental functioning are also indicated.

TAT. This technique often supplies the flesh and sinews of the personality picture. Whereas the Rorschach may illuminate internal conflicts, the TAT can spotlight projection of these conflicts externally. Here, the testee reveals how he thinks in words and even in syntax. Mood, actual techniques of dealing with people, emotions, fantasies, familial and social relationships, and the like, are often delineated in the TAT.

Draw A Person (DAP). Human figure drawings can present a multilevel picture of self-concept in its relationship to sexual and social role. Their particular contribution to a battery is a non-verbal index of conceptualization and one which is especially sensitive to the presence of distorted judgment (or its reflection in motoric performance) that may not have permeated to the verbal level. DAP also can be useful in indicating the body image concept.

MMPI. The MMPI is a procedure that can present the defensive network of the personality and the characteristic techniques the person has in handling affect and tension. It can also provide information with respect to adaptive ego resources. As a personality inventory, it is keenly sensitive to the social desirability implied to the testee by the various items and is very much structured by the situation and the examiner. Accordingly, each person has to assume a set or a role so that a manifest level is tapped, probably associated to the person's defensive maneuvers. The empirical results and underlying determining tendencies in each subject, related to this test, throw light on adaptability as well as deviant thinking (variations from the norm).

Interpersonal Checklist (ICL). The ICL is a measure that indicates the conscious presentation of the self to others and also can be utilized to contrast this presentation with how one would like to be, or how one believes others see him. There is a representation that ranges from adaptive to maladaptive attitudes.

WAIS. This test is one of the best assessments of intelligence. Moreover, since it is a scale that includes eleven subtests measuring a variety of verbal and performance skills, it also serves as a diagnostic tool. Discrepancy among scores from one test to another, intra-test scatter, configuration of test and qualitive aspect of answers shed light on personality dynamics.

Interview. Depending on the technique, skill, and theoretical orientation of the examiner, the interview can provide a comprehensive, multidimensional, and multilevel source of information. It also can be used to establish a relationship, foster the proper evaluation climate, and can and ought to be a therapeutic contact. That is, a depth interview explains as it uncovers, juxtaposes events and behavior, relates current modes of action with genetic material, and permits expression of affect and self-evaluation.

Group techniques. The trainee must be versed in group techniques for two reasons: 1) to economize his time and energy while evaluating large groups of subjects, and 2) amass and compare test data providing numbers and norms not available in individual testing. The MMPI, ICL, and DAP not only can be employed as group techniques but, in combination, can serve as a screening battery. The latter have particular efficacy in outpatient and clinic services.

3. *Supervision and field experience*

The essence of supervision and field experience, insofar as diagnostic training is concerned, is the proficiency with which the trainee learns to utilize testing techniques and communicate them in a report.[3,10,16] Ideally, the teachers of these skills in the universities should be clinicians who have proven themselves in the field.

Good supervision is as important an element of clinical training as any that could be listed. Just as the churning out of crisp research papers on, say, the perceptual distortion of schizophrenics does not necessarily make an adequate instructor in psychopathology, the "sharp" clinician does not necessarily make a good supervisor. "How to supervise" is not taught in the universities. That is why some field training programs hold inservice institutes in this area. (*See* Chapter 10.)

The supervisor has the herculean task, in a year or less, to encourage the trainee to season his academic base with applied skills, to speculate and speak to his convictions but maintain good clinical caution, and to amass a wealth of loosely integrated information which he must communicate in literate, cogent, and *simple* language. In this task, fortunately, the supervisor can rely on several devices: a) have the trainee observe an experienced examiner administer, score, and work up a test battery; b) observe (preferably via one-way screen) and critically evaluate the trainee's test administration; c) have the trainee present to psychology and interdisciplinary staff conferences; d) have the trainee present at an informal meeting of his peers. (*See* Chapter 10).

No technique can replace the supervisor's astuteness and patience, and the trainee's ability to change and grow. The student must be encouraged to dig out information and present it in a standard enough manner so as to be convincing to his colleagues but not replete with trite generalities; he must also be encouraged to paint a vivid picture of his testee's personality without being idiosyncratic or wildly speculative.

To attain such goals, or at least to approach them, it is necessary that the trainee be exposed to a wide range of normal and psychopathological populations. The major responsibility for exposure to normal subjects lies in the universities. In the field, a wide spectrum of populations may be seen through rotating assignments and in workshops. (*See* Chapter 10 for description of the New Jersey Centralized Training Program in Psychology.) In the final analysis, however, with the huge variety of populations involved—normals, character disorders, neuroses, transient maladjustments, psychoses, physically disabled, young, old, physical illness, different cultures, different socioeconomic representation—the trainee must seek experiences for himself for years after he has become a clinician.

INNOVATIONS FOR TRAINING

Luciano L'Abate

Change, improvement, and progress cannot occur unless we question: a) the assumptions under which we are operating as clinical psychologists, b) the training that takes place in producing clinical psychologists, and c) the techniques we use in our diagnostic operations. We cannot look to the future with progress in mind unless we question what we have taken for granted in the past and unless we abandon inefficient and inappropriate methods.

In a way, clinical psychology finds itself in the place of the neurotic patient who is too diffuse to know his identity, too anxious to consider more efficient ways of operating, and too rigid to change his old, repetitive, and compulsive rituals. Innovation, therefore, cannot take place unless we are able to cast a hard, critical look at our diagnostic practices, realizing and accepting without repression or denial the "neurotic" problems that beset the profession. Once entrenched defenses and maladaptive habits are overcome, these problems can be dealt with, and possibly more appropriate courses of action can be suggested.

Progress in diagnosis can occur a) by improving the accuracy and efficiency of the tools we already have and b) by adding new and more adequate tools and perhaps abandoning old ones. How else can progress occur? Scientific progress is based on the development of new, more accurate, and more efficient probe bodies. That is one aspect of science that cannot be divorced from technology; the same applies to clinical psychology and especially diagnosis. Only through the improvement of techniques can the profession change. Training, therefore, should be directed toward exploring new techniques of analysis together with the old tried and true. There is a need for young, clinical psychologists and graduate students to learn a variety of diagnostic skills: all of the new techniques for the detection and measurement of cerebral deficit, of intellectual functioning, and of personality in children. There is a vast area of need for training of a technical and of a scientific nature at the predoctoral level.

Multidimensional diagnosis

Cronbach in considering the two disciplines of experimental and correlational psychology has argued[6] (*see* p. 676) that "no observed criterion is truly valid and . . . simultaneous consideration of many criteria is needed for a satisfactory evaluation of performances." In supporting this thesis, he cites Miller's[26,27] contention that a variety of experimental means are needed to study changes in motivation.

The same methodology holds in diagnostic testing. Examples

of recent comparisons of the relative efficiency of a battery of tests are available in studies of brain damage.[17,18] By comparing either old tests or new ones, both studies indicate the importance of a variety of tests to deal with such a heterogeneous variable as brain damage. The same approach holds in the study of Winter and Stortroen, comparing several indices to differentiate psychotics from normals with various MMPI indices. As these authors comment[33] (*see* p. 222):

"It would be exceedingly useful to have available a series of studies comparing the efficiency of various psychological measures in making pertinent decisions, thus hopefully relieving the busy clinician of much routine work. Unfortunately it looks as if for some time to come, real life diagnosis will be the end product of a combination of hard facts, intuitive judgment, experience with local norms, guesswork and error."

Among objective screening tests, the MMPI exemplifies best of all the need for a multidimensional approach to diagnosis. After the failure of the heroic last-ditch effort of the Meehl-Dahlstrom rules[24] to discriminate psychotic from neurotic profiles, this test can be relegated to the place it deserves in group screening *with* a battery of other tests.[11,23,33] Historically, its triumphs and its failures have taught us a great deal. It still remains a useful screening and research tool. Now we are ready to use it with other techniques.

Looking to future approaches

There are at least two directions that can be taken to increase the diagnostic accuracy and effectiveness of the clinical psychologist to meet increasing diagnostic demands and needs for multidimensional diagnosis, namely: a) group testing and screening and b) individual testing through the laboratory method.

Group testing and screening. Here the skill of the clinical psychologist consists of screening out obviously deviant individuals, as in the military services and more recently in the Peace Corps. However, screening should be based on a multidimensional view of psychopathology. One should be able to detect individuals who are deviant: a) intellectually; b) emotionally; c) cerebrally; and d) in more restricted, not necessarily psychiatric and more possibly academic settings—vocationally. Group screening methods appear crucial especially in child guidance clinics with waiting lists of one year and longer.

Group screening could be performed, therefore, using standardized batteries of tests rather than a single test. For instance, with children under 15 years of age one could use various combinations of batteries dependent on age, sex, and specific setting or purpose of the screening. With children below 8 years of age one could use Frostig's test of perceptual development and drawings. From 6 years on, sentence completion tests, the California tests of mental maturity and personality, and Jastak's Wide Range Achievement Test could be added. With children older than 8 years one could use, among others, Rogers Test of Personality Adjustment and Rosenzweig's Picture Frustration Test. With literate adults, one could use batteries of tests based on Leary's Interpersonal Theory,[21] including the MMPI and the Interpersonal Checklist, or sentence completion tests and group tests based on conceptual systems theory,[13] or just empirical instruments like Q-sorting and the California Personality Inventory. For intellectual functioning one could use proverbs and vocabular scales, the Shipley-Hartford scale and/or Raven's Progressive Metrices. Other devices to screen for brain damage could be adopted, like lantern-presentation of visuomotor tests and the like.

On the basis of this first step and very brief reports on the degree of "normality" in intellectual, emotional, and organic functioning encountered in the individual, further, more individualized testing could take place if indicated and a second diagnostic step undertaken. This step could be performed through the laboratory method.[19,20]

The laboratory method. The laboratory method implies that the administration and scoring of a standard battery of tests should be relegated to specially trained technicians, while the clinical psychologist retains the functions of training and supervising technicians and of interpreting and reporting battery-based test results. By sharply separating technical (test administration and scoring) from professional (supervision, interpretation, and reporting) skills, the diagnostic efficiency and usefulness of the clinical psychologist is enhanced. He can be of more and hopefully better service to more patients and to more referring agencies at a truly professional level than he could before.

One may question the use of a standard battery of tests where, for instance, a series of brain-damage tests are routinely administered to all patients that are evaluated, even if the possibility of brain damage is exceedingly remote. From the viewpoint of the clinical psychologist interested in calibrating his instruments, such standard procedure is not at all wasteful. On the contrary, these are the very patients that would eventually furnish the best form of control, either through individual matching or through mean group comparison for patients who are eventually diagnosed, on a basis other than psychological testing, as showing cerebral dysfunctions. These patients would probably be drawn from the same population, very likely with the same socioeconomic background, as the experimental patients. By the same token, organics would perhaps function as controls for experimental patients whose main differentiating category would be emotional psychopathology.

Group screening and the laboratory method envisage a wider use and knowledge of tests than perhaps psychologists have been taught traditionally. Their technical training may have been limited by teachers with doubtful clinical experience who have taught a restricted number of tests and provided narrow exposure to the number of diagnostic problem areas. For instance, only recently, and specifically through the efforts of Reitan's laboratory,[30] have psychologists been able to see the usefulness of their tests in the assessment of psychological deficits due to neurological dysfunctions, immaturities, and traumas.

Assumptions and assertions

If clinical psychologists want to be scientists they will need to abide by the rules of the scientific game. It is necessary for professionals to be trained first of all as scientists and secondly as professionals, rather than mixing up these two aspects. The differentiation should make it possible for clinical psychologists to be trained as scientists by psychologists during their period of predoctoral training and by clinical psychologists during their postdoctoral training period. This assertion and differentiation is based somewhat obliquely on at least two overlapping assumptions that are presented as further assertions.

A science is as good as its technology. Present training of clinical psychologists is analogous to training soldiers to shoot with the World War II rifle while a lighter, more rapid-firing and just as accurate weapon is now available. We should train our students with the latest instruments available that appear more accurate and more efficient then some of the older tests. Unfortunately, as long as we operate traditionally, divorcing service from research activities, we cannot compare the various types of validities of newer tests. We are trapped in stagnation. Change in a science parallels change in its technology.

A technology is as advanced as its instruments. If we use the traditional Wechsler scales, TAT, and the Rorschach and make no provision in our *modus operandi* to try out new techniques, it is obvious that progress cannot take place. While we are keeping the same tests and refuse to adopt new promising ones, testing them according to accepted criteria and methods of validation, we remain static as a profession; we preclude change. Technical change can occur (and this point has been belabored) within the framework of scientific intersubjectivity, where one's data and methods of operation are open to another scientist's investigation and probing. Without this primary criterion, clinical psychologists may be relegating themselves to function as practitioners, and by definition remain "closed systems" who use the same techniques and are unwilling to consider and utilize new ones. This statement does not mean that practitioners should not be produced in clinical psychology. On the contrary, the vitality of a science may well be gauged by the vitality of its practitioners. We need to produce and better equip practitioners who will be able to exploit a wide range of techniques efficiently and who hopefully will continue to feed back their findings based on new samples and different clinical problems.

Predoctoral training: scientific

In considering various aspects of predoctoral training in diagnosis, as they are summarized in Table 1, one should sharply differentiate among pure, applied, and technical aspects of scientific training. By "pure" is meant whatever is divorced from specific application or subject matter, like statistics, research methodology, and electronic computers. Essentially this background is of a general rather than of a specific nature. "Applied" refers here to the more specific subject matter and content areas studied (developmental, social, psychopathological, etc.). The "technical" aspect implies essentially the type of probe bodies used (tests of intelligence, brain damage, psychopathology, etc.).

TABLE 1   PARADIGM FOR PREDOCTORAL TRAINING IN DIAGNOSIS: SCIENTIFIC CURRICULUM

Pure	Applied	Technical	
Statistics	Developmental	Tests for intellectual functioning	D I S
Research methods	Personality	Organic deficits	S E R
Electronic computers	Social	Personality and psychopathology	T A T I
Philosophy of science and/or neuroanatomy	Psychopathology	Vocational	O N

From the viewpoint of a tripartite division of scientific endeavor, departments of psychology have emphasized sufficiently the first two aspects, the pure and the applied, relegating the technical aspect to a minor role in the overall graduate curriculum. This deficiency is responsible for many criticisms[1] that have been voiced about the quality of clinical training and its de-emphasis in major departments of psychology.

Training in diagnosis therefore should be directed to fulfilling these three overlapping but different aspects of scientific training. Each of these aspects of training, according to emphasis, produces different types of psychologists who are concerned with different aspects of the diagnostic process. These different aspects, for instance, could be illustrated in terms of a statistician who will be interested in some kind of clinical problems but whose major interest is essentially of a statistical nature, as against the clinical psychologist who would be interested in different types of diagnostic methods or the practitioner who will essentially be concerned with specific applications of techniques.[14]

Pure curriculum. The predoctoral training of clinical psychologists should not be different from the training of experimental psychologists. Both learn to rely on probe bodies, that is, the techniques and instruments that are necessary to test scientific hypotheses. Experimental psychologists may learn to test with mazes or memory drums while clinical psychologists learn to use intelligence and personality tests. The more varied the experimental armamentarium of the experimental psychologist, the greater the number and kind of hypotheses that he can test.[26,27] The major difference between the experimental and clinical field lies in the type of probe bodies used and in the types and complexities of hypotheses searched. The tools are different, the scientific and theoretical assumptions are the same. At the technical level, predoctoral training therefore should be directed toward the understanding, construction, administration, and research of probe bodies.

The distinction between clinical and other kinds of psychological specializations, therefore, is based on the types of probe bodies used and the way they are applied. Consequently, a clearer line between scientific and professional training needs to be drawn, and some differentiation among various aspects of training in clinical psychology should be arrived at.

Applied curriculum. If a student wants to extend his knowledge in any experimental area he should be given time and credit to pursue whatever experimental courses he may desire. In fact, he should have sufficient freedom to extend his knowledge in whatever elective he may desire, from neuroanatomy to anthropology. Yet the core curriculum should remain the same. Greater emphasis should be given to developmental and social courses. In this regard, formal courses in developmental psychology should be extended to include basic knowledge of theory and research. Specifically, developmental psychology should give greater emphasis to the contributions of such men as Piaget, Werner, and Erikson who, on the whole, have been de-emphasized by the more commonly used American textbooks.[13]

Social psychology should be thought of in terms of concepts that are more pertinent to clinical psychology, such as person perception, the formation of interpersonal perception, personality impression, etc. For the clinical psychologist who plans to go into group work, a knowledge of research on group dynamics would be invaluable. Unfortunately, group therapists possess an extremely limited knowledge of experimental social psychology. In fact, if students know from the beginning of graduate training that they want to go into group work, perhaps their training should be undertaken in departments of social psychology.

A further area to be included in a curriculum of this type would be psychology of language and semantic analysis, especially as it relates to problems of interprofessional communication and report writing. A course of this type would cover theory and research as well as application. Knowledge of semantics and problems of language and style should be viewed as the necessary background for efficient and effective communication. Without this background, report writing becomes a separate skill that is learned outside of academic training. Such a skill should have a thoroughly academic background at the same level as learning to write research papers. Of course, applied courses should be offered in a sequence that illustrate different views of a particular clinical activity. In this type of course, there should be a meeting of theory and practice, showing how theoretical formulations apply to patients and to the instruments used to describe them.[22,31]

Technical curriculum. It follows from the preceding arguments and assertions that psychologists will need to become acquainted with more tests than in the past. At the predoctoral level, the technical aspect would be learning the background and rationale of each test, its mode of administration and scoring, and its mechanical and essentially statistical background. There is the need, therefore, to create a wider range of courses devoted specifically to keeping up with research on old tests and creation of new techniques.

Assuming that all students would have received an introductory course on tests and measurements (notwithstanding regional differences in training[29]), the technical curriculum would consist of the following courses:

A. Intelligence Testing
   1. Groups
     a. children
     b. adolescents
     c. adults
   2. Individuals
     a. by age (children, adolescents, adults)
     b. by handicap (verbal, motor, etc.)
   3. Special clinical settings
B. Testing for cerebral and organic deficits. This course would not be devoted to group testing but to the types of measures suggested by Korman and Blumberg,[17] L'Abate *et al.*,[18] L'Abate,[19,20] and Reitan.[30]
  C. Personality and psychopathology
   1. Groups (objective, projective) and settings
     a. children
     b. adolescents
     c. adults
   2. Individuals and settings
This section may require two courses, one devoted to objective techniques and the other to projective techniques.
  D. Vocational maladjustment. This area should be part of the curriculum in counseling psychology. Sometimes vocational tests are taught in courses on tests and measurements. There is a need to relate educational deficits especially in children as well as vocational maladjustment in adults to the three previous areas of intellectual and cognative functioning, cerebral deficits, and psychopathology.[19,20]

Postdoctoral training: professional

The pros of postdoctoral training. This type of training is based on the assumption that group screening and the laboratory method furnish useful paradigms for diagnosis and for research in clinical psychology.

Postdoctoral training in clinical psychology has many assets and, at least to this biased observer, very few liabilities. Training a person with a Ph.D. allows better selection, at least as far as the academic preparation of the clinical psychologist is concerned, and perhaps as far as the motivational basis for his work. As a consequence, there would be fewer clinical psychologists who have no terminal degree and only a questionable professional and academic preparation.

Postdoctoral training would make clinical psychology a profession on a par with any other profession. Without this safeguard (the Ph.D. degree), clinical psychologists will always struggle between the role of insecure psychometricians and that of mature professionals. Better selection means better training. Training of this sort would be concentrated in a few but well-equipped professional institutes, as is the case at present in a few settings for postdoctoral training.

The advantage of postdoctoral training centers independent of psychology departments would lie mainly in their competitiveness. If entrance into this type of training is on a competitive basis, regardless of university affiliation but on the student's own merits and curriculum, the rejection of students from such programs may be a clear reflection of their inadequate training and should reflect on the department that trained them. In this fashion, postdoctoral training centers may be able to control the type of training that is necessary predoctorally. An example of postdoctoral training in psychodiagnosis is presented in Table 2.

Diagnostic training would be based on the interpretations of test results by integrating whatever has been acquired predoctorally in terms of rationale and background for each test. How is one test consistent within itself and with other tests in the battery? How are test and battery results consistent with external behavior? The ultimate part of postdoctoral professional training would then consist of the reporting of these results. (Postdoctoral training in general as well as reference to diagnosis in particular is discussed in Chapter 6. Eds.)

The teaching of interpretative skills. Three recent studies have indicated that although experience is necessary for clinical accuracy, judges without experience but with special training can quickly learn to make fairly accurate discriminations. In Grebstein's study[9] three groups of judges varying in amounts of clinical experience predicted IQ levels from Rorschach protocols just as well as a multiple regression equation and better

TABLE 2   PARADIGM FOR POSTDOCTORAL TRAINING IN DIAGNOSIS:
PROFESSIONAL CURRICULUM

Time allotted for each activity	
First year	
Psychodiagnostics (practice and supervision)	50%
Conferences, rounds, etc.	25%
Psychotherapy and supervision	25%
Second year (optional?)	
Advanced psychodiagnostics:	
Practice with less supervision and more independent role	25%
Conferences, rounds, etc.	25%
Psychotherapy or other special skills (group work, at discretion of individual intern)	25%
Research	25%

Diagnostic skills acquired during training
1. Interpretation of battery results: a. intra-test consistency b. inter-test consistency c. extra-text consistency
2. Report writing and professional consultation

than chance. Predictive accuracy did not increase significantly with amount of clinical experience. Oskamp[28] found that undergraduate students can be taught to discriminate between psychiatric and medical MMPI profiles almost as well as experienced clinicians. Furthermore, statistical predictions based on the Meehl-Dahlstrom rules required "fully as much caution in their usage as does clinical prediction." (p. 22)

In attempting to answer his own question on whether expertness can be taught, Oskamp suggests that a brief period of training in MMPI usage "may equal the results of years of clinical experience" as long as this training is based on specific methods with immediate feedback. Furthermore, training in the actuarial method "markedly improved" the judges' appropriateness as well as their accuracy. As Oskamp adds:

"Clinical training programs for fledgling psychologists could well use a number of multi-objective prediction tasks to speed the development of internal norms. By contrast, the usual clinical training procedure of building by norms through prolonged study and analysis of a few cases over a long period of time and often without feedback of results is scientifically unsound, inefficient, and wasteful of many skilled man hours." (p. 21)

It would appear from Oskamp's conclusions, therefore, that clinical psychologists may be as inefficient in their interpreting as they are in the time they take up in performing relatively unskilled chores, such as test administration and scoring.

Weiss[32] found that psychologists predict significantly more accurately than physical scientists when the amount of information available to them is meager. However, when the amount of information available to both groups is increased, physical scientists perform more accurately than psychologists.

These three studies suggest one profound implication for future training that is in keeping with innovations suggested in this chapter. Instead of a great deal of time being spent with one single instrument, training time could be exploited more efficiently by having students learn more techniques. Of course, this course of action may smack of superficiality and facility. All one can reply is to ask for more studies to support the contention that depth of knowledge of one instrument is a far more relevant factor to emphasize in training than extensity. The burden of proof remains on those who support this position. Of course, this conflict could be solved by asking that each psychologist become thoroughly familiar and knowledgeable with each instrument he uses.

Initial group screening and subsequent individual testing through the laboratory method imply knowledge of a wider range of tests, as well as more extensive knowledge of each test than one would suspect. Acquiring interpretative skills would imply becoming familiar and comfortable with "blind" evaluation of test results, especially if the objective aspects of test results are emphasized.[19]

Report writing and consultation

Training in report writing should be oriented toward an awareness of various levels of abstractions and complexity not only in psychological functioning but also in written communications of clinical psychologists. Psychologists, working in medical settings, for instance, are forced to face, not without frustration and some pricks to their pride, the dichotomously concrete thinking of physicians, whose only concern can be very often relieved by a few direct statements: yes, the patient does show signs of cerebral dysfunction; no, the patient is not psychotic. In other words, diagnosticians need to differentiate not only among levels of abstraction of their patients but also of professional people with whom they work. (It would be helpful if physicians or agencies requesting psychological studies would indicate the length of the report desired. This simple device may save a great deal of work on the part of the zealous clinician without detracting one iota from his unique professional contribution.)

Training in report writing, therefore, would be concurrent to training in blind evaluation of test results. Once the clinician starts using objective criteria, like cutting scores,[25,30] indices, and configurations based perhaps on combinations of sub-indices[33], "blind" evaluation should become an objectively communicable process which is repeatable within each setting and from one clinical setting to another.

Another differentiation that needs to be made in report writing pertains to duMas' suggestion[8] that the clinical psychologist who is serving two masters at the same time, namely science and society, must concern himself with formal, empirical, and societal statements. The nature of formal and empirical statements may range from false to doubtful to true. Societal statements pertain to recommendations which are based on strictly probabilistic grounds. He needs to make them but their truth cannot be really ascertained on either logical or practical grounds.

Creation of technical courses

The obvious need for a subprofessional specialty of technicians demands the creation of professional schools, not for clinical psychologists, as some have suggested[1], but for psychological technicians. Professionally they would be equivalent to many ancillary medical specialties, such as medical and x-ray technicians, physical and occupational therapists, etc.[19]

If experiences in military services[12] and the author's experience in teaching part-time volunteer technicians at St. Louis Children's Hospital[20] are relevant criteria, depending on the level of education and intelligence of the technician, it would take approximately four to six months for them to become acquainted and comfortable with the verbatim administration of test batteries.

Best results are obtained by outlines in specially constructed manuals about a) clinical rules, b) types of desirable behavior on the part of the technician while testing, c) suggestions for shortcuts in recording, and d) clear instructions as to types of tests administered routinely by age of the patient and type of handicap.

Courses of this type imply that the clinical psychologist be first of all acquainted and experienced with the tests he is going to teach to technicians. Secondly this type of training will tax and test the psychologist's perception of his own role. He is going to be a teacher and a supervisor of individuals who do not have the formal background of the interns and graduate students with whom he is familiar. However, this activity can be extremely beneficial to the psychologist. He learns to see his patients through the eyes of technicians, and once he becomes more comfortable working with them, he may then wonder why he did not use them before.

Perhaps there is no need to create formal technical courses as yet. Clinical psychologists who feel comfortable in assuming this responsibility may have to rely on the time-tested method of informal and individual instruction to especially selected individuals. As the laboratory method gathers impetus, the creation of formal courses for psychological technicians may become a reality. Perhaps medical schools may become the settings where courses can take place. In settings of this type there would be a sufficient number of psychologists to teach and to assume responsibility for in-training supervision. This training would acquaint technicians with a variety of patients. Courses would be limited to the administration and scoring of group and individual tests with no knowledge on the technician's part of what the results may possible mean. This aspect of training is comparable to that of the x-ray technicians. They learn to follow instructions as to the specific type of x-ray desired and are sufficiently acquainted with the apparatus to obtain as good results as the radiologist.

Conclusion

In considering the assumptions under which we are operating as clinical psychologists, one can see that the traditional division of science versus profession implied in our activities as clinical psychologists would disappear if clinical psychologists were trained in diagnosis first as scientists and secondly as practitioners. Although our scientific (pure and applied) background is sufficient, we fail mostly in our technical training which is restricted to an inefficient use of a few old, tried, and not always true tests. Enlargement of technical training to include a wider number of group screening techniques and individual test batteries administered by technicians or assistants should help clinical psychologists achieve a greater degree of professional integration and usefulness. If we wish to be true consultants and professionals, we cannot waste our time performing time-consuming technical tasks.

Learning more appropriate, efficient ways of working should allow clinical psychologists to leave behind a neurotic condition which up to now has been handled either by avoidance; by performing more satisfying tasks, like psychotherapy, for which we are not specifically trained; by passivity; by having junior psychologists perform testing; or by complete rejection and retreat into the ivory tower of teaching or the sanctum of the laboratory. By assuming new ways of operating, clinical psychologists may achieve a *rapprochement* between psychology as a science and as a profession. The gap would only become wider if clinical psychologists persist in the *status quo*.

REFERENCES

1. Aronson, M.L., *et al.,* Clinical alumni statement on doctoral training. *newslt. Div. Clin. Psychol.,* 1962, *15,* 7-10.
2. Bass, Bernard M., and Berg, Irwin A., *Objective approaches to personality assessment.* Princeton: Van Nostrand, 1959.
3. Blank, Leonard, *Interrelationships of psychological reports with psychotherapy.* Unpublished manuscript.
4. Blank Leonard, and David, Henry P., The crisis in clinical psychology training. *Amer. Psychol.,* 1963, *18,* 216-219
5. Brower, D., and Abt, L. E. eds., The psychodiagnostic test battery. In *Progress in clinical psychology, Vol. III.* New York: Grune & Stratton, 1958, 28-85.
6. Cronbach, L. J., The two disciplines of scientific psychology. *Amer. Psychol.,* 1957, *12,* 671-684.
7. David, Henry P., and Blank, Leonard, eds., *Manpower and psychology: Joint responsibilities of universities and states.* Washington, D.C.: Government Printing Office, 1963.
8. DuMas, F. M., Clinical statements as scientific propositions and social decisions. *J. Consult. Psychol.,* 1955, *19,* 255-258.
9. Grebstein, L, C., Relative accuracy of actuarial prediction; experienced clinicians and graduate students in a clinical judgment task. *J. Consult. Psychol.,* 1963, *27,* 127-132.
10. Gurvitz, Milton S., *The dynamics of psychological testing.* New York: Grune & Stratton, 1951.
11. Gynther, M.D., A note on the Meehl-Dahlstrom rules for discriminating psychotic from neurotic MMPI profiles. *J. Clin. Psychol.,* 1963, *19,* 226.
12. Harding, G. F., and Cravens, R. B., Military clinical psychology. *Amer. Psychol.,* 1957, *12,* 89-91.
13. Harvey, O. J., Hunt, D. E., and Schroeder, H. M., *Conceptual systems and personality organization.* New York: Wiley, 1961.
14. Holtzman, W. H., Can the computer supplant the clinician? *J. Clin. Psychol.,* 1960, *16,* 119-122.
15. Holtzman, W. H., *Inkblot perception of personality.* Houston: Univ. of Texas, 1961.
16. Klopfer, Walter G., *The psychological report.* New York: Grune & Stratton, 1960.
17. Korman, M., and Blumberg, S., Comparative efficiency of some tests of cerebral damage. *J. Consult. Psychol.,* 1963, *27,* 303-309.
18. L'Abate, L., et al., The diagnostic usefulness of four potential tests of brain damage. *J. Consult. Psychol.,* 1962, *26,* 479.
19. L'Abate, L., The laboratory method in psychodiagnosis of adults. Ms. unpublished.
20. L'Abate, L., The laboratory method in psychodiagnosis of children. Ms. unpublished.

21. Leary, T., *Interpersonal diagnosis of personality: a functional theory and methodology for personality evaluation.* New York: Ronald Press, 1957.

22. Luchins, A. J., Integration of clinical and experimental theoretical psychology through core courses. *Psychol. Rep.,* 1955, *1,* 221-246. *Monogr. Suppl.*

23. Lykken, D. T., and Rose, R., Psychological prediction from actuarial tables. *J. Clin. Psychol.,* 1963, *19,* 139-151.

24. Meehl, P. E., and Dahlstrom, W. G., Objective configural rules for discriminating psychotic from neurotic MMPI profiles. *J. Consult. Psychol.,* 1960, *24,* 375-387.

25. Meehl, P.E., and Rosen, A., Antecedent probability and the efficiency of psychometric signs, patterns, and cutting scores., *Psychol. Bull.,* 1955, *52,* 194-216.

26. Miller, N. E., Effects of drugs on motivation: the value of using a variety of measures. *J. N. Y. Acad. Sci.,* 1956, *65,* 318-333.

27. Miller, N. E., Experiments on motivations: studies combining psychological, physical and pharmacological techniques. *Science,* 1957, *126,* 1271-1278.

28. Oskamp, S., The relationship of clinical experience and training methods to several criteria of clinical prediction. *Psychol. Monogr.,* 1962, *76,* No. 28 (Whole No. 547).

29. Peskin, H., Unity of science begins at home: a study of regional factionalism in clinical psychology. *Amer. Psychol.,* 1963, *18,* 101-104.

30. Reitan, R. N., *The effects of brain-lesions on adaptive abilities in human beings.* Indianapolis: Ind. Univ. Med. Center, Dept. Surgery, 1959, Ditto.

31. Tyler, F. B., Integrating scientific and professional training at the graduate level. *J. Clin. Psychol.,* 1963, *19,* 116-120.

32. Weiss, Janis H., Effect of professional training and amount and accuracy of information on behavioral prediction. *J. Consult. Psychol.,* 1963, *27,* 257-262.

33. Winter, W. D., and Stortroen, M., A comparison of several MMPI indices to differentiate psychotics from normals. *J. Clin. Psychol.,* 1963, *19,* 220-223.

Training for Psychotherapy

GORDON F. DERNER

Psychotherapy is a practice based on psychological principles and, therefore, is an essential part of psychology. For many years, but since World War II with increasing momentum, psychologists have devoted themselves to psychotherapy practice. At least one state law, New York, specifically authorizes the practice of psychotherapy by psychologists. The APA has made many public statements acknowledging psychology's role in psychotherapy. The *Shakow* Report and the *Boulder* Conference recommended psychotherapy training as an essential part of clinical psychology education.

University and/or professional school program

University departments of psychology have had to accommodate to the student whose role-model is not the professor or the laboratory scientist but the humane person giving help, solace, and scientific zeal to those problems of suffering called personality disorders. Some universities have disclaimed for themselves and sometimes even for other universities any stake in the training of students with forthright professional practice goals. As psychology emerges in its professional direction, the training for practice may become the responsibility of a professional school. The professional school for psychology, however, must be based in the best tradition of practice which develops and is remolded on a firm ground of scholarly theory and research. Although psychotherapy can be practiced on a limited basis as a technical skill, therapy then becomes essentially subprofessional. Full training requires extensive educational and experiential back-

175

ground. Psychologists should be trained at the full professional level which requires doctoral and postdoctoral training and experience. The course of training and supervised experience will take at least five and possibly nine years. Programs of a shorter period have been suggested but they usually entail curtailment of the curriculum in general psychological science and psychodiagnostics, with greater emphasis throughout on therapy practice. In sharp contrast are university programs which oppose professionalization in psychology and curtail clinical training (often placing responsibility for such training outside the university) and concentrate the educational program on research.

There has also been some movement to make psychotherapy a new profession onto itself. Such a plan could very well remove psychotherapy from the rigors of scientific study so necessary for its development. Additionally, with the enormous need for psychotherapists, there is the restriction which would inevitably come from the smaller numbers to be trained and the limitation of the practice of psychotherapy by those commonly called the mental health professions: psychology, psychiatry, social work, and other professions as well. Rather than launch a new profession, it would seem desirable if all professions now training psychotherapists reexamine their programs and expand their training facilities. Psychology is in a particularly advantageous position because the body of theory of psychotherapy is psychology, the university where psychology is taught offers a scholarly climate and research-mindedness, and professional vigor is available in many younger and energetic psychologist-psychotherapists.

The university has a responsibility either through departments of psychology or a new type of professional school to further the training for therapy practice by psychologists. The key to this practice is supervised therapy of exemplary quality.

Prerequisites for training

Six factors contribute directly to the quality of the practice. They are 1) supervision, 2) the extent of practice in time, 3) the intensity of practice, 4) the range of human problems brought to the therapist, 5) the opportunity for evaluation and experimentation, and 6) the opportunity for professional exchange with coworkers.

It is a peculiarity of some academic institutions, mental hygiene clinics, and mental hospitals that persons appointed as supervisors often, and with good reason, do not feel, and are in fact not, qualified for their supervisory responsibilities. The supervisor should be a person of maturity, with an extended period of practice himself, and preferably be a Diplomate in Clinical Psychology of the ABEPP. He should be actively engaged in the practice of psychotherapy. Wherever possible analytic training or other substantial postdoctoral training should be expected to have been obtained by the supervisor. As a practitioner himself, he will be aware of the practical problems faced by his trainees, be prepared to accept responsibility for his trainee's practice, and be cognizant of the subtle nuances of therapy activity. As an experienced therapist he can afford the luxury of calm alertness to problems but will be prepared to deal with therapeutic crises. His assurance and skill will be helpful and supportive to the neophyte. The experienced therapist also can afford to experiment and develop new ideas and methods. He is not made anxious by deviations from "orthodoxy," and so can communicate a spirit of inventiveness and adaptability in the application of technique.

In the beginning of training in therapy practice, supervision will require step-by-step review of the particular patient's difficulties, careful establishment of goals, and then an outline of the therapeutic procedure. Tape recordings and actual observation through a one-way vision mirror or participation in the interview afford the most effective methods for supervision. The supervisor can demonstrate through his supervision how therapy is conducted. This is not to suggest that supervision is envisioned as therapy. In supervision those problems of the therapist which interfere with the therapy are examined. If the problems cannot be dealt with as here-and-now issues but require intensive personal investigation, then therapy for the therapist is indicated, not supervision.

With intensive supervision, the full hour of therapy is reviewed—exchange by exchange. As supervision progresses and the neophyte therapist develops skill and awareness in the therapeutic process, the supervision can concentrate on increasingly subtle issues of dynamics and technique. The student may then choose selections from the therapy hour, rather than all exchanges, for close examination. The tape recording may be used selectively for intensive study, and a typescript or summary may suffice for other parts of the hour. Gradually the apprenticeship tapers off although all therapists find it necessary, from time to time, to consult a colleague on their therapy. An interesting innovation has been used by the Atlanta Psychiatric Clinic group in which a colleague is brought into the therapy session to help the therapist become aware of elements of transference and counter-transference. Good supervision will encourage the willingness to be alert continuously to one's practice no matter how experienced one becomes. The quality, experience, and skill of the supervisor in teaching methods of therapy, humanity, and critical but positive attitudes toward treatment is the key to the development of therapy skills and also therapy development.

The time it takes to mellow into that stage in which full responsibility for psychotherapy can be assumed by the therapist depends, in part, on the individual. The period of supervised practice must be of sufficient length, that is not less than three years and, more likely, five years. In the usual clinical psychology program, supervised practice is begun in the student's third year, during his internship.

If the university then maintains a therapy program of high quality, as a fourth-year clerkship, the student will be well along toward professional competence. A more desirable arrangement would have the student take didactic work in therapy during his second year and remain at the university for his third year during which he could begin his therapy practice under university supervision. His fourth year would then be spent on an internship where his experience in psychotherapy could be broadened.

In either arrangement he would have at least two years of supervised therapy practice in his predoctoral program. By having experience in an outpatient clinic (not just a university counseling center where he would see only young adults) and an inpatient service, he would encounter a wide range of human problems, possibly including children and adults, character and emotional disorders, relatively normal persons and special cases like retardation.

The student should be encouraged to try many methods. The model of psychotherapy based upon psychoanalysis is probably the most widespread but other methods should be considered. Recent advances in operant procedures and conditioning should lead to exploration and critical evaluation of these methods.

Evaluation and self-evaluation should be continually encouraged. Critical concern about methods used reflects a frame of mind devoted to improvement of professional practice. Experimentation is welcome but must proceed in a planned way. Opportunity to evaluate new ideas in therapy practice can often be afforded by consultative visits from experienced therapists who have definite points of view. If new methods that are quite different from those used by the supervison are introduced, the supervisor needs tolerance for the difference. He can help the student therapist to be willing to experiment or he can deaden his interest by a doctrinaire point of view.

Case conferences and therapy seminars with students and supervisors holding differing viewpoints can sharpen thinking about therapy. While informal exchange is one source of learning, organized seminars can offer structure for critical thinking. Such seminars do not need the anti-therapy devil's advocate but they do need an atomsphere of the scholarly search. Debates may get heated but if the focus is on mutual learning the debate can fulfill the important task of continuing critical examination of theory and method.

The first two years of therapy practice would therefore be in the context of scholarship and research which is the forte of the university. The beginning of therapy practice would become a central part of the student's predoctoral education. (*See also* Chapter 5.). The course of study for practice in psychotherapy at the predoctoral level would include supervised practice as well as a suitable breadth of academic training. An additional two to four years of supervised experience and, where feasible, postdoctoral training is needed to become an independent practitioner.

The postdoctoral training (*see* Chapter 6) is not to be viewed as a substitute for predoctoral training or a make-shift arrangement to make up for inadequate predoctoral training. Postdoctoral training should build on a firm base of acquired predoctoral therapy training.

Predoctoral training must not be a mere introduction to psychotherapy but must include a substantial beginning for practice. It is a curious phenomenon that the descriptions both of the university practicum and the internship often state that the goal is to give the student an introduction to psychotherapy. One wonders who gives the advanced experience.

The course of study on the predoctoral level to prepare for psychotherapy practice requires all the usual training for clinical psychology as well as the training in psychotherapy per se. The *Shakow* Report and the *Boulder* conference outline the general academic background. Specific course content should include general and clinical psychology theory, research and statistics, biological and sociological bases of behavior and didactic clinical courses, supervised practicums and case conferences.

The whole field of psychological knowledge is potentially pertinent to clinical practice. However, choices of emphasis must be made. These will vary from program to program. A particular program will probably function best when it uses the talents of faculty and staff members who have interests that may potentially be related to the clinical areas. Such faculty members will be most helpful to the neophyte therapist when they than offer a view toward fuller understanding of the therapeutic process rather than demeaning clinical practice. Generally, areas such as learning, perception, and motivation can be central to understanding and planning therapeutic interventions. The limitations of knowledge in many areas are a handicap but they need not lead to nihilism. A wholesome questioning of "pure knowledge" concurrent with a questioning of "applied knowledge" will give the student perspective. A cynical view of psychotherapy on the part of his professors may discourage the student from proceeding with the study of therapy or he may revolt against "academic psychology." In the former case the possibility of his contribution to therapy vanishes. In the latter he may fail to enrich his practice through the trying of new ways; he may not reevaluate his theory of practice and may establish a gulf rather than a bridge between his activities and those of many of his colleagues. Although the basic areas of psychology can become a rich background for therapy, it must be made clear that much of psychology is not directly or indirectly, presently or maybe even in the future, applicable to psychotherapy.

Among theory courses which are directly relevant for the psychotherapy student are developmental psychology, social psychology, personality theory, psychopathology, and psychodynamics.

Developmental psychology should cover the knowledge of human psychological growth from birth to death. With increasing knowledge growing out of genetics, even prenatal issues become important. Certain crucial periods of life are particularly important for the therapy student.

Social psychology affords an understanding of the individual beyond the intrapsychic or interpersonal level. Applications of group dynamic theory to group psychotherapy are self-evident, but there are many other applications. Problems of the adolescent in psychotherapy, for example, may often be seen most fruitfully in the context of his social group rather than as an intrapsychic event.

Personality theory extends psychological knowledge into the area most directly pertinent to clinical practice. Complications brought on by philosophical issues, such as the nature of man, humanist versus mechanistic views of behavior, and focus on the observable versus metapsychological constructs, impose a substantial burden on the professor who is preparing the student for psychotherapy practice. Two approaches appear to be helpful: either to review several theories critically and help the student develop a personal theory of personality or to teach a single theory in depth, albeit critically. The first approach places the burden on the teacher to discourage an eclecticism which may be self-contradictory or just personally pleasing rather than substantially integrated. The second approach, which permits consistent and orderly investigation, can also lead to a dogmatic and doctrinaire position which makes questioning intolerable.

The course in psychopathology should be more than psychiatric nomenclature. The therapy student needs to know psychiatric language and the nosology of emotional disorder. He needs to know about treatment methods other than psychotherapy and when they are helpful. He should know about the biochemical methods, electric shock treatment, hospitalization, and environmental manipulation. The study of psychopathology requires clinical demonstrations. It must serve as a basis for therapeutic planning not for psychiatric name-calling.

Psychodynamics, or the study of human motives, is central to human understanding. To date the insights of Freud serve as a basis for most psychodynamic investigation. Freud did not allow his old ideas to prejudice him against new ones, and in turn the student of Freud will need to go beyond Freud. He can be well served with a thorough familiarity with Freudian theory as a starting point for exploration into the complexities of human behavior and for attempts at changes in behavior. Some later theorists offer important elaborations, extensions, and reformulations. Sullivan is particularly noteworthy because of his empiricism, operationalism, and clinical grounding. Murray also offers a substantial formulation of psychodynamics which is based on intensive research.

Research methods and statistics are required to make psychotherapy a scientific endeavor rather than simply an artistic pursuit. There is a need for more efficient, more dependable, more available, and financially more reasonable methods of psychotherapy, especially when viewed from a community mental health perspective. Only research can improve the procedures and insure more satisfactory outcomes. The value of research-mindedness in therapy is evident if we think of distinguished psychologists as diverse as Freud, Rogers, Ellis, Mowrer, Kelley, and Wolpe.

Research training for the therapist will probably have its greatest impact if, in addition to exposure to laboratory-oriented research, he receives clinical research training.

Biological and sociological sciences give the therapy student a frame of reference. He needs to know something of physiology and, increasingly so, neuropsychology. These areas need to be studied (in conjunction with clinical presentations) in their applied areas, i.e., clinical medicine and clinical neurology. The sociological studies should include anthropology as well as sociology. Knowledge of sub-cultures is particularly important for the psychotherapist. Studies of literature and the great myths may aid the therapist in gaining insight into human behavior and methods of behavioral change.

Experience should be obtained with normal as well as abnormal people. A good place to begin work is in the public schools where a wide range of children and adolescents can be observed. During the student's first year a series of seminars that bring together diagnostics with clinical field experiences will start him on his way toward becoming a therapist. The clinical work should continue in a variety of settings, such as a university counseling center, a child guidance clinic, a mental hygiene clinic, a mental hospital. It is crucial to the training that all work is carefully supervised.

In his years at the university, the student should spend about half of his time in clinical pursuits. During his second year he should begin didactic courses in psychotherapy, both theory and method. Case conferences, seminars, and supervised practice focusing on therapy will continue throughout the predoctoral period.

While predoctoral training will need to accept professional practice as one of its goals, the postdoctoral program will probably have practice as its primary goal. The curriculum should include theoretical courses, technical courses, case conferences, research courses, and supervised practice—all designed to help the therapist attain therapeutic effectiveness. He will need to be sensitive to the cultural, philosophical, and personal forces within himself and his patients. This demands personal maturity on a high level which often can be obtained only through personal therapy for the therapist. With the rationale similar to that of the predoctoral program, the critical appraisal of theory and method with alertness to the many unsolved problems in psychotherapy needs to be constantly emphasized. A scholarly atmosphere is desirable. It allows evaluation, examination, and the pursuit of new ideas as well as learning the old ones. Thus, the program can be carried out best in the tradition of the university. At present two such university programs exist, one at New York University and the other at Adelphi University. The programs extend over several years of training with specialized courses, extensive supervised practice, and personal therapy.

The extension and intensification of predoctoral programs

with clear professional objectives that will go hand in hand with programs devoted to research objectives seems very likely. In keeping with such a development, more university-based post-doctoral programs for research and for practice also seem likely. A combined predoctoral and postdoctoral program in a professional school also seems on the horizon. The development of the professional school may fulfill the promise made that "promotion of human welfare" is one of the objectives of psychology.

Society has accepted psychology's role in psychotherapy. Psychology must continue to improve its contribution to psychotherapy, both with more well-trained practitioners and more research. The effectiveness of the research will be dependent upon the quality of training of the practitioner.

Specialized Training for Research

Leslie Phillips

Introduction

In clinical psychology the concept of research includes the development of new knowledge and new methods in the area of mental health programming. As noted in the report[16] on the *Stanford* Conference, "Present knowledge of the nature, etiology and treatment of mental illness and of the factors involved in the establishment and maintenance of mental health is so inadequate that research must be given highest priority," and ". . . opinion favored placing higher priority on research and on the development of preventive programs" (p. 128).

Research and development in mental health can be considered the unique and distinguishing function of the clinical psychologist. If undertaken on a wide scale, mental health research and development would set the clinical psychologist apart from other types of psychologists, and would distinguish him also from members of other disciplines in the mental health field.

The writer proposes, and will attempt to demonstrate from available evidence, that clinical psychologists as a group, however, have failed to fulfill this task of research leadership in mental health programs. It is this failure, I believe, rather than any general failure in research productivity which endangers the unique identity of the clinical psychologist. This is contrary to the kind of criticism that has been leveled at this profession.[8,9] What evidence I have been able to discover will be adduced in support of the proposition that graduates of clinical psychology programs are not uniquely deficient in the production of traditional forms of research. Rather, they have not fulfilled the hope that clinical psychology would make major contributions to research and the development of new forms of mental health programs.

Since there is ambiguity in the assessment of the success or failure of clinical psychology as a profession, and since this assessment is dependent to some extent on one's definition of a clinical psychologist, it is necessary to clarify the criteria for this category of worker. The broadest classification used in this chapter will restrict the title of clinical psychologist to those obtaining a doctorate in this discipline. Within this totality there exist at least three clearly recognizable groups: a large group which may be taken to include those who go into clinical practice, whether public or private (this includes also those primarily active in university clinics); a much smaller group who join an academic faculty, and whose prime function is teaching or the direction of a university clinical training program; and a small residual group whose dominant activity is to carry on research programs in clinical settings.

The second (academic) group tends to become involved in those types of research which can be identified as falling within the current framework of psychology, e.g., perception, personality, learning. The research productivity of these people tends not to contribute, directly at least, to the innovation of new clinical procedures. It is to the first and third groups that we must look for new contributions to mental health programs.

We will first discuss the sequence of graduate education as this has been operative for most clinical students. To anticipate the findings detailed below, we shall examine why this training fails to develop the kind of leading cadre to which the psychology profession has aspired. The writer takes a pessimistic view of the likelihood that any decisive change for the better can be brought about on a national scale in the graduate education of the clinical psychologist. Consequently, there is little warrant to expect any substantial change in the role and status of the practitioner members of this profession. Because of the barriers which hinder the further development of graduate education in clinical psychology, the writer proposes that the establishment of postdoctoral programs of training for clinical research may well be the most feasible approach to the fulfillment of the professional aspirations which have been expressed for clinical psychology.

The last section of this chapter will be devoted to an analysis of the requirements of such programs, illustrated by the postdoctoral training in research provided at Worcester State Hospital.

Graduate Training for Research in Clinical Psychology

As noted above, the professional identity of the clinical psychologist remains highly ambiguous. This ambiguity is inherent in the original definition imposed on him. The source of this difficulty has been outlined by Kenneth Clark[2] as follows:

"Psychology today is trying to succeed in a social experiment which has resulted only in failure when tried by others. We are striving to keep within the same social structure the creators of psychological knowledge and the professional persons who apply this knowledge to human problems; in older disciplines, such as physics and biology, separation has been the rule, rather than the exception. We are willing as a group to try to make the experiment work, and are willing to pay some appropriate price to achieve the continuance of the union, for we believe that at our current state of knowledge the practitioner requires close association with the researcher, in order that he may learn more about the development of the science; but the researcher also needs to be in close communication with the practitioner, in order that the problems on which he works may have some relation to the world in which the problems are being faced in a day-to-day situation" (p. 121).

Sharp criticism has been leveled at the product of our national effort in the training of clinical psychologists. An adequate review of these programs and any suggestions for their modification requires that we take cognizance of those critical assessments which have already appeared in the literature. We shall turn to these first.

Publication rate of the clinical psychologist. A major criticism has been that clinical psychologists are not productive as investigators, using publication rate as a criterion. I believe this interpretation of a sparse research productivity among clinical psychologists is based on an inadequate reading of the record.

Critics have failed to consider the publication rates of other psychologists and other scientists. When such controls are instituted, the deficiency of the clinical psychologist in the publication of scientific papers is by no means clear.

Illustrative of the criticism directed at clinical psychologists, Kelly and Goldberg[8] have reported that a sample of 167 clinical Ph.D.'s drawn from former VA trainees were "not contributing much to the current literature of psychology" (p. 18). These psychologists were first studied in 1947 as predoctoral students and re-evaluated in 1957, some seven or eight years after most had received their doctorates. In this period, 47% had failed to publish and another 23% had but one publication to their credit. The top 10% of this group had produced five or more titles.

Levy[9] also expressed concern over the non-productivity of the clinical Ph.D. He studied a group of 781 persons whose dissertations were listed by Rabin in his paper "Doctoral dissertations in clinical training programs: 1948-1953." Levy searched the Psychological Abstracts from 1948 through 1960 for published entries under the names of these individuals. The group studied by Kelly and Goldberg were part of Levy's population. Since doctorates were awarded to members of this group over a span of six years (1948-1953), it seems reasonable to assume that the average time period post-Ph.D. until 1960 was approximately 10 years. In this interval, 28.9% of this group had not published, and another 19.2% had only one publication each to their credit, 48% thus producing either zero or one paper. The top 10% of the group accounted for 45% of all published titles, or an average of 17 publications for each member. Levy viewed this performance as a reflection on the doctoral training program in clinical psychology and commented that ". . . we might pause to consider whether the fact that approximately 30% of a population purportedly trained in research methodology and indoctrinated in the importance of research and communication have produced not a single publication requires any revision in our image of the clinical psychologist and his training" (p. 246).

Although Levy was aware of data provided by Dennis[4] in 1954 that would be pertinent for comparison, he made inadequate use of these. Dennis examined the productivity of several groups of psychologists active professionally from 1887 to the early 1950's. He observed that the total number of publications in each group tended to be the work of a relatively small proportion of that group. In each one of his four samples, the less productive half contributed 15% or less to its total output. Dennis was not concerned with the issue of absolute productivity, and therefore did not report average number of publications for all his groups or their segments. However, he provided sufficient data to permit the calculation of a few comparisons to the publication productivity of present-day clinical psychologists.

Dennis' first group was composed of all psychologists listed in Murchison's Psychological Register who were born prior to 1879 and who were living in 1932. Dennis counted the total publications of each of these 160 individuals up to age 50. The top decile in productivity produced 47% of all titles, an average of 89 papers. The lower half of the distribution, however, produced an average of only 2.7 titles.

It is not possible to calculate absolute productivity for any of the other groups reported on by Dennis. His fourth group consisted of all persons who published between 1887 and 1900 in the only two American psychological journals of that period. Dennis noted that in this group, *all of whom—obviously—had published at least one original article,* each man in the bottom half of the productivity distribution had published only one article. We have no evidence on the number or proportion of psychologists who failed to publish during this same period. We must remember that academic pursuits, including original investigation, was a way of life in this early period of American psychology, with none of the "distractions" of professional practice, and must further recognize that the educated segment of American life, including psychologists, represented a far smaller and select element of the total population. With these considerations in mind, I propose that the case is by no means proved that today's clinical psychologists are less productive in original research than were the academic individuals who worked in an earlier period.

The low research productivity of such a large proportion of today's clinical psychologists does not appear due to any peculiarity of the breed or of their training, but appears quite generally in all of psychology. Dennis noted, for example, that the most productive person in his first sample of 160 psychologists produced more papers than all 80 individuals who made up his lowest five deciles of productivity. Further, data from other disciplines show that this phenomenon of productivity restricted to the few holds generally among the sciences. Approximately 75% of investigators in all sciences who produce one original paper do little more. It is the 10% of productive writers who are responsible for one-half the world's scientific literature.[11] It follows that criticism cannot realistically be leveled at present-day clinical psychology training as failing to produce research-oriented investigators unless this charge is directed at graduate education in psychology generally, and indeed in all fields of science.

Research and Development in mental health and the clinical psychologist. A more directly pertinent question is whether the production of research papers by individuals holding a doctorate in clinical psychology is evidence that clinical psychologists are fulfilling their role as investigators and creators of new forms of mental health programs.

At the beginning of this chapter, a distinction was drawn between graduates of clinical psychology programs who work in academic posts and those who work in practitioner settings. The publications of the former will not be likely to represent direct contributions to mental health programs. The question, then, is whether the latter, who represent the great majority of clinical psychology doctorates, have contributed their share to mental health advances.

Both the 1947 *Boulder* Conference[13] and the 1955 *Stanford* Conference[16] considered the question of the contribution which psychology might make in the mental health field. The *Stanford* Conference, in particular, concentrated on an area of increasing concern for a number of professional disciplines; that is, the need to explore the many social and community factors which might operate as aids or detriments to mental health.

The conviction was expressed that, in the foreseeable future, no available methods of treatment would be able to meet all community mental health needs. The prediction was made that the development of new methods of treatment and prevention would soon become of immediate concern. Two conclusions were reached: 1) that research into the factors operative in the maintenance of an individual's mental health is the prime necessity in this expanding field, and 2) that clinical psychologists, with their specialized training in research procedures, should play a leading role in these innovations.

Nevertheless, in a survey of clinical psychologists conducted in 1960, Kelly[7] still found his modal respondent spending the greater part of his working day in intensive individual psychotherapy with adult patients either in a medical setting or in private practice. He expressed himself as ". . . deeply concerned about several discrepancies between the image of the clinical psychologist whom we talked about training at the *Boulder* Conference and the clinical psychologist mirrored in our survey findings" (p. 9). Based on his data, Kelly posed as a major issue "What sort of public image is clinical psychology developing for itself and is it the public image which we seek" (p. 10)?

That we are not creating a profession dedicated to research and innovation in the therapeutic function was noted by Pratt[10] who pointed out in 1961 that of ten major books recently published on changing clinical practices in the mental hospital, none has a psychologist as a senior author, and only two have a psychologist as one of its junior authors.

Other data also indicate that psychologists in clinical settings fail to play a leading role in therapeutic innovation. Psychologists have taken pride in the fact that members of their profession serve as principal investigators on more research grants supported by the NIMH than any other profession. In 1961, for example,[18] psychologists held 54% of all regular grants of NIMH, while psychiatrists, biologists, and social scientists shared only between 11 to 13% in each of these disciplines. It is true, that, on the average, psychiatrists directed financially larger grants, but even in terms of monies awarded, 45% went to psychologists and only 22% to psychiatrists.

Interpretation of these figures, however, must be tempered by the fact that 79% of regular NIMH grants were allocated to colleges and universities, and that 80% of all psychologists to obtain such funds were affiliated with academic institutions. Only 10% of these psychologists were affiliated with hospitals and

clinics. Unpublished data for the fiscal year 1962 only mildly
modify this bleak picture:

". . . the actual research activities sponsored by the research grant
program are more heavily represented in clinical settings than would
appear to be the case. In nearly one-fourth of the projects supported,
for example, hospitals provided the setting and the support for the
research—including the use of patients, data, and facilities."[15]

The NIMH awards a class of project grants (Title V) ". . . for
the purpose of conducting studies and demonstrations which will
promote the development of improved methods of care, treatment, and rehabilitation of the mentally ill, and stimulate the
growth of interest and development of skills in mental health
programs."[18] Here is a type of program that closely parallels the
stated objectives for psychologists in mental health work. Clinical psychologists should be active in these functions if they are to
live up to the aspirations which have been expressed for their
profession. Unfortunately, it is precisely in this field of function
that psychologists appear as a minority group. In 1961, for
example, psychologists held only 21% of such grants, while
psychiatrists directed 37% of all Title V grants awarded, with
social work, a thoroughly applied profession, being responsible
for nearly as many grants as psychology. (See Chapter 2.)

How has it come about that psychology has failed to live up to
its own aspiration of providing leadership in the development of
new forms of mental health programs? Tryon[17] has suggested an
answer with which the present writer thoroughly agrees:

"Administratively, the clinical psychologist got himself into the
worst possible situation. He came under the complete administrative
control of the medically trained psychiatrist. Few psychiatrists
understood what psychologists were trained to do, hence understandably administered psychologists in the very terms that the
psychologists accepted for themselves, namely, as "little psychiatrists"—and poorly trained ones at that. Now, what the psychologist
was trained *for* was to do r*esearch,* a very high status function which
he could perform with considerably greater understanding and
experience than the psychiatrist, and a function badly needed, considering the state of ignorance in the field of mental health. I feel sure
that until the psychologist gets himself *autonomously* in the role of
research worker in mental disorders, his professional lot in clinics and

hospitals is going to continue to be an inferior and unhappy one," (pp. 138-139; italics in original).

How, in fact, did the clinical psychologist get himself into the unfortunate situation described by Tryon, and why has he failed to live up to his self-ascribed role of investigator, when of all disciplines active in the mental health field he is the best trained in research?

The reasons are multiple and complex, some originating in the clinical psychologist himself and in his pattern of professional existence, some in the established sequence of graduate training and the value system of academic psychology. Most central, however, are the divergences between academic and clinical psychologists in *Weltanschauung* and value systems, differences which divide these groups prior to graduate education, through the graduate years, and in the postdoctoral period. We must remember, too, that the relation of clinician to academician is initially and most critically that of student to professor. In the formative years of the clinician, it is he who is schooled by the academician and it is the academician who holds a most decisive power over the subsequent professional status of his student, i.e., whether or not he shall achieve a doctorate.

Let us briefly review the well-known discordance between the clinical student and his professor through his career in graduate school. Characteristically, clinical students (usually as a group constituting more than half the student body) are attracted into psychology through a desire to help people, to become members of a healing profession. Faculty members see it as their duty to knock this "nonsense" out of the students for they visualize psychology as a science, a body of knowledge about laws, not men, to paraphrase a precept of the legal profession. Their objective is to create experimentalists, and, hopefully, scholars.

During the graduate years, the clinical student is exposed to two divergent sets of pressures; one from the university department, the other, from his practicum and internship experiences. Let us examine these in some detail.

The university faculty typically educates the student by exposing him to courses in methodology, laboratory experimentation, statistics, and so forth, as well as to theoretical courses in personality and more academic aspects of psychology. Note that the traditional program of study stresses intrapsychic phenomena, as is appropriate for conventional concepts about the nature of psychology. But note also that the sphere of the intrapsychic does not conform to the newer fields in which innovations in mental health program development are taking place, e.g., psychopharmacology, neuro- and psychophysiology, and family and community structure and organization.

As expressed by Strother[16] in his summary of the *Stanford* Conference:

"More emphasis will need to be placed on the importance of a broad social science background. Knowledge of the cultural and social factors involved in personality development and in behavior will be as essential as knowledge of the structure and functions of the human organism. Both on the undergraduate and on the graduate levels, greater familiarity with the concepts, methodologies and data of cultural anthropology and sociology must be encouraged" (p. 128).

Further,

". . . Familiarity with the instruments, methodologies, experimental designs and statistical techniques presently utilized in the psychological laboratory will not be sufficient. A great deal of exploratory research and the development of new tools and methods will be required before a critical attack on many problems in the field of mental health will be possible. Investigations must be carried on in the clinic, the hospital, and the community as well as in the laboratory. Consequently the student must develop skills in field, as well as in laboratory research. Interdisciplinary research, too, is becoming essential and some experience with the problems of communication and coordination involved in such research would be useful" (p. 129).

For the most part, university psychology has not incorporated these fields of study into the clinical curriculum. The reasons are probably multiple. They do not fit the conventional concept of psychology; typically, they lie outside the sphere mastered by the faculty; they are "messy" fields for research; and in any case, the active investigators on the faculty are often already involved in psychological projects more easily carried out on a university campus, projects which may well be supported by NIMH grants.

It will be remembered that the majority of regular NIMH awards go to psychologists, and the bulk of these are given to colleges and universities. It is likely, therefore, that the small segment of clinical psychologists who publish regularly on new research are mostly those holding academic appointments.

Traditional programs in clinical psychology provide for one full year of graduate education to be spent in some clinical institution obtaining direct experience with deviant populations. This exposure to clinic function provides the contact with human problems that is so essential for meaningful future research by the student. The internship experience itself, however, is primarily practical in nature, consisting largely of diagnostic and psychotherapeutic experience. Clinicians rightfully claim that the work of future investigators must be built on adequate clinical knowledge, and that the traditional internship is the minimum requirement for its achievement. Nevertheless, the internship might be a time when the student could be exposed to a critical analysis of institutional programs and to discussions of the theoretical issues involved in established clinical procedures. Most often, however, the student is indoctrinated into existing clinical programs without opportunity to explore possible alternatives.

In order to achieve some integration of the clinical practicum with an opportunity for research experience, it has been suggested[3,14] that some aspects of research training be assigned to the staffs of clinical agencies. Typically, this does not come about for several reasons. Psychologists in clinical centers are, for the most part, not involved in research, nor is there a tradition of investigation in these institutions upon which this activity can be built. Further, the university faculty who will be responsible for supervising the research experience of their students are likely to hold research grants for which the services of graduate students are required. Since the faculty determines who will achieve the doctorate, and how quickly, students find it expedient to become involved in those projects to which members of the academic staff are committed.

In any case, the present psychology staffs of both university faculties and clinical centers are typically unable to provide the kinds of training which will permit those students able to develop new types of clinic and community programs to fulfill their promise. Most clinical students today go into non-academic settings for which their rigorous theoretical and methodological academic education in interpsychic phenomena is inappropriate. For the most part, they find job opportunities which focus on the application of those clinical skills which they have learned through practicum and internship experiences. Consequently, in such settings they appear most adequately trained in precisely those areas least valued by the faculty—psychotherapy, personality evaluation, and diagnosis.

In clinical centers, the initiation of a research program or a change in established procedures would, at best, be an uphill fight. Since the clinical student's original objective was that of helping people and healing the sick, and since in the clinic he enters a center dominated by just such a value system, it is no wonder that we so often see a "return of the repressed," i.e., the reappearance of the clinical values which the student temporarily suppressed within the academic setting. In their university training, clinical psychologists had to accept a program of training which they did not want, so that they might acquire an academic title which is inappropriate but necessary for current professional practice.

The writer recognizes that this analysis of training for research in graduate programs in clinical psychology is rather depressing. More positive aspects of training for research in this field have been noted by Garmezy[5] and must be included to provide some balance. He noted that clinical doctoral dissertations increasingly make use of psychiatric populations in the composition of subject samples. He reported also that in isolated instances across the country clinical graduate students have been given an opportunity to participate in research-oriented seminars in clinical centers which are attended by established investigators. Garmezy also commented that some of the clinically most meaningful research of the last few years has come from non-clinical sources. He cited as examples such work as Hebb's investigations of the effects of sensory deprivation, the cortical stimulation studies of Olds, Miller, and others, and that of numerous investigators in the fields of child development and family structure.

Nevertheless, the split between academic and practicing clinical psychologists is so deep and wide that it is difficult to foresee these two groups actively working together in large numbers toward the systematic development of newer forms of clinical procedures. So long as these two types of psychologists are split apart it is likely that the graduate education of clinical students will also remain bifurcated. The writer proposes therefore that postdoctoral programs of training for clinical research and innovation are a possible method for providing clinical psychologists capable of leadership in mental health programs. We now turn to a discussion of the requirements for such postdoctoral programming.

Postdoctoral training in clinical research

As we have noted, training for the doctorate in clinical psychology currently does not encompass all the skills required for the complexities of today's large-scale research enterprises in the field of mental health. It provides a certain basic research sophistication, but cannot equip its candidates for full professional competence. The requisite demands in time and money would be inordinate. The training necessary to permit a sophisticated attack on the problems in the field of mental health requires a mastery of theory and methodology in the border fields of psychophysiology and psychopharmacology, or alternatively in social psychology, sociology, public health administration, and family and community organization. (Yates and Ross[19] suggest a course consisting of 30 two-hour seminars divided into research in 6 content areas: memory and perception, neurophysiology, verbal learning, information theory, personality association, and preconscious perception. Research articles are extensively utilized.—Eds)

The facilities now available for the development of clinical investigators seem to be neither sufficient in number nor adequate in scope for the large corps of professional research personnel essential for today's and tomorrow's requirements in the clinical field. One current source of training lies in participation in the project of an established investigator. The aims of any one project, however, are typically exacting and restricted, and committed to relatively specific time-limited objectives. In these circumstances, independence is circumscribed, experience is likely to be narrow, and the requirements of education for investigation are typically limited by the goals of the particular study itself. Nevertheless, this is a route commonly taken toward the role of the independent researcher.

An alternative path to professional autonomy is that of a postdoctoral research fellowship. A stipend permits the recipient to follow his own particular research interests, and this is all to the good. Nevertheless, there are drawbacks to this form of support also. Particularly unfortunate is the emphasis on the fellow's dedication to a specific and limited piece of research, one within the abilities and resources of a new doctorate working alone. This fellowship structure is the antithesis of that required for a future career as an independent investigator, in view of the dominance of large-scale studies in the borderline fields of clinical investigation.

The Worcester training program. At Worcester State Hospital our postdoctoral training program in research is built around another alternative to that of the apprentice role and the postdoctoral research fellowship. The postdoctoral fellow works within an ongoing program which ranges from biochemistry to crosscultural studies in psychopathology. We attempt to keep some balance between projects directed toward the innovation of new types of therapeutic programs, such as remotivation, family treatment, or rehabilitation, and investigations of a more abstractly theoretical nature, e.g., cognitive styles, psychophysiological interrelations, or genetics.

The setting, Our postdoctoral training program is placed within a setting which provides two major advantages to both staff and students:

1. As part of a clinical complex, investigators have direct access to adult psychiatric inpatients and outpatients. Through close working relations with the staffs of other community agencies, access is also provided to child guidance clinic cases, as well as to a wide variety of children and adults drawn from the general population.

2. Because the psychologist works as a member of an established research and training organization, his relations with his clinical colleagues are explicitly those of a cooperative, mutual

acceptance aimed at the joint development of new orientations in treatment.

The writer is convinced that a research organization which exists in conjunction with a clinical facility must incorporate a spectrum of investigation which ranges from the abstract-theoretical to the more directly applied, and this for two reasons: a) existence of this spectrum of studies maintains for both the clinical and research staffs a clear image of the investigator in a role independent of that of the practitioner, and b) both abstract-theoretical studies and demonstration projects can profit from easy and informal interchanges of their respective investigators.

The program. Within the program of our Research Institute of Life Sciences at Worcester we stress a freedom for the post-doctoral fellow to develop his own investigative interests. In the main, we reject the philosophy of training supported by the Estes Park Seminar[1] (ETB of the APA), which proposed that skills in research are best learned in an apprentice role to an established investigator. We agree that these skills will best be learned in an atmosphere saturated with the spirit of inquiry, but we feel it important to stress also that from the beginning the fellow is embarked on a career of independent investigation. (Holzberg[6] advocates such autonomy for research training of interns. This work, however, is supervised and he encourages the intern to devote regularly spaced time to his research rather than patching a crazy-quilt schedule of diagnosis, therapy, and research.—Eds.)

With some years of experience in postdoctoral training we have come to articulate what the objectives are in a program of research training at the postdoctoral level. Clearly, it cannot be intended to duplicate the academic program of the graduate years, nor can its primary purpose be simply to fill in gaps in the student's knowledge of his field of interest. We have come to realize that the main focus of our program should be to permit and encourage the postdoctoral fellow to achieve independence of his student past, to acquire an identity as an independent professional investigator.

The main objective of our program, then, is the transformation of the student's self-concept from that of apprentice to that of master of the trade of psychological investigation. The problem of status change has psychological overtones, but the means for its accomplishment are of a very practical nature. A set of complex skills needs to be mastered for successful achievement in the field of clinical research. The student must know more than theory or methodology, and be beyond simple technical skill in statistics.

Professional research competence requires sensitivity in the recognition of a problem for investigation; an ability to assess its significance and to weigh the value of its solution; know-how in devising an economic methodology; ability to mobilize resources effectively and efficiently; perseverance in carrying the project to a conclusion; decisiveness and will-power in terminating a study at an appropriate end-point; and an ability to organize data and their interpretation lucidly in written form for journal presentation. These skills are the stock in trade of the professional investigator; but they are not inborn nor are they ordinarily established at the time a doctorate is acquired.

Compared to the magnitude of the tasks which require both theoretical solution and experimental demonstration in the clinical fields, the size of the available cadre of professional personnel is woefully small. It is essential, then, that individual psychologists committed to clinical research learn to maximize the effective use of their time. This requires a decision as to those research activities in which the direct participation of the professonal psychologist is essential and those which can be carried out by auxiliary personnel or machines.

The postdoctoral fellow must learn, then, how to weld nonprofessional personnel into an effective research instrument. At Worcester we have found that this learning is characteristically a long, arduous, and trying experience. To accomplish this task we try to provide the resources necessary for independent professional activity to the extent that the postdoctoral fellow can make constructive use of such facilities.

Studies have been undertaken in industry in which it has been observed that approximately half the work-time of engineers can be saved, and the work thus eliminated can be performed as well or better by much less advanced workers. In psychological research, too, we have found that many of the routines often undertaken by professional psychologists can be completed successfully by people of lesser training. Technicians can be taught to carry out even complex testing programs, including the arranging of test schedules, testing proper, scoring, the tabulation of data, and its analysis or its programming for computer analysis. The research psychologist can then reserve for himself time to formulate the hypotheses to be tested, their required methodology, organization of the resrach team, data interpretation, and the preparation of reports for publication.

The achievement of these skills which mark the independent investigator requires hard practice. In essence it represents the transformation of a graduate student from a skilled apprentice, the role usually played today by the doctoral candidate vis-à-vis his faculty advisor, into an autonomous director of a project team. For we must recognize that the day of the lone investigator in clinical research and its allied fields is largely gone. Indeed, research in all the major scientific disciplines is now dominated by large-scale investigations.

The choice of students. While the encouragement of individual initiative is the *sine qua non* of an effective program of training in research, its success ultimately is dependent on the type of person trained. Our experience in postdoctoral education is that relatively few individuals can take advantage of a setting of freedom. When the social context of learning is unstructured and without definite guidelines for work, control and direction must come from within. The uncertain student, the one waiting for inspiration, the disorganized, the plodding and pedestrian thinker, the passive and apathetic drifter, the flitting dilettante, do not succeed in an atmosphere of permissiveness and freedom. The task of research is a hard master, it demands unswerving commitment to an idea; hardness and firmness in its undertaking; perseverance, doggedness, ingenuity, stubbornness; denial of insurmountable difficulties; and an unflagging drive for completion. These qualities can scarcely be taught, certainly not at the postdoctoral level. They must be brought to the fellowship program as part of one's baggage. They can be neither given nor even simply encouraged in the student who does not already in large measure possess them.

Administrative considerations in the training of research personnel. Particular problems exist for programs which are directed primarily at the training of research workers for mental health work. Until recently, all research fellowships of the Federal government were awarded centrally. Even now only a fraction of the Federal stipends are allocated to students majoring in fields outside that of clinical psychology. In contrast, clinical stipends are awarded by the institution at which the student is in training. This difference in stipend source has a number of critical consequences.

First, it may be observed that the establishment of a system of predoctoral stipends in clinical psychology awarded by the training institutions themselves has helped to establish and foster systematic programs of training for clinical skills. The consistent assignment of such stipends to universities and other institutions has led them to accept a prime responsibility for the development of training programs. This has stabilized and enhanced the level of these programs; it has led to an increase in their number and an expansion in the number of students who go into them. There has thus emerged on the national scene a clearly recognized and systematic predoctoral training sequence in clinical psychology.

With stipends in clinical psychology at the postdoctoral level now being awarded by institutions, there have also emerged a number of specialized postdoctoral training programs for practitioners. Over the past few years some agencies to whom such stipends are available have created a two-year formal sequence of advanced training.

There has been no such concurrent development in training for *research* in clinical psychology. It is true that for a number of years predoctoral research fellowships have been available, but they have had no such decisive impact on developing a corps of professional workers for mental health research as clinical stipends have had on providing practitioners skilled in diagnostic testing, personality evaluation, and psychotherapy.

At the postdoctoral level, in particular, there is as yet no established tradition of formal training in mental health research. Had teaching grants and stipends under local administration been available for training in clinical research, the writer is confident that effective programs in this area would have been developed. Institutions, however, find it difficult to establish systematic training programs in research, for there exists no dependable financial base for their operation.

It must be recognized that like all practicum training, post-doctoral education for clinical research is a highly expensive procedure. In addition to staff time for consultation, we have deemed it essential at Worcester State Hospital to provide equipment for experiments, funds for subjects, clerical and secretarial help, and research assistants for the use of the postdoctoral fellow, insofar as he learns to make effective use of these resources. His experience with the direction of such facilities serves as a bridge to a subsequent career as an independent investigator. The costs of providing such resources for each post-doctoral fellow run high and in our experience can total as much as $5000 per year. This, of course, is in addition to the fellow's own stipend. When we consider that the fellowship can and probably should extend over a period of three years or more, it can be seen that a fellowship program in mental health research represents a very substantial financial investment.

Society is making demands on the profession of psychology which we cannot hope to meet in the foreseeable future. However, our science is relatively unique among disciplines in that it possesses the skills to study its own values and goals and the ways in which these may be optimally achieved. It must soon find an answer to the question of whether it is possible to continue to maintain some balance between investigation on the one hand, and application on the other, within the confines of an increasingly diversified and expanding discipline.

It must be recognized that most fields of science are today undergoing a rapid transmutation into applied professions. We have only to cite the experiences of mathematics, physics, and biology and their involvement in the space-age, and of economics, sociology, and anthropology in the worlds of domestic and international politics. These divisions of science have, of necessity, worked toward some resolution of the issue of their role as theoretical disciplines versus their role as fields of application. What can be learned of relevance to psychology and its training procedures from the internal changes within these other disciplines? Certainly we must recognize that the issues facing psychology in the immediate future are not unique but part of the general transformation of the relation of science to society.

References

1. American Psychological Association, Education and Training Bd., Ad Hoc Comm., Education for research in psychology. *Amer. Psychol.*, 1959, *14*, 167-179. (Estes Park Seminar).
2. Clark, K. E., The summary of progress. In *Training for research in psychology*, K. S. Bernhardt, ed. Toronto: Univ. of Toronto Press, 1961, 119-123.
3. Coons, W. H., Training for clinical research. In *Training for research in psychology*, K. S. Bernhardt, ed. Toronto: Univ. of Toronto Press, 1961, 99.
4. Dennis, W., Productivity among American psychologists. *Amer. Psychol.*, 1954, *9*, 191-194.
5. Garmezy, N., Some problems related to training for research in clinical psychology. Paper read at APA, New York, Sept., 1957.
6. Holzberg, J., Research training during the internship. In *Training for clinical psychology*, M. H. P. Finn and F. Brown, eds. New York: International Universities Press, 1959, 120-138.
7. Kelly, E. L., Clinical Psychology—1960. *Newsletter, Div. of Clin. Psychol.*, APA, 1961, *14*, 1-11.
8. Kelly, E. L., and Goldberg, L. R., Correlates of later performance and specialization in psychology. *Psychol. Monogr.*, 1959, *73* (12, Whole No. 482).
9. Levy, L. H., The skew in clinical psychology. *Amer. Psychol.*, 1962, *17*, 244-249.
10. Pratt, S., Of myth and models: An agonizing reappraisal. Paper read at APA, New York, 1961.
11. Price, D. J. de S., A calculus of science. *International Science & Technology*, 1963, *15*, 37-43.
12. Rabin, A. I., Doctoral dissertations in clinical training programs: 1948-1953. *Amer. Psychol.*, 1954, *9*, 114-116. Cited in L. H. Levy, The skew in clinical psychology.
13. Raimy, V. C. ed., *Training in clinical psychology*. New York: Prentice-Hall, 1950.
14. Rodnick, E. H., Training for research in the mental health field. In *Psychology and mental health*. C. R. Strother, ed. Washington, D.C.: APA, 1956, 93-109.
15. Segal, J., Personal communication. May, 1963.
16. Strother, C. R. ed., *Psychology and mental health*. Washington, D.C.: APA, 1956.
17. Tryon, R. C., Psychology in flux: the academic-professional bipolarity. *Amer. Psychol.*, 1963, *18*, 134-143.
18. U. S. Department of Health, Education and Welfare, *The research grant program of the National Institute of Mental Health* (1961). Bethesda, Md.: 1962.
19. Yates, M., and Ross, J., A new approach to training in research design. *Amer. Psychol.*, 1963, *18*, 214-215.

Training Within A State Program

LEONARD BLANK

HENRY P. DAVID

Of steadily growing importance are the clinical psychology training programs developed in the states. Their growth is reflected in the annual reports of the Conference of Chief Psychologists in State Mental Health Programs (available from the Secretary of the conference, Dr. Jerry W. Carter, Jr., NIMH, Bethesda 14, Md.) and the accreditation of independent intern training centers. As one example we shall describe the New Jersey program. In its diversity of facilities and its spectrum of psychology functions it is typical of state systems. It is unique as the only state-coordinated APA accredited program with a Director of Training.

History

The training of clinical psychologists has been an integral function of the New Jersey State Department of Institutions and Agencies since the 1920's, coordinated by the State Chief Psychologist. With the mushrooming of psychologists' positions, functions, and demands for training, it became exigent to assign training responsibilities to a full-time person, particularly after a Centralized Training Program had been initiated in the state in the 1950's and when a core group of facilities within this program was accredited by the Education and Training Board (ETB) of the APA. With these considerations in mind and the fact that New Jersey annually appropriated in excess of $25,000 for Junior

Reprinted with modifications from: Training within a State program. *Welfare Reporter*, 1964, *15*, 1.

Fellowships in Psychology,* NIMH was requested to grant monies
to support a full-time Director of Psychology Training. The initial
objectives were:

1. In the absence of accredited graduate university training
facilities in New Jersey, to attract "home" qualified residents
enrolled in doctoral programs at out-of-state universities.

2. To collaborate with the State University in developing a
graduate training program in clinical psychology which would
meet the criteria of accreditation by APA and provide suitable
field placements.

3. To offer consultation to affiliated community mental health
clinics, which looked to the Centralized Training Program for
guidance in developing their own training programs.

A three-year grant was awarded July 1, 1961 (Training Grant
5TL-7291-03CL in Clinical Psychology) and a full-time director
appointed. His assignments have included responsibility to co-
ordinate and integrate the APA accredited psychology training
programs, strengthen other training centers to the point where
accreditation might be requested, develop joint efforts with
Rutgers, the State University, facilitate interdisciplinary training, and promote closer collaboration with neighboring universities and affiliated clinics.

For the first two years of the grant, there were 21 Psychology
Junior Fellows from 13 different universities, including several
from abroad (Japan, Holland, England etc.) at seven core and
nine affiliated facilities. All were enrolled in doctoral programs
or were postdoctorates. Three of the trainees were Public Health
Fellows with appointments emanating from the grant.

Diversity of facilities

In New Jersey, as in most state systems, psychologists work, and
are trained, in mental hospitals, correctional centers, schools for
the retarded, community and child guidance clinics, training and
research institutes, and a variety of other agencies. The Psychology Junior Fellows have opportunities to learn about the mani-
fold functions of a psychologist as well as to have contact with

*These fellowships are awarded as training assignments and have been ruled
tax exempt by the United States Treasury.

multifarious populations in these varied settings. Unlike a private agency, university clinic, or some government facilities, the choice of assignment in a coordinated state program is not restricted to a particular agency with a specific population. To describe the New Jersey Program, we offer the standards for training, adopted by the Psychology Training Committees.

Standards for Training of Psychology Junior Fellows in the New Jersey Centralized Training Program

I. Philosophy of the training program

A. The fellowship provides a field situation for the Fellow wherein he may obtain professional clinical experiences. It is assumed that his basic psychological knowledge, insofar as theory and conceptualization are concerned, will be established in the university. However, the fellowship will provide an opportunity for developing and implementing psychological skills in the actual practice of psychology.

B. The facility engaged in training benefits by the stimulation of inquiry engendered in such programs via the new ideas and perspectives of the Fellow, interaction with universities and consultants, the influence of teaching and training in keeping abreast of professional developments, and the necessity of maintaining the highest standards.

C. Maximum training standards and diversified experience will be promoted by a centralized program in which all fellows, irrespective of facility to which assigned, will participate in joint seminars and workshops and have their selection, assignment, and evaluation coordinated by the Director of Psychology Training.

II. Areas of training

A. *Psychodiagnosis.* The Fellow should have the opportunity to interview, evaluate, write reports, and attend staff meetings on as varied a group of patients as are typically seen in the agency (or agencies for concurrent assignments). It is the responsibility of the supervisor to insure the greatest variety possible along such dimension as age, severity of illness, sex, diagnostic category, and so on. On the other hand, diversity of patients should not be attempted at the expense of a reasonably intensive experience with a sufficient number of patients. To maximize diversity of experience, practicums and workshops will be arranged at various installations to acquaint the Fellow with the different types of cases handled by specialized facilities. Implementation of these aims may be achieved with the following techniques:

1. General interdisciplinary staff case presentation. Fellow participates in these presentations.

2. Departmental psychology case presentation. Fellow participates and/or presents to the psychology staff.

3. Fellow presents at the Junior Fellow seminars.

4. Workshops at different facilities exposes Fellow to various populations and participation with diverse personnel.

B. *Psychotherapy.* The Centralized Program provides an introduction to major therapeutic procedures (such as individual, group psychotherapy, brief and intensive psychotherapy, and so on). This training shall provide an *introduction* to psychotherapy when the supervisor judges the Fellow is ready for such an experience.

1. Fellows will be expected to have had course work in psychopathology and theory and practice of psychotherapy. (*See* VI A. Items 1, 2, and 3.)

2. Psychotherapeutic training consists of the usual methods of presenting process notes and/or tape sessions to supervisors, case conferences, seminars, and so on, for individual treatment. For group treatment, collaboration and discussion with a more experienced therapist and "a group on groups" conferences might be added.

3. A journal club in psychotherapy on a psychology departmental and/or entire Centralized Training level is encouraged.

4. Case and continuous psychotherapy case presentations are encouraged at the Junior Fellow seminars.

C. *Research.* While clinical situations are utilized to employ evaluative and rigorous thinking, experimental psychological techniques are not overlooked in the fostering of a research attitude and suitable projects.

1. The Fellow may be required to complete a paper to be submitted to his supervisor and to the Director of Training. Some possibilities follow:

a. An experiment in any area of psychology designed, executed, and written up by the Fellow under supervision.

b. A report of the Fellow's role in any ongoing departmental or other project. This role should be more than that of a technician.

c. A theoretical paper.

d. A critical review on any area.

e. An intensive diagnostic and/or therapeutic investigation of any particular clinical case, in which the student shows how experimental methods (such as, the hypothetical-deductive method) have been applied.

f. All or part of the Fellow's dissertation may be utilized in his research experience and reported on.

2. Up to 20% of a Fellow's time, when warranted, may be allotted to research.

3. Staff are strongly encouraged to involve Fellows in research projects as at least junior members, giving credit in publications, mention in newsletters, and participation in psychological conferences.

III. *Supervision*

The supervision of the Junior Fellow is the cornerstone of the centralized program. While the supervisory process will vary from one facility to another, the following standards are set:

1. A minimum of 3 hours per Fellow for the first six months; this may be diminished gradually for the remainder of assignment.

2. At least two different supervisors during the course of assignment; this offers diversity of supervisor experience and also provides the Fellow with a wider choice of references and the Junior Fellow program with a broader basis of intern evaluation.

3. The supervisory responsibility is borne by a person with a doctorate or ABEPP in clinical psychology.

4. All of the Fellow's supervisors as well as the Training Director, meet on a regular basis.

5. Collaboration with other disciplines is encouraged and particularly with respect to training in psychotherapy.

6. The Training Director is available for consultation and will make every effort to assist in providing consultants, additional training opportunities for supervisors, and so on. Supervisors take an active and continuous part in in-service supervisory training programs.

IV. *Communication and interdisciplinary relationships*

1. Emphasis is placed on the Fellow writing reports in such fashion that jargon is minimal and communication to the various disciplines made clear and meaningful.

2. The Junior Fellows will attend and present at interdisciplinary and at psychology staff meetings.

3. Joint meetings and activities with psychiatric residents and social work trainees is encouraged for the Psychology Fellows.

V. *Identity and professional practice*

1. Fellows are required to attend psychology departmental meetings on a regular basis. Such matters as ethics, professional practice, discussion of articles in the *American Psychologist,* and so on, will be discussed at these meetings.
2. Fellows are encouraged to attend association meetings and conventions.

VI. *University responsibilities*

A. *Preparation of students for field assignments*
1. Provide foundation courses in psychology necessary to the training of any psychologist (such as, experimental psychology, motivation, learning theory, research methodology, and so forth).
2. Provide foundation courses in psychology necessary to the training of any clinical psychologist (such as, personality theory, abnormal psychology, test and measurement, developmental psychology, and so forth).
3. Provide technique courses as necessary background for Fellow experience (that is, in at least such of the following: individual intelligence testing, projective techniques, statistics, theory and practice of psychotherapy, and so forth).
4. Carefully and continuously screen students so that those who reach the fellowship level are fully capable of continued professional activity in psychology.
5. Actively participate with training centers in joint supervision of fellows. (See below, items 1c, 2a-b).
B. *Implementation of university-training center liaison*
1. Selection of Fellows.
   a. Fellow is appointed only with the express approval of the university department or advisor responsible for his overall training.
   b. No fellow is appointed until he has successfully completed certain required background courses. It is suggested that the following courses or experiences be considered as minimal requirements for fellowship training: a master's degree in psychology, including courses in statistics, individual intelligence testing, projective techniques, and counseling or psychotherapy techniques. (cf. VI A 1-3).

c. Fellow is considered for appointment when a full resume of his background and training has been submitted to the training center.

d. Fellow is appointed only after the training supervisor with whom he will work has reviewed his vita, interviewed him, and given his approval.

2. Communication

a. An evaluation* of the Fellow's experience is prepared by the training supervisor and sent to the university advisor after six months and at termination.

b. To promote mutual participation in, and involvement with, the development of the Fellow, familiarization with each other's program is encouraged between the university and training center. Whenever possible, meetings are held between university and agency supervisors, and continued communication, at least via correspondence, will be the rule. The Training Director makes every effort to expedite such communication.

VII. *Facilities*

A. Training and research facilities of the New Jersey State Department of Institutions and Agencies are available to the Fellow. This includes Central Office consultation in all of the mental health disciplines, medical and psychology libraries at the various agencies, research and computer equipment, tape recorders, duplicating devices, and secretarial assistance.

B. General Considerations

1. Preference will be given to candidates from APA accredited universities.

2. Fellow assignments will be made on a concurrent or rotational basis when feasible.

3. Fellows will begin their assignments in September whenever possible.

Special training features

In addition to the Psychology Training Director, there are other special features to the New Jersey Centralized Training Program in Psychology:

Junior Fellows meetings. All of the Junior Fellows in the Centralized Program, as well as trainees in affiliated agencies,

* See rating form at end of chapter.

meet regularly during the academic year. In the meetings, they have as a resource consultant a senior psychologist (the Training Director) who does not have a direct supervisory relationship with them. The discussions range from professional problems encountered at assignments to specific research findings. The Fellows rotate in presenting psychological evaluations and case material. The climate engendered in this context stimulates professional growth somewhat differently from that of the typical psychology departmental staff conference which is usually more hierarchically structured and limited in population material.

Junior Fellows colloquia. Six or seven times a year, the Junior Fellows have an opportunity to interact on an informal basis with a distinguished psychologist. The colloquia are also planned to provide a structure for the Fellow's field experience. (Thus, 1962-63 colloquia were divided between presentations in psychotherapy and diagnosis.)

*Junior Fellows workshops.** Every year Junior Fellows attend a series of workshops in the areas of mental hospitals and clinics, retardation, and correction. The philosophy of these workshops is to expose the Fellow to as wide a spectrum of patient populations and psychologist functions as possible. Case material illustrating common diagnostic and treatment problems is presented and ongoing research in these areas is discussed by accomplished psychologists, and Fellows are encouraged to participate freely in the workshops.

Combined staff conferences. Several times a year the staff psychologists and Junior Fellows meet with psychologists from other facilities. Typical of such programs are the workshops in the Holtzman Inkblot Technique and in the MMPI, held in 1962-1963.

New Jersey seminars in psychology. In co-sponsorship with Princeton and Rutgers Universities and with the Educational Testing Service, the New Jersey State Department of Institutions and Agencies has in past years presented lectures and informal discussions by distinguished psychologists.

*For a detailed presentation of these workshops *see* the January 1964 issue of the *New Jersey Welfare Reporter,* "Workshops for Junior Fellows in Psychology," Blank, L., et al.

Advantages of state system training

In New Jersey, every Psychology Junior Fellow has the resource of the Training Director. Thus, every Fellow has in the Director a person primarily interested in his training and who can mediate between the service needs of the agency and the academic emphasis of the university. The Junior Fellow has an opportunity to participate in a program broader than any one facility can offer. He also is in contact with peers from a number of universities and with a variety of assignments.

Staff training

Staff psychology training is another important function of state training. How to supervise is not part of the university curriculum; nor are diagnosis, therapy, and the application of clinical research to a wide range of disorders taught fully in the schools. The New Jersey Psychology Training Program has instituted supervisory workshops and the Training Director serves as consultant to the staff psychologists in institutions and agencies.

The Joint Commission Report in Mental Health has recommended the broadening of roles for clinical psychologists and their increasing functions in community mental health programs. The New Jersey Psychology Training Program has already begun to place Junior Psychology Fellows in community agencies, assist these facilities in efforts to qualify for ETB accreditation, and the Training Director has consulted with the entire professional staff of such agencies in matters of training, diagnosis, therapy, and research.

Application for fellowships

In the State of New Jersey, the applicant for a Junior Fellowship in Psychology is asked to give information on:
    College and graduate school attended and degrees obtained
    Subject of M.A. thesis (if any) and advisor
    Status of doctoral program
    Subject of dissertation (if selected) and advisor
    Psychological experience (psychotherapy, testing, etc.) and supervisor

Related experience (teaching, camp counselor, etc.)

Psychological tests in which systematic training has been received and approximate number of persons examined with each test

Three persons familiar with applicant's psychological background and experience

Papers published or read at professional meetings

Areas of clinical psychology in which applicant is particularly interested (e.g., delinquents, retarted children, psychotic adults)

And, less formally, applicant's professional and other interests, special abilities, long-term aims, etc.

RATING FORM FOR JUNIOR FELLOW IN PSYCHOLOGY

This form, used in the New Jersey Department of Institutions and Agencies, is based to a large extent on the rating forms devised by Dr. James Page and his colleagues in clinical psychology at Temple University.

Part I Psychodiagnosis, Psychotherapy, and Research

Directions: Since the final objective is a well-trained and competent clinical psychologist, we wish to evaluate "absolute" competence, rather than competence in terms of level of current training. As a guide in planning further training for the Fellow, we are interested in ascertaining how far along he is in meeting professional standards in particular areas. Station personnel reviewing the ratings are expected to "correct" for the Fellow's level of training thus far. If the rater is uncomfortable using "absolute" criteria in evaluating beginning students, he may wish to modify his rating of "unsatisfactory" by adding "due to limited experience."

The asterisk (*) in a column or side heading means that the rater should explain his evaluation.

1. TEST ADMINISTRATION: Familiarity with and accuracy of test administration and ability to relate meaningfully to patient and test situation. Check appropriate space.

	Intelligence	Tests: Objective Personality	Projective	Other
Good	_____	_____	_____	_____
Fair	_____	_____	_____	_____
Unsatisfactory*	_____	_____	_____	_____
Don't know	_____	_____	_____	_____
Outstanding*	_____	_____	_____	_____

2. TEST SCORING: Accuracy of Scoring. Check appropriate space.

	Intelligence	Objective Personality	Projective	Other
		Tests:		
Good	_____	_____	_____	_____
Fair	_____	_____	_____	_____
Unsatisfactory*	_____	_____	_____	_____
Don't know	_____	_____	_____	_____
Outstanding*	_____	_____	_____	_____

3. INTERPRETATION OF TEST DATA: Level and accuracy. For each type of test go down the list and check as many items as apply.

Description	Intelligence	Objective Personality	Projective	Other
		Tests:		
Don't know	_____	_____	_____	_____
Inaccurate*	_____	_____	_____	_____
Accurate but superficial	_____	_____	_____	_____
Stereotyped--textbookish	_____	_____	_____	_____
Too speculative	_____	_____	_____	_____
Misses main points	_____	_____	_____	_____
Inferences from other sources "attributed" to test data	_____	_____	_____	_____
Integrates all data-- presents coherent picture	_____	_____	_____	_____
Satisfactory--pertinent	_____	_____	_____	_____
Exceptionally insightful*	_____	_____	_____	_____

4. WRITING REPORTS: Rate each item by entering check mark in appropriate space.

Description	Rarely	Occasionally	Frequently
Poorly written (grammar, style)	_____	_____	_____
Rambling--too general	_____	_____	_____
Misses main points	_____	_____	_____
Esoteric terminology	_____	_____	_____
Good interpretation+	_____	_____	_____
Integrated--meaningful	_____	_____	_____
Well-written	_____	_____	_____

+Differentiates between conscious and unconscious; overt vs. phantasy functioning.

5. CLINICAL BACKGROUND: Providing frame of reference for test interpretation and case summary.

	Test--Ability to use personality theory	Treatment--Ability to use theory of abnormal psychology
Good		
Fair		
Inadequate*		
Don't know		
Excellent*		

6. COUNSELLING AND PSYCHOTHERAPY: Place check mark in appropriate spaces.

Individual

	Control of situation	Rapport	Degree of perceptiveness	Competence
Good				
Adequate				
Unsatisfactory*				
Don't know				
Excellent*				

Group

	Control of situation	Rapport	Degree of perceptiveness	Competence
Good				
Adequate				
Unsatisfactory*				
Don't know				
Excellent*				

7. CASE CONFERENCES AND STAFF PRESENTATION: Participation

Good	Adequate	Unsatisfactory*	Don't know	Excellent*

8. RESEARCH: When pertinent, comment on Fellow's ability to formulate problem, structure experimental design, collect data, handle statistics, communicate findings, etc.

9. WORK RELATIONSHIPS:

	Good	Acceptable	Unsatisfactory*	Excellent*
Ethical standards	____	_____	_____	_____
Promptness--punctuality	____	_____	_____	_____
Effectiveness in planning time	____	_____	_____	_____
Dependability in handling assignments	____	_____	_____	_____
Does share of "chores" willingly	____	_____	_____	_____
General attitude	____	_____	_____	_____
Productivity	____	_____	_____	_____

Part II Personality and Interpersonal Traits

1. Personality Traits: The intent is to evaluate the personal fitness of the Fellow, particularly with respect to certain temperament traits. Since it is assumed that each trait, if present to an extreme degree in either direction of the continuum, may impair professional competence, ratings in the middle area are considered more desirable than ratings at the ends. A Fellow should be rated by comparing him with either "most" Fellows or "most" clinical and counselling psychologists. Marks indicating ratings may be placed anywhere among the continuum.

Check frame of   _____   Most Fellows
reference used:
                      _____   Most clinical and counselling psychologists

Rigid
Compulsive |__|____|_____|__|__|_____| Disorganized
                         Flexible   Suggestive

Irresponsible |__|____|_____|__|__|_____| Perfectionist
                       Responsible

Exceeds author- |__|____|_____|__|__|_____| Dependent; Requires
ity; Know-it-all   Independent   "spoon-feeding"

Tense |__|____|_____|__|__|_____| Phlegmatic
                        Relaxed

Domineering |__|____|_____|__|__|_____| Submissive
                      Give and Take

Cold, |__|____|_____|__|__|_____| Sentimental
Insensitive   Friendly   "Gushy"
                     Understanding

Inhibited, |__|____|_____|__|__|_____| Impulsive,
Overcontrolled   Controlled   Erratic
                      Adaptiveness

2. SUPERVISOR-FELLOW RELATIONSHIP: Brief comment stating attitude, reaction to supervision, progress being made, etc.

3. INTERPERSONAL RELATIONSHIPS: In general, how does Fellow get along with others. Enter check mark in appropriate space.

	Good	Fair	Unsatisfactory*	Don't know	Excellent*
Other Fellows					
Psychology Staff					
Psychiatrists and M.D. Staff					
Other Personnel					
Patients					
Conjunctive Therapists					

4. OVER-ALL IMPRESSION: As compared with other Fellows at his (her) level whom you have supervised, how would you rate this person?

	Percentile Rating			
	Lowest 25	25 - 50	50 - 75	Top 25
Current level of competence				
Potential for developing into a good clinical psychologist				

Graduate Training Abroad

Henry P. David

Interest in graduate training is shared by psychologists everywhere. It is the purpose of this chapter to survey, insofar as feasible, graduate university training and supervised practicum facilities in fifty-seven countries outside the United States. Included, to the extent of available information, are names and addresses of universities, degrees obtained and length of time required to obtain them, comparisons with American degrees, comments on curriculum content, and notes on practicum facilities. Following an overview, the reports are arranged alphabetically within major geographic areas, most of which are introduced by brief commentaries.

The material presented is based primarily on extensive communication with correspondents, most of them abroad. Their names are cited in the text and their addresses appear in a listing at the end of the chapter. Observations gathered on personal travels and discussions with colleagues are also included. While translations and edited papers were resubmitted for revision to the correspondents, corrections and additional information would be greatly welcomed for future editions.

If this chapter renders a service, it will be due to the dedication of colleagues who share the ideal of international cooperation.

Overview

As will be apparent from the following reports, concepts of clinical psychology and professional practice differ from country to country. The model of an accredited doctoral level graduate training program with an approved internship, enjoying massive governmental and private support, appears unique to the United States.

One of the difficulties in making international comparisons is the varying approach to professional practice, job specifications, and academic training. In many countries the term "clinical" has been equated with "applied" psychology, where traditionally a Ph.D. has not been considered a prerequisite for advancement. Patterns of education differ and the stage at which professional practice begins varies widely. Requirements may be more or less systematized and of shorter or longer duration than in the United States. A doctorate may be granted in recognition of a truly scholarly or research contribution, or awarded for a lesser effort when combined with many years of dedicated service. Comparing degrees obtained in one country with those given in another is particularly cumbersome, and requires a knowledge of local conditions to evaluate academic credentials and practicum experience.

The APA and the International Union of Scientific Psychology have long been aware of the difficulties of communication. With the support of the NIMH, a small Planning Conference on International Opportunities for Advanced Training and Research in Psychology was arranged at La Napoule, France, in the summer of 1962. It was suggested that, to facilitate compilation of international resources, future reports from individual countries should include a short account of the ages between which primary and secondary education is given; a statement of the requirements for entry to university; an account of university education, including course, examination, thesis, and language requirements, with special reference to the stage at which courses in psychology begin and to the proportion of time which is given to courses in psychology at different stages; an account of arrangements for training and of facilities for research work outside the universities, particularly in view of the emphasis on non-university methods of training in many countries, and an account of the stage at which a person becomes recognized as a psychologist, by whom recognition is conferred, and whether there is legal recognition and protection.

In viewing the international scene, American psychologists

are not always fully aware of their own role. According to the 1957 *International Directory of Psychologists* (now in revision), some 70% of all self-styled psychologists live and work in the United States, and the percentage rises to 80% if only Ph.D's are counted. As of 1957, and probably as of this writing, six out of seven Ph.D. psychologists contribute their professional talents to the United States. It is hardly surprising that American psychology is perceived as a Goliath and that colleagues abroad are sensitive about the attention, if any, their contributions receive. The situation is further complicated by the opinion of some that the per capita research productivity of psychologists is far greater outside the United States.

Demand for professional services is growing at such a rapid rate all over the world that many countries are exploring expanded uses of non-medical personnel. Psychologists are assuming additional administrative responsibilities. In Japan they frequently head clinics for children and provide the major professional resource in rehabilitation and correctional centers. In the emerging countries of Africa, psychologists have been assigned a leading role in social and industrial planning, and in the selection and training of candidates for higher education. Where resources are limited, professional personnel tend to be characterized by the breadth of their activities rather than specialization.

While the use of tests continues to be viewed as a primary responsibility of the clinical psychologist, particularly in diagnostic work and assessment of training capabilities, there is growing recognition that the application of techniques standardized in one country to a totally different population on another continent is questionable at best. Efforts to translate or adapt Western instruments have been initiated in many lands. The importance of original contributions has been demonstrated by the work of the American Institute for Research in Nigeria.

Individual and group psychotherapy by qualified psychologists are more often encouraged than not, especially in children's centers and in working with delinquent or disturbed youths. Freud's theories have long divided academicians and professionals. Increasingly, emphasis has been placed on neo-Freudian and other depth therapies, such as phenomenology and existentialism, and on learning theory-oriented behavior therapies. In most countries psychoanalysis is associated with private institutes which do not necessarily restrict membership to any one profession. There is, however, growing recognition that traditional one to one therapist-patient relationships are unlikely to resolve major mental health problems, and that manpower shortages alone demand more training in the areas of mental health consultation and working with other groups. In the emerging countries, the basic question is likely to be one of who can be of service now, on what basis and with whom, rather than who has had what traditional prerogatives.

EUROPE

Just as there is no American brand of clinical psychology, European approaches vary according to local interests and academic traditions. Except for the children's area, European universities rarely offer professional programs. Few provide opportunities for practicum training and some are still bound to philosophy. In the absence of academic leadership, independent schools and professional societies have assumed a major role in clinical training, certification, and legislative efforts, particularly in Switzerland. When their own country offers less opportunity, many students study English and discuss American publications.

Dynamically oriented psychologists frequently tend to be physicians who seldom identify with clinical psychology. While numerous psychiatrists hold that psychotherapy should be restricted to medical practitioners, psychologists are often encouraged to engage in therapeutic activities, especially with children and adolescents. In Poland they have been invited to join the psychiatric association.

In contrast to the United States, many European countries place less emphasis on the doctorate as a requirement for clinical positions. For example, few Scandinavian psychologists have a Ph.D., which is generally considered a research or scholarly degree. In the Soviet Union the Ph.D. is awarded in recognition of major contributions, often in mid-career. Occasionally, the non-medical doctorate is more easily obtained and may be equivalent to an American M.A. A knowledge of local standards is essential to fully evaluate a European psychologist's credentials.

Austria

The three major Austrian universities (Graz, Innsbruck, and Vienna) offer graduate training programs in clinical psychology or a "diploma." The Ph.D. degree is awarded in the traditional experimental areas, primarily in perception, neuropsychological research, and learning. While courses in psychological evaluation are given, there is limited interest in practical applications and professional services.

There is no clinical psychology intern training program in Austrian institutions at the present time. Practicum experience usually consists of on-the-job training. There are opportunities to attend lectures at university clinics, and those particularly interested and qualified may obtain "private" training at psychoanalytic institutes.

Correspondent: *John L. Wallace,* St. Cloud, Minn.

Belgium

Of the four Belgian universities, Louvain has given special degrees in psychology since 1945 and Brussels since about 1950. Liège started a psychology program in 1962. Ghent currently offers a degree in "Vocational Guidance and Selection." All four provide opportunities for clinical training with children and adolescents, and, to a lesser extent, with adults.

In Belgium, the basic university degree is the "candidate," which is roughly equivalent to the American B.A. After two or three years of successful graduate work, the student becomes eligible for the "Licencié," which is roughly equivalent to Master's degree with thesis. The doctorate is awarded after further scientific work. The degree required for professional practice is the "Licencié" in psychology.

In Brussels and Louvain (and the same will soon apply to Liège), the graduate student is permitted to specialize in particular areas, including clinical psychology. However, the degree given is in the broad field of psychology. While each university is responsible for establishing its own standards for psychology training, these are roughly equivalent.

Practicum facilities are frequently associated with university training programs. Clinical work with patients requires fluency in either French or Flemish. Among the university centers are:

Centre médico-psychologique, 407 Chaussée de Louvain, Schaarbeek, Brussels (Prof. P. Osterrieth);
Clinique médico-pédagogique du Brabant, Avenue du Jonc 2, Uccle, Brussels (Dr. Jadot Decroly);
Neuro-psychiatrische Kliniek, Guinardstraat 14, Ghent (Prof. De Busscher and Dr. Wens);
Consultation psychologique de l'enfant, Service de Psychologie de l'Université de Liège, Place du 20 Août, Liège (Dr. Husquinet);
Medisch-psychologische Kinderkliniek, De Merodelei 1, Antwerp (Prof. R. Dellaert);
Consultation d'hygiène mentale, Hospital St. Pierre, Brusselse straat, Louvain (adults), (Prof. Rouvroy and Dr. Buyse).

Correspondent: Joseph *Nuttin,* Louvain

Czechoslovakia

In Czechoslovakia psychology is studied on entry to the university. While psychology is a separate discipline, departments and institutes of psychology are included in philosophical faculties. Training in clinical psychology is available in the departments of psychology of Charles University, Prague; Purkyne University, Brno; Palacky University, Olomouc; and Comenius University, Bratislava.

Until 1953 the Ph.D. was awarded after completing four years of study, passing prescribed examinations, and acceptance of a dissertation. Since that time a new title "Promovany psycholog" (Prom. psych., i.e., diploma psychologist) has been established, requiring five years. A thesis must be defended and a state examination passed.

The graduate degree in psychology is the Candidate of Science, which usually requires at least five years beyond the Prom. psych. and also includes a thesis. The highest degree is Doctor of Science, which may be reached ten or twenty years after the Candidature. A doctoral thesis must be successfully defended; there is no other examination.

Postgraduate training is organized outside the universities. Special courses in psychodiagnostic methods were recently given by the Czechoslovak Psychological Society. Longer-term training in professional areas is coordinated by the ministries within whose competence psychologists are employed. The Ministry of Health supervises the training of clinical psychologists. Supervised practicum experience has been provided at the psychiatric clinic of Charles University, Prague; Purkyne University, Brno; Comenius University, Bratislava; and the psychiatric hospitals of Dobrany, Brno, Kromeriz, Pezinok, and Vel Ke Levare.

Since 1957 the Medical Institute for Postgraduate Study in Prague has arranged courses for clinical psychologists. Seminars were also organized in Bratislava by Comenius University and the Slovak Psychological Society.

Correspondents: *J. Hoskovec*, Prague
J. Diamant, Prague

Denmark

Denmark has two universities but a psychology program is offered only in the Psychology Department of the University of Copenhagen. Until 1944 the "magister artium" (mag. art.) was the only university degree in psychology. Emphasis was, and still is, on experimental psychology in preparation for university teaching careers or pure research. Approximately six to eight years are required before passing the final examination (magisterkonferens). The mag. art. is probably close to the American Ph.D.

With the growing demand for training in applied areas of psychology, the university degree of "candidatus psychologiae" (Cand. psych.) was established in 1944. The approximately six years' study program was reorganized in 1960 and now permits specialization in clinical psychology, similar to university degrees in medicine and law. In addition to formal courses and examinations, a candidate must have practicum training in different fields and write an acceptable thesis, which again closely corresponds to the American Ph.D.

The Danish Ph.D. is rather rare, requiring a major research endeavor which must be accepted by a committee, published, and defended in a six-hour oral university examination. As of 1963 about ten of the 330 Danish psychologists have a Danish Ph.D.

Major clinical centers (and their chief psychologists) providing supervised practicum or intern training facilities are:

The Child Guidance Clinic of the University of Copenhagen (Bodil Farup)
The Department of Psychiatry, University Hospital, Copenhagen (Lise Ostergaard)
The Department of Child Psychiatry, University Hospital, Copenhagen (Merete Clausen)
The Department of Pediatrics, University Hospital, Copenhagen (Helle Hopfner Nielsen)
The State Hospital, Risskov, Jutland (Alan Mogensen)
The Department of Child Psychiatry, State Hospital, Risskov, Jutland (Lise Haslund)
The Detention Center for Criminal Psychopaths, Herstedvester (Erik Hoeck-Gradenwitz)

With the burgeoning demand for clinical psychologists an internship is not required for a staff appointment. However, most younger psychologists request supervised experience before accepting more responsible positions.

Correspondents: Karen Berntsen, Copenhagen
Lise Østergaard, Copenhagen

Finland

Chairs of psychology exist at the Universities of Helsinki and Turku, and also at the University of Jyväskylä (School of Education), and the School of Social Sciences at Tampere. The University of Åbe, which is located in Turku, has a small Institute of Psychology; since it has mainly Swedish-speaking students, the official language is Swedish.

The degrees awarded by Finnish universities include a Candidate of Humanities, which takes three to four years, and the Candidate of Philosophy, which generally takes five to six years. Many psychologists continue towards the Licentiate which may require about two additional years. A Ph.D. degree is unusual and requires extensive scholarly research.

Correspondents: Martti Takala, Jyväskylä
Isto Ruoppila, Jyväskylä

France

Higher education in France includes several types of institutions, the major ones being the seventeen "académies" located in the larger cities. Each "académie" has a university with faculties of letters and human sciences, law and economics, medicine, and pharmacy. A number of institutes attached to the universities offer instruction in less traditional areas and have some administrative autonomy.

Approximately 65% of French students attend the University of Paris (Sorbonne). Attached is the Institute of Psychology which offers training in research and applied areas, including school, abnormal and social psychology. Although under the jurisdiction of the Faculty of Letters, courses are given in the building of the Faculty of Medicine. The Division of Pathological Psychology is headed by Daniel Lagache, an eminent philosopher, physician and psychoanalyst. Courses in clinical psychology are usually given by psychologically-trained psychiatrists and psychologists with a psychiatric background. The professional chair is occupied by Mme. Juliette Fayez-Boutonnier.

Students with their "Bachot," equivalent to two years of college, are accepted at the Institute after passing a competitive examination. Compared to the first years of college, the number of laboratory hours is greater, courses are less theoretical and general, and student discussion and participation more extensive since class size is much smaller. Teaching is done not only by professors but also by practitioners and researchers. Psychological philosophy is secondary to scientific orientation.

The French higher educational system may perhaps be best described in the context of the "cycle system." The completion of the baccalaureate at the end of the lycée period marks the starting point for all higher education in France. The student then undertakes the "premier cycle" at the University, the so-called propaedeutic year. This is a year of intensive general study (liberal arts type) including an honors thesis and a stiff set of year-end exams.

Upon completion of this work, professional education in one's chosen specialty area begins. This is the so-called "deuxième cycle." In psychology, the "deuxième cycle," if negotiated successfully, culminates in receipt of the "license" which is something of the journeyman psychologist's degree. Though technically achievable in two years, a three- to five-year effort is more usual. To receive the license the candidate must qualify in five prescribed areas, by dint of coursework and very rigorous exams. The five areas are as follows: general (including learning, perception, abnormal, etc.), child, social, and comparative psychology. The program is identical for all license candidates. General and child psychology must be passed first, and then the other three exams must be taken. For each area a total of 6½ hours of exams must be taken (3 hours written, 3 "practicum" and 30 minutes oral). If any one section of the exam is failed the candidate may not be admitted to succeeding ones and must start the exam sequence all over again. The practicum exam is based on a distributed list of functions which the candidate is expected to be able to perform. These exams, totalling 32½ hours, are very searching. The average license class each year at the Sorbonne is 300 (about 75% women); of this total perhaps no more than one-third complete the program successfully. Graduates are considerably better grounded than American M.A. psychologists; they have completed all course work and any degree beyond this point is essentially a research degree.

After the completion of the license (deuxième cycle), the superior candidate may advance to the next level, "troisième cycle." There are three kinds of doctorates. The doctorate "du troisième cycle" involves a major research study or series of studies generally greater in magnitude and scope than the typical American Ph.D. thesis, requiring perhaps three years, and culminating in the publication of a monograph or volume. The "doctorat d'état" requires five to ten years and two theses, a "thèse complémentaire" and a "thèse principale." The former, which is usually a research thesis, may actually be the one used for the troisième cycle degree or one of similar magnitude. The latter is a magnum opus, generally broad in scope, of a theoretical-conceptual nature, and culminating in the publication of a major volume. It would be unusual to find a Frenchman who had completed the troisième cycle before the age of 30, or one who had completed the "doctorat d'état" before the age of 40. Each of these facts of life has obvious implications for the pace at which French psychology can develop.

A third degree, the "doctorat d'université" is most frequently reserved for students from abroad who, on arrival, are credited with the equivalent of a license and, with limited sponsor contact, complete a thesis within a year. It should not be considered equivalent to an American Ph.D. and is certainly not on a par with the "doctorat du troisième cycle."

A clinical program with a standard internship in an approved setting is probably non-existent in France. While it is possible to obtain some practicum experience in psychiatric hospitals and clinics, this is largely limited to diagnosis learned through on-the-job training. There is no formal supervision in psychotherapy.

Correspondents: Victor D. Sanua, New York, N.Y.
Emory L. Cowen, Rochester, N.Y.

Federal Republic of Germany

The Federal Republic has eighteen universities, each of which has a Department of Psychology, and four institutes of technology providing some courses. None offer a clinical psychology training program in the American sense.

Systematic training in certain areas of clinical psychology began in 1950 when Professor Bondy opened the first child guidance clinic in the Psychology Department of the University of Hamburg. Students in their third and fourth year are trained by a professional team (child psychiatrist, psychologist and social worker) in intensive diagnostic studies with emotionally disturbed children. Although no training is offered in psychotherapy or in psychoanalysis, students can make the necessary arrangements outside the department. Particular emphasis is placed on the team approach, on interdisciplinary supervision, and on effective communication of diagnostic impressions and observations. In the absence of a widely accepted German language textbook, students are encouraged to acquire a reading knowledge of English.

With the continuing establishment of child guidance and mental health clinics, the universities of Freiburg (Dr. Heiss), Munich (Dr. Lersch), Goettingen (Dr. Duhm) and Saarbrükken (Dr. Spreen) followed the Hamburg example by opening training facilities in clinical psychology. The orientation is predominantly theoretical, with limited practicum experience in diagnostic and therapeutic work with children and adults. Systematic training in clinical research is available in Marburg (Dr. Duecker: pharmacological studies) and in Hamburg (Dr. Hofstaetter, Dr. Bondy: standardization of tests and their clinical application.)

Most of the psychology students at the eighteen universities work for the Diploma in Psychology. Introduced in 1941, the Diploma in Psychology (as well as in other specialties) is regulated by state laws which are practically the same in the ten states of the Federal Republic and in West Berlin. The minimum requirement is eight semesters (i.e., four years) of academic studies; many students take ten to eleven semesters. Requirements include a scientific thesis, the passing of specialty area oral and written examinations, and completion of three internships to be served during vacation periods. Quite frequently a "Diplom Psychologe" has training equivalent to that of most American M.A. level psychologists. There is no special degree for clinical psychology.

In general, a diploma is required for admission to doctoral candidacy. During the last decade only about 20% of all students have continued their studies to the Ph.D., mostly those intent on academic careers. Requirements for the Ph.D. usually include at least two semesters of further study after the diploma, acceptance and publication of a dissertation, and extensive examinations in psychology and two other sciences of the student's choice.

Supervised practicum and intern training facilities are offered in clinics and hospitals attached to the previously mentioned universities. The university department generally assigns students to these practicum centers for six months during their academic training and for one year after receiving the diploma. Because of the relatively limited number of non-university training facilities, practicum is rarely arranged elsewhere. The one-year internship is not mandatory, though students are advised to take it after their diploma.

Correspondents: *Hildegard Hiltmann,* Freiburg
Hans J. Priester, Princeton, N. J.

German Democratic Republic

Professional training and specialization in medical psychology may be obtained at the psychological institutes of Humboldt University in East Berlin and at the Universities of Leipzig and Dresden. A fourth institute is to be established at the University of Jena. Allowing for individual differences in the personal orientation of the respective directors, academic requirements in all three institutes are largely similar and follow the pattern of other German universities. Primary focus is on training for research. The diploma course lasts five years, followed by an additional four years for those relatively few who continue to the doctorate.

Training in medical psychology at Humboldt University, East Berlin, is facilitated by extensive modern laboratories and by a kindergarten for disturbed children who can be continuously observed and studied through one-way screens and other recording media. A non-medical director is in charge with a psychiatrist available for consultation. Much of the research is topological and Lewinian in orientation, with a modified Gestalt methodology prevailing. The majority of students, after receiving their diplomas, go into clinics, industry, or some form of teaching. Research is emphasized as an integral part of their responsibilities.

The Institute of Cortical-Visceral Pathology and Therapy of the German Academy of Science in East Berlin is engaged in efforts to integrate clinical and experimental techniques within a framework of Pavlovian physiology and psychology. Recognizing that Pavlov was concerned with all forms of activities, not just conditioning, in his attempts to formulate the principles of higher nervous functioning, Pavlovian concepts have been applied at a variety of physiological and psychological levels. Sleep therapy, which in accord with these principles is regarded as a form of protective inhibition, is practiced extensively. At first, sleep is induced by means of barbiturates and similar agents, then, using placebos and a variety of pleasant conditioned stimuli (interspersed by drug reinforcements from time to time), a conditioned sleep response pattern is gradually introduced.

Medical psychology in the German Democratic Republic is part of the state service; there is no private practice. Communica-

tion with colleagues is facilitated through the German Psychological Society and other professional associations whose activities
transcend the borders between East and West.

Correspondent: *Cyril M. Franks,* Princeton, N.J.

Greece

Practically speaking, there is no training in clinical psychology
in Greece. Of the few professional psychologists in the country,
most were trained in other European countries and a few in the
United States. Only one holds a Ph.D. in clinical psychology,
awarded by an American University.

None of the Greek universities has a psychology department
and no degrees are granted in psychology. There is no postgraduate training in clinical psychology. What in the United
States might be considered supervised practicum is offered at the
Athenian Institute of Anthropos, a recently established non-profit
organization for research and postgraduate training in the behavioral sciences. Currently, such training cannot be considered
the equivalent of an internship. Initial efforts are devoted to test
standardization for the Greek population.

Correspondent: *Vasso Vassiliou,* Athens

Ireland

Although psychology has always been taught at Irish Universities, it has been attached to departments of philosophy; there has
never been a Chair of Psychology in its own right. It was not
until the post-World War II period, when Rev. Prof. E. F.
O'Doherty occupied the Chair of Logic and Psychology at the
University College, Dublin, that psychology became a separate
department. The first course in applied psychology was officially
initiated in 1958. It is a three-year program, with the third year
devoted to research and thesis work, for the M. Sc. in psychology. A similar program has been developed at University College, Cork. A Ph.D. in psychology is possible six terms after
graduation.

Correspondent: *John McKenna,* Dublin

Italy

Italian universities are composed of academic "faculties." At this writing, no Faculty of Psychology exists and none is officially planned, despite the need expressed by psychologists. While some aspects of psychology are taught in the 18 full-fledged universities, courses are widely dispersed among faculties of philosophy, fine arts, law and medicine. There are few permanently appointed professors of psychology; many courses are given by non-psychologists. Teaching facilities and laboratory and library resources in institutes of psychology are generally limited. Most clinical psychologists tend to be physicians.

After a minimum of four years' study, university students are eligible to become candidates for a doctorate in one of the humanities; there is no official degree below the Ph.D. level. Standards for a degree are extremely varied from department to department within a school and between schools. In unusual instances an Italian Ph.D. may be equivalent only to an American B.A.; in other cases, the years of additional training may be comparable to an American Ph.D. An M.D. requires at least six years.

Within the university structures, there is a variety of postgraduate (specialization) schools, each of which, like a new faculty, must be authorized by the government. Two postgraduate schools of psychology have been established at Milan and Genoa for students holding an M.D. degree; three more are planned, with one open to non-physicians. These schools offer a diploma of "Specialist in Psychology" after successful completion of a three-year course.

In Italy clinical psychological training is usually apprentice training received largely in a university institute of psychology or in university psychitric clinics whose directors are favorably disposed toward psychology as a science. The usual form of practical training is personal and pyramidal. There is one director salaried by the state. Everyone else in his "institute" is an assistant, with skills varying from diplomate to college senior. Students (often already holding an M.D. or Ph.D.), who are admitted to training, consider themselves fortunate if they receive unpaid experience for several years. They are called "volunteer assistants" and engage in all sorts of "on the job" work, beginning with clerical tasks. Those able to secure part- or full-time remunerative positions, in addition to their clinical apprenticeships, manage to exist. If they show considerable promise and have publications (always with the authorization of the institute's director), they may be given some financial support and after a few years receive an academic salary. Positions of security and comfort are, however, dependent on obtaining the "Libera Docenza," a series of oral examinations at the ABEPP level, plus publications.

Correspondents: *Franco Ferracuti,* Rio Piedras, Puerto Rico
Luciano L'Abate, Atlanta, Ga.
Luigi Meschieri, Rome

Netherlands

Psychology training is available at all of the universities in the Netherlands, namely, the Municipal University of Amsterdam, the Free University of Amsterdam, and the Universities of Groningen, Leiden, Nijmegen and Utrecht. The "doctoral" course of studies is composed of two parts and requires approximately seven years; it is about equivalent to the American M.A. The first part (candidate's courses) is usually taken within 3½ years and may be followed by an equal period of study for completion of all qualifications.

While there are some differences in the training offered by the several Dutch universities, these are gradually diminishing. No basic differences exist in training at the candidate's level, but some chance for differentiation is offered during the second part of the studies leading to qualification. At the end of the qualification period, the student must satisfactorily complete a research project.

No additional course work is required for the Ph.D. The candidate works with his senior professor in planning and completing an extensive research study which must eventually be defended in public and published before a degree can be awarded. Although there is an increasing tendency to work for the Ph.D., it is not required for clinical appointments.

At all the universities, clinical psychology students must complete three to six months practicum courses in university psychiatric clinics or other institutions. At Leiden and Utrecht, a portion of the practicum is spent in the university psychological centers. At several universities all psychology students, whether clinical or not, must work three months in a psychiatric center.

Membership in the Netherlands Institute of Practicing Psychologists (NIPP) is granted after the student has completed his studies and has taken a year or more of practicum work under the supervision of NIPP member. The year of training and supervision can be completed in any institution where it is possible for a NIPP member to provide supervision. Although most psychologists continue their work in the area in which they have been supervised, this is not required; some go to work in industry after finishing supervision in a clinical setting.

Correspondents: J. T. Barendregt, Amsterdam
A. Gravestein, Amsterdam

Norway

Of the two universities in Norway, only the University of Oslo has a program in psychology. In accordance with the 1959 education law, the Oslo program is divided into two parts and usually requires about six years of study after the "artium" examination. The first part consists of general psychology including laboratory experiences in experimental psychology, tests and measurements, and theories of personality, along with examinations in the related fields of biology, physiology, psychiatry and sociology. The second part consists of more advanced training within a special area chosen by the student. Courses are given in clinical, developmental, social, and experimental psychology, and in counseling and psychometrics. It is required that students take courses from two fields of which one is chosen as the major subject (entailing two semesters of study) and the other as a minor subject (entailing one semester of study). The first semester of the course in clinical psychology is technically oriented and provides an introduction to a basic battery of psychodiagnostic tests along with general clinical methods (interviewing, organizing of clinical case material, etc.) The second semester places emphasis on theory, general systematic study, and more advanced diagnostic work based on this expanded theoretical background. Students also study central topics in psychopathology and the principal features of psychotherapy.

In addition to the required courses, it is necessary during the second part of the study program to take nine months practicum at a university-approved institution. The candidate must also deliver a scientific paper before he can present himself for the final examination ("embetseksamen"). Successful completion permits the use of the title "candidatus psychologiae" (Cand. Psychol.), a degree somewhere between the American M.A. and the Ph.D.

Although the University of Oslo awards a Ph.D., there is no academic program leading to this degree, either in clinical psychology or any other field. If a student aspires to the doctorate (and few do), he must first complete studies for the Mag. Art. or Cand. Phil. He must then produce a scholarly work, get it published as a book, submit it to the faculty, have a faculty committee judge the work suitable for a Ph.D. thesis, give two public lectures, and be examined on the thesis and defend it orally. Because professional employment and advancement in Norway are not dependent on the doctorate, only a minority of clinicians have the Ph.D., perhaps 5 to 10%. Even on the faculty of the University, less than half of the staff members hold Ph.D.'s

The required practicum in the second part of the university study program consists of nine months of clinical psychological work at an approved clinical institution. There are seven such facilities in or around Oslo, including mental hospitals and out-patient centers for both children and adults. The university pays the assigned supervisor, usually the senior psychologist at the institution.

Only one institution in Norway has developed a program of post-university training. The Child Psychiatry Institute (Munkedamsveien 87, Oslo), founded in 1953 by the late Dr. Nic. Waal, has a three-year program of supervised study in child psychotherapy and child guidance for clinical psychologists.

Informal supervision is given to psychologists working at "lower" levels of competence at most of the large institutions. Requirements of the Norwegian Psychological Association for attaining "specialist" competence in clinical psychology include two years of supervised clinical work at an approved center, working a minimum of two hours per week under supervision.

Correspondents: *William Rabinowitz,* University Park, Pa.

Bjørn Killingmo, Oslo

Poland

The development of Polish psychology has been intrinsically tied to the fate of the country, with its most recent renaissance after the 1956 convention of Polish psychologists. There is no division of graduate and undergraduate training. The psychological curriculum extends over five years and leads to the M.A. degree, which is granted to persons who write a dissertation and pass an examination. Clinical psychology is one of several fields of specialization; others include general and experimental, developmental and educational, and industrial psychology (which in Poland is often called "psychology of work").

While there are psychology departments in at least eight Polish universities, M.A. and Ph.D. degrees in psychology are granted primarily in three: Warsaw, Poznan and Krakow. Though all give degrees in clinical psychology, the only chair in clinical psychology, held by Prof. Andrzej Lewicki whose interests center on problems of pathopsychology, is at Poznan University. In Warsaw there is a Department of Clinical Educational Psychology, directed by Docent Halina Spionek, and in Krakow a Department of Educational Clinical Psychology with Docent Maria Susulowska as its head. At the Catholic University in Lublin, students may choose courses in clinical psychology, but they do not get degrees in this field.

Although there is no formal center for supervised practicum or intern training in Poland, the facility most approaching that status is the Laboratory of Clinical Psychology in J. Babinski State Hospital for Nervous and Mentally Ill in Krakow-Kobierzyn. Organized in 1950 by Dr. Mieczyslaw Choynowski, who was its head for ten years, it has been directed since 1960 by Dr. Zenomena Pluzek. It provides short internships for psychologists working in mental hospitals and for psychology students from various universities. Well supplied with tests, it offers excellent opportunities for supervised training and diagnostic studies.

Since 1956 some courses in diagnostic techniques have been

sporadically organized by the Central Dispensary of Mental Health in Warsaw and by the Mental Hygiene Association, under the direction of Prof. Maria Kaczynska. Since Poland lacks properly validated and standardized tests, the Ministry of Health and Social Care established in 1961 a Laboratory of Clinical Psychology, affiliated with the Psychometrical Laboratory of the Polish Academy of Science which endeavors to facilitate test research.

Correspondents: *M. Choynowski,* Warsaw
Z. Pluzek, Krakow

Portugal

There is no doctoral training program in clinical psychology in Portugal, either in the universities (which are governmental schools) or in the privately operated "superior institutes." A Medical Degree or a Licentiate in Philosophy (Psychology), given at the universities of Lisbon and Coimbra, are equally accepted for postgraduate training in clinical psychology in private practicum centers.

The Faculty of Letters at the Universities of Lisbon, Coimbra, Porto since 1962, Luanda since 1963, Louenco Marques since 1963, give courses in educational sciences which are considered the equivalent of a B.A. degree. This is not, however, sufficient for entrance to graduate training. Plans for a Ph.D. program in psychology are being contemplated for the universities and have been supported by the Portuguese Psychological Society.

The Instituto de Orientaco Profissional, Faculdade de Letras, Lisboa, has a three-year program in vocational counseling, which includes some training in diagnostic testing. A diploma is awarded. The Instituto de Filosofia—Centro de Psicologia Aplicado, Faculdade de Letras, Lisboa, offers postgraduate training, without diploma, in testing procedures.

The Portuguese Society for Neurology and Psychiatry, through its group analytic section, has for several years provided training in group analytic techniques in clinical settings to medical and non-medical graduates.

Correspondent: *Maria Rita Mendes Leal,* Lisbon

Spain

Clinical psychology as an independent profession is just beginning in Spain. Only the School of Psychology and Psychotechnics at the University of Madrid offers a Diploma in Clinical Psychology. This diploma is given after two years of study; the first year provides basic courses and the second year specific information in clinical areas. Tentative plans have been initiated for the University of Barcelona. Some supervised practicum training is available through personal arrangements with the psychiatric services of universities or private sanataria.

Correspondent: *Jose L. Pinillos,* Valencia

Sweden

All Swedish universities (Göteborg, Lund, Stockholm and Uppsala) offer graduate training in clinical psychology, usually in cooperation with varied state institutions and hospitals. There are two categories of psychologists in Sweden: Assistant Psychologist and Psychologist. Appointment as Assistant Psychologist requires passing a university examination (filosofie kandidat), which generally takes about three years plus a supervised practicum of at least six months. To reach the "Psychologist" level, candidates must study for approximately three additional years toward a "filosofie licentiat" examination and complete an extensive research project which corresponds rather closely to the American Ph.D. A Swedish Ph.D., which is much less common, requires a further two years of pure research and is usually a prelude to a university career.

Practicum is usually arranged outside the universities at psychiatric facilities for children or adults attached to medical faculties and general hospitals. Specialized training with children may be obtained at the Erica Foundation in Stockholm and in children's centers. There are also opportunities to gain experience in youth hostels, homes for addicts, and correctional settings.

At least six months of supervised practicum are needed for a certificate of competence as an Assistant Psychologist. The Swedish Union of Psychologists requires experience in two of the following areas: educational psychology, occupational psychology, and clinical psychology. To facilitate placements, the Union has established committees to act in an advisory capacity to practicum centers. Qualified psychologists are members of the Swedish Psycho-Aanalytic Society which since 1954 requires the status of 'psychologist' for acceptance in psychoanalytic training by non-medical personnel.

Correspondents: Gösta Frobärj, Göteborg
Margareta Garai, Stockholm

Switzerland

Clinical psychology is scarcely recognized in the nine Swiss universities. Frequently it is still considered a part of philosophy, with little interest either in empirical and experimental research, or in classical psychoanalysis, Jung's individual psychology, psychological testing and graphology. Freudian and Jungian psychotherapists and graphologists have had to establish their own training centers and professional schools.

While graduate training for the doctorate degree, with some coursework and research in clinical psychology, is available at four Swiss universities, none offer training in psychotherapy. At the University of Geneva, Prof. Jean Piaget and Bärbel Inhelder direct the Institut des Sciences de l'Education; Prof. A. Rey heads clinical training. Emphasis is on child psychology. Courses are taught in French. Prof. E. Montalta is Director of Training at the Institut für Pädogogik, Heilpädagogik and Angewandte Psychologie, University of Freiburg i. Ue. Focus is on school and educational psychology. Courses are given in German and French. At the University of Zurich, Prof. Ulrich Moser is lecturer in clinical psychology; special interest is on psychodiagnosis. Courses are in German. Prof. Richard Meili is Director of Training at the University of Bern. Emphasis is on psychological testing and developmental psychology; courses are taught in German.

Courses in clinical psychology are available at the universities of Basel, Neuenburg, and Lausanne, and also at the Federal Institute for Technology in Zurich and the Hochschule St. Gallen for Economic and Social Sciences.

Specialist training, leading to a diploma, may be obtained at the Institute for Applied Psychology in Zurich, and at other centers established by the several psychotherapeutic schools. The Swiss Society for Psychology and its Application certifies training in clinical psychology and gives diplomas for experience with the Rorschach and Szondi tests. The Swiss Graphological Society also offers training and certification.

Although most training institutions require at least some practicum experience, few facilities have close relationships with the universities. Supervised practicum experience can be obtained in homes and institutions for children and adolescents, school services, educational guidance centers and in a very few psychiatric clinics and hospitals. The Institut für Psychohygiene Biel (Prof. A. Friedemann) also offers supervised experience.

Correspondent: *Fred Schmid,* Zurich

Union of Soviet Socialist Republics

While there are psychology departments in all the universities and pedagogical institutes of the Soviet Union, the major centers are in Moscow, Kiev, Leningrad and Tbilisi. Basic undergraduate training requires about five years, with heavy emphasis on biological sciences. There are also courses in sociology and the philosophy of dialectical materialism as well as special seminars reflecting the particular research interests of the professors.

Beginning with the fourth year, students have to do theoretical and experimental work. During the last year most time is given to a diploma thesis, which eventually must be defended in departmental assemblies. There is some question whether this work is closer to an American B.A. thesis or the M.A.

Some students continue their training for approximately three years or longer as postgraduate "aspirants" in universities or research institutes. Every aspirant is associated with a specific laboratory and during these three years has to write a dissertation for the degree of Candidate of Science, which may range in equivalence from below M.A. to near Ph.D. About one hundred Candidate degrees are awarded annually. A limited number of psychologists eventually write a dissertation for the degree of Doctor of Science, based on independent research.

Practicum is arranged through the university departments of

psychology and the institutes; there is no clinical psychology intern training program in the American sense. Research and practicum are usually available in the Institute of Psychology, Moscow, the Institute of Defectology, Moscow, and institutes affiliated with the USSR Academy of Medical Sciences, and the RSFSR Academy of Pedagogical Sciences.

Correspondents: *A. R. Luria,* Moscow
Ivan D. London, Brooklyn, N.Y.

United Kingdom

University postgraduate courses have been developed at Belfast, Edinburgh, Glasgow, Leeds, London, and Manchester. A non-university course is given at the Tavistock Clinic in London. As of 1963, the University of London-Maudsley Hospital Program offered two courses, a 13-month diploma course and a two-year master's course. All graduates are encouraged to continue to the Ph.D., which is strictly a research degree, and about 15% do so, usually requiring about another two years.

The Maudsley program may perhaps be best described by indicating its training goals. Graduates are expected to give opinions on any question of treatment and management of a patient, provided those opinions represent the application of working hypotheses derived from psychology and are, therefore, a distinct contribution to the armory of ideas at the disposal of the clinical team. These opinions may be "off the cuff," informally given in discussion, or may be formalized. In the latter event the psychologist would read up on a particular topic which is relevant to the policy of his unit and make a full report to his colleagues of the outcome of his studies. For example, it might be necessary to consider what is known concerning the effects of certain drugs upon intellectual functions of patients who are being discharged on a maintenance dose of that drug. Ideally, the clinical psychologist's contribution in clinical discussion should represent the distillation of what the whole of experimental and general psychology has to offer with regard to etiology, treatment and management of a patient.

Maudsley-trained psychologists are expected to carry out

uncontrolled observations of the behavior of patients, whether in terms of the patient's own report or the reports of the patient's associates. Such uncontrolled observations are distinguished from the use of unvalidated variables which only have a hypothetical or highly attenuated relationship with the criterion variable. It would seem that it is one thing for the applied scientist to make uncontrolled observations of criterion variables (i.e., having content validity) and another thing to draw far-reaching conclusions from the observation of non-criterion variables.

The psychologist should only use, routinely, measures which conform with the minimum requirements of validation and calibration. Strict application of such requirements means that there are very few acceptable instruments, such as some cognitive tests, several learning tests found in literature but not on the market, and interest schedules. At the Maudsley the Rorschach is rarely used, aside from Piotrowski's findings concerning prognostic signs of schizophrenia. The MMPI and most personality inventories are considered to have too low reliabilities for application to an individual case. Instead, attention has been turned increasingly to the use of measures of specific content of an individual patient's mind, e.g., the clinical application of Kelly's Repertory Grid, Osgood's Semantic Differential, and Shapiro's Personal Questionnaire.

The psychological manipulation of psychological dysfunction should be the center of the psychologist's role and he should, ideally, be primarily concerned with problems of psychological treatment and management. It is necessary for the psychologist to be expert in the application of working hypotheses derived from the experimental work on the processes of learning, opinion change, and affective experience to the treatment and management of psychological dysfunction. This involves a knowledge and experience of such techniques and methods as relaxation, desensitization, negative learning, and rational psychotherapy, plus some ability to relate ongoing work to the ideas of psychoanalysis.

Research is part of the clinical psychologist's service work at the Maudsley. It is expected that he can design applied research projects with the same confidence with which he would carry out a cognitive test and that he should endeavor to work in such a way as to be continually acquiring information about the usefulness of his efforts.

These views tend to be identified with the clinical psychologists working at the Institute of Psychiatry in the Maudsley and Bethlehem Royal Hospitals. This development at the Maudsley Hospital, however, is no accident. There are a substantial number of departments in the country which are fully committed to working strictly on applied science. It is, therefore, difficult to assess the relative strength of the main trends in the country as a whole.

Correspondent: *M. B. Shapiro,* London

Yugoslavia

Undergraduate and graduate training in psychology is offered in the major Yugoslav universities of Belgrade, Ljubljana, and Zagreb. The basic program usually requires four years and includes a thorough grounding in experimental psychology and psychometrics, in addition to training in philosophy, education, logic and physiology. Upon completion of oral and written examinations, plus successful defense of a thesis, the candidate is awarded a diploma and may use the title of "diplomate in psychology." The Yugoslav university program is usually considered equivalent to training at the M.A. level in the United States.

Most graduates of the basic program either go into applied work or become teachers of psychology, philosophy, and logic in the senior grades of high school. Those who become recognized through their research and publications may be invited to enroll in doctoral programs, where they eventually qualify for the degree of "Doctor of Psychology." Although this degree is awarded for the successful defense of a doctoral thesis, it is also a reward for high professional achievement.

Although Yugoslavia does not have a graduate training program in clinical psychology, practicum training is given through course work in the universities. Supervision is generally by staff psychologists in mental hospitals, clinics, schools for the retarded, and correctional centers.

Correspondent: *Nicholas Kopatic,* Vineland, N.J.

MIDDLE EAST AND NORTH AFRICA

Among the Arab countries of the Middle East and North Africa, (Algeria, Egypt, Iraq, Jordan, Kuwait, Lebanon, Lybia, Morocco, Saudi Arabia, Syria, Sudan, Tunis, and Yemen), only Egypt offers formal training in clinical psychology. While the American University in Beirut, Lebanon, has an active Psychology Department, primary interest is in traditional experimental areas. There is increasing research in mental measurement. Graduate psychology training in the other Arab countries is strongly influenced by European traditions and emphasizes educational services.

Egypt (*United Arab Republic*)

Graduate training programs in clinical psychology have been developed at Ain-Shams University in Cairo, Cairo University, and Alexandria University. In 1955 the first Center for Social Research in Arab Countries was established, which in 1960 became the National Center for Social and Criminological Research in Cairo.

The Department of Psychological and Sociological Studies, Faculty of Arts, Ain-Shams University in Cairo, was the first Egyptian educational institution to adopt the term "clinical psychology" and offer training patterned after that available in the United Kingdom and in the United States. Undergraduate students share a common first year, begin to major in either psychology or sociology during the third year, and join in seminars during the fourth year. Practicum training is mandatory during the senior year for clinical psychology students. Faculty members who represent a broad range of psychology facilitate the adaptation of American or English tests for Arab communities, and promote psychological services in mental health centers and government facilities. A professional Diploma in Psychological Services may be awarded after two years' graduate study and practicum. Work for M.A. and Ph.D. is research oriented.

The Department of Mental Health in the College of Education at Ains-Shams University is similar to graduate departments of clinical psychology in the United States. Training in diagnostic testing and therapy is provided in the Psychological Clinic administered by the Department. Both M.A. and Ph.D. programs have been developed. The M.A. usually requires a minimum of one year course work plus two years for a thesis. An additional three years is needed to complete the Ph.D., including defense of a dissertation.

Psychology occupies a major place in the Department of Sociology, Faculty of Arts, Cairo University. At the graduate level, M.A. and Ph.D. programs are offered, as is a Diploma in Psychological Services. Alexandria University continues to maintain the integration of psychology, sociology, and anthropology with philosophy and logic. Although it offers no practicum training, Alexandria does have M.A. and Ph.D. programs which permit a clinical orientation and encourage research in psychology.

The National Center for Social and Criminological Research includes a psychological clinic, laboratory, and library. University professors supervise research, including development of pertinent psychological tests. The annual budget offers scholarships for graduate training in Egypt and abroad.

While there is no accredited clinical psychology intern training program in Egypt, practicum facilities are arranged by the university departments in approved centers or affiliated clinics. Supervision in psychological testing and rudimentary aspects of psychotherapy is usually by senior staff members or university faculty. The National Center for Social and Criminological Research has been a particular resource for research training related to "social planning" and problems encountered in the socialization of Egypt, e.g., prevention and rehabilitation of juvenile delinquents, prostitutes, drug addicts, etc.

Correspondent: *Moneim A. El-Meligi,* Princeton, N.J.

Israel

None of the three Israeli universities awards Ph.D. degrees in clinical psychology. The oldest and best established Israeli university is the Hebrew University of Jerusalem, Kiryat Ha Universita. The Department of Psychology developed very slowly and there are only a few courses in clinical psychology While the department grants an M.A. degree in psychology, i has no training facilities for clinical work, except for brief assignments to the psychiatric institutions of the Ministry of Health.

The second Israeli university, Bar-Ilan University of Ramat-Gan, founded in 1955, set its Department of Psychology from the very beginning toward a clinical orientation, especially on the M.A. level. There are several courses matching the American curriculum of clinical training. Recently, the Tel-Hashomer Government Hospital agreed to provide clinical training facilities under the supervision of the two chief psychologists of the psychiatric department. There is a plan to extend these facilities to other institutions of the Ministry of Health. However, such training does not provide the Bar-Ilan graduate with the possibility to work independently in clinical psychology.

The third Israeli university, the University of Tel-Aviv, created a Department of Psychology two years ago. Only a B.A. degree is granted; although some courses necessary for clinical training are given, no clinical training is available.

There are no centralized supervised practicum or intern training facilities in Israel. The Clinical Section of the Israel Psychological Association is currently preparing a program of clinical training for its members and candidate members. This training will be organized within those institutions where independent or chief clinical psychologists are able to give supervision and teaching to the trainees. At the present moment, institutions of the Ministry of Health and the Hadassah University Clinic, Jerusalem, offer on-the-job training facilities.

Taking into consideration the special needs of mass immigration to Israel, the Ministry of Health carried out, since 1958, a training program based on scholarships for clinical psychologists newly arrived from Eastern European lands. These were largely M.A. psychologists with a theoretical and practical background different from that used in Israel and the Western Hemisphere. The training program was of one year's duration and enabled the new immigrants to adjust professionally while maintaining their social status and mental well-being. By 1963 all these trainees had become fully employed clinical psychologists. In 1961 the Jewish Agency, together with the Ministry of Labour and the Ministry of Education, established a training fund for psychologists and the Ministry of Health continues to provide the practicum training facilities. Some combined educational and clinical training is provided on a smaller scale by the Youth Immigration Department.

Correspondent: Edith Falik, Tel Aviv

Turkey

As of 1962, psychology departments exist in Orta Dogu University in Ankara and Istanbul University. Neither offers any graduate training in clinical psychology. Plans have been initiated at Orta Dogu to start a Master's program during 1964-65. Courses are given on essentials of psychological testing, projective and individual tests, counseling, and abnormal psychology. A counseling service has also been opened which offers field practice to psychology students.

The Psychology Department at Istanbul University is located in the Faculty of Letters and Arts. It offers three main certificates to its students, namely, in social, general, and experimental psychology. With the aim of providing general knowledge in all areas of psychology, courses are offered in perception, learning, personality, attitudes, emotions, psychological testing, and psychoanalytic theory.

After receiving the Master's, a graduate student may work toward the Ph.D. Although there are no course requirements, as in the USA, advanced study usually takes at least three years plus acceptance of a dissertation on a topic in experimental psychology.

A psychology internship program on the American model remains to be developed in Turkey. The Psychology Department of Istanbul University allows students to take a three-month course and practicum at the Psychiatric Clinic of the Medical School, where they have an opportunity to gain experience, although very limited, in the administration and interpretation of basic psychological tests.

Books on clinical psychology are not available in Turkish. Students have to master a foreign language to supplement or increase the knowledge given by the psychology departments or in practicum assignments. The first Turkish text on psychological testing was recently published by Dr. Cansever.

Correspondent: Gökçe Cansever, Istanbul

MIDDLE AND SOUTH AFRICA

The term "Middle Africa," as used by UNESCO, includes most of Africa, that is, all except the Arab countries to the North (Egypt, Lybia, Tunisia, Algeria, and Morocco), the Portuguese territories and the Republic of South Africa to the South.

In Middle Africa, that vast area encompassing about thirty countries, many of them newly independent, there were nineteen universities in 1960. Over 70% of the faculty members were born and trained abroad, mostly in Great Britain, France, Belgium, and the United States (in that order). The African nations are making extraordinary efforts and sacrifices to expand their educational facilities, to teach their children to read and write, to send increasing numbers through secondary schools, and to provide university training for their ablest students.

While education is vital to economic and social development plans, primary emphasis is on producing educators, engineers, managers, agricultural experts, and physicians. Psychology has priority only to the extent to which it contributes to state plans and the development of talented manpower.

Cameroons

It was reported at the 1962 La Napoule Conference that the reunited former British and French Cameroons have as yet no institution of higher learning. While English and French are both considered official languages, it appears that French will predominate. Financial resources are very limited and initial educational efforts are focusing on teacher training with some interest on psychological testing and measurement.

Congo

In June 1960, independence came with unexpected suddenness and without preparation to a country whose 900,000 square miles are nearly equivalent in area to Western Europe. Among the 14 million native population, there was not a single Congolese physician, lawyer, or engineer; there were only fourteen college graduates.

At the time of our visit in 1961, there were no psychiatric facilities for non-Europeans. Psychotic Congolese remained in their villages. Juvenile delinquency was rising, fostered by large-scale unemployment, ineffective government controls, and loosening family ties. While Belgian psychologists had taught in Elizabethville and Leopoldville, their activities focused mainly on personnel selection and social-anthropological studies. In December 1962 one Belgian missionary psychologist had returned to Louvanium University in Leopoldville; there is no information about Elizabethville. While there are no present prospects for establishing a clinical psychology training program, the Congo (and other emerging African countries) constitutes a vast laboratory for studies in the public health approach to mental health, particularly as individuals leave a relatively sheltered tribal community for the beckoning attraction of the rapidly industrializing but impersonal and frequently stress-inducing cities.

Ghana

As of January 1963, there was no undergraduate or graduate training in any field of psychology in Ghana. Psychological activities at the University of Ghana in Legon are generally limited to teaching in the education and sociology departments, psychological testing, and research. The Psychological Testing Unit at the University participates in the West African Aptitude Test Development Program and in the screening and selection of candidates for government, education and training schemes. It is staffed by an M.A. psychologist, aided by two assistants and a $20,000 Ford Foundation grant for a two-year period. In 1963 four Ghanaians completed their M.A. training at the University of Pittsburgh to facilitate national standardization for Ghana of aptitude tests developed in Nigeria by the American Institute of Research. The M.A. psychologist currently in Ghana will be sent to the United States for Ph.D. training. Meanwhile, through the U. S. Agency for International Development, recruitment has been initiated for a Professor of Psychology to direct the Department in Legon.

Correspondent: *George Soloyanis,* Accra

Nigeria

The primary focus of university programs in Nigeria is on teacher training. At the University College in Ibadan, psychology is taught at the undergraduate level and there is an active testing program; postgraduate research emphasizes developmental and educational approaches. Provision for psychological courses have been made at the University of Nigeria in Nsukka, where there is a psychological testing program under the office of the Dean of Students.

There are no clinical psychologists in the strict sense of the word in Nigeria. Neither a graduate training program nor traditional practicum facilities have been established. However, the Neuro-Psychiatric Centre at Aro Hospital, located just outside Abeokuta, has become well known for its "village system" of community care for the mentally ill. It was established by Dr. T. Adeoye Lambo in 1954, who, in 1962, became the first professor of psychiatry at the University College Medical School.

Correspondent: *Thomas A. Wickes*, Enugu

South Africa

The only major university currently offering a full-fledged course in clinical psychology is the University of Witwatersrand, Milner Park, Johannesburg. The degree conferred is a Master of Arts or Master of Science in clinical psychology. The denominational Potchefstroom University for "Christian Higher Education" has recently instituted a clinical course. It is likely that similar courses will soon be availabe at the universities of Cape Town, Pretoria, and Stellenbosch. A Master's degree enjoys fairly high status in this country, entailing at least five years' full-time study and practical work, together with the production of a full-length thesis.

The only institution which currently offers an internship in clinical psychology is the Transvaal Provincial Neuropsychiatric Center, Tara Hospital, P.O. Box 13, Saxonwold, Johannesburg. Applicants for this 18-month internship must have a Master's degree in psychology and are subjected to an intensive screening procedure. An attempt is made to provide a many-sided training program including the handling of cases under mentorship, but no examination is conducted relating to the experience gained.

It should be added that, apart from formal clinical courses, most of the large universities have a child guidance or other mental health clinic where psychology graduates receive training which renders them eligible for registration by the South African Psychological Association.

Training facilities in South Africa are affected by the formidable sociopolitical problems facing that divided land. The South African Psychological Association's 1961 decision to admit to membership the small number of non-European psychologists resulted in considerable professional dissension. Governmental policy favors separate associations for the different races. With 3 million Europeans living amidst 12 million Africans, the reigning political doctrine clouds the otherwise promising picture of clinical psychology in South Africa.

Correspondent: *Arnold Abramowitz,* Cape Town

SOUTHEAST ASIA

Many developments in Hong Kong, Indonesia, Malaya, Singapore, Taiwan, and Viet Nam have been influenced by the psychology prevailing in the European countries which until recently controlled a large part of Southeast Asia. Indonesian psychologists have been deeply influenced by the Dutch, those in Malaya have drawn on the experience of the British, while French influences are still reflected in Vietnam. Hong Kong shows both British and Chinese influences while Taiwan has retained little from the Japanese because psychology is in the hands largely of those who came from the mainland more than a decade ago.

At their state of development, these countries do not have professional groups with sharply circumscribed roles as is the case in the United States. The result is that anyone who was trained as a clinical psychologist may work in many phases of psychology and completely outside of psychology. Likewise, someone with limited training in psychology but extensive training in quite another discipline might be found working as a psychologist. Professional persons are characterized by the breadth of their activities rather than by their narrow specialization since this is the only way they can earn a living.

Clinical psychology, such as it is, seems to be getting its start in the educational setting in much the same way as in the United ·States. At the present time the contribution is primarily in the assessment of ability. In most of these countries there is also some attempt to use psychological tests in the armed forces. But only now is an attempt being made to develop tests appropriate to the cognitive processes of the subjects concerned. This is made more difficult by the presence of many dialects in each of these countries. Using tests developed in other countries has never been satisfactory, a realization that is becoming increasingly clear. In Indonesia, at least, this realization has been extended to questioning the validity of psychodynamic formulations developed in Western cultures. The picture then is of a limited number of psychologists in each of these countries, who have received their graduate training abroad and who are performing a wide range of psychological activities using Western instruments. Diagnostic work is their principal concern, with little opportunity or tradition for either psychotherapy or research.

Correspondent: *George M. Guthrie,* University Park, Penna.

Burma

Two Burmese universities offer a two-year M.A. degree in psychology. The University of Rangoon has a separate Department of Psychology, headed by Prof. Hla Thwin (Ph.D., Columbia). At the University of Mandalay, a smaller and newer institution, Dr. Sein Tu (Ph.D., Harvard) is Professor in the Department of Psychology and Philosophy.

While there is no separate degree in clinical psychology, relevant course work with an associated practicum can be taken; a graduate student could major in clinical psychology and minor in experimental psychology. One difficulty with clinical courses and practicum at this time is the lack of an experienced clinical psychologist to supervise clinical training at the university as well as at the internship or practicum center.

Student interest in psychology has been demonstrated by a

continually increasing enrollment over the years in both lower level and advanced courses. Among those who become "majors" and advanced degree candidates, a growth of interest in clinical training has been marked.

Although there are no staff psychologists in non-university institutions, the Government Mental Hospital at Tadagalay, near Rangoon, is used for practicum experience and is the logical place for intern training to develop. A branch of the hospital is to be established in Mandalay. Field training facilities would then be conveniently located near both universities. The hospital psychiatrists have urged the University of Rangoon to train clinical psychologists and it is expected that full- or part-time interns would be welcome.

Correspondents: *Julian Wohl*, Toledo, Ohio
Hla Thwin, Rangoon

China

Direct communication with psychologists in the People's Republic of China is difficult for the United States. However, Chinese medical and psychological journals are available in the Library of the Academy of Medicine in New York City and elsewhere. Articles are frequently published in English, less commonly in Russian; Chinese contributions generally have English and Russian summaries. A report of trends in Chinese psychology has also appeared in *Psychologia,* an English language journal dedicated to psychology in the Orient and edited by Prof. Koji Sato in Japan. Written by Prof. Pan Shu (Ph.D., University of Chicago), Director of the Institute of Psychology, Academia Sinica, Peking, and Past President of the Chinese Psychological Association, this report, quoted with permission, makes the general observation:

"Since the Liberation, psychologists in China have been intensively studying Marxism as well as the Soviet psychology and Pavlov's theory. Profiting by the experience of Soviet psychologists in building up the dialectic Materialist Psychology, Chinese psychologists fully realized that, in order to shake off the ideological and methodological influences of the Idealistic Psychology of Capitalist countries, and in order for psychology to take up its share of important tasks in Socialist Reconstruction, it is necessary to reconstruct a scientific psychology upon the basis of Pavlov's theory in accordance with Marxist principles."

In considering the Chinese scene, it must be recalled that many senior Chinese psychologists received their training in the United States and that few know the Russian language, or are very familiar with Soviet psychology.

More recent Chinese publications suggest considerable competition between Western and traditional Chinese medicine, with the latter apparently gaining the upper hand, as of 1963. Particularly popular at the moment are traditional acupuncture (needle therapy) and cauterization, modernly viewed as a form of shock treatment.

While there is no current information on clinical psychology training and practicum facilities, it is known that China is experiencing a great shortage of professional personnel. Conceivably, the traditional Chinese methods of treatment are attractive because time required for training is far less than in the West.

Hong Kong

The University of Hong Kong offers some training in psychology as part of the program in education. At least one staff member has a Master's degree from an American university; a second was trained in England. A small child guidance clinic has been conducted in conjunction with offerings in developmental psychology.

Correspondent: *George M. Guthrie,* University Park, Penna.

India

In India, students who complete all college B.A. requirements are eligible to join the University School for postgraduate study. The M.A. usually takes two years. The Ph.D. generally requires at least two more years plus independent research for a dissertation.

Although Indian universities have no doctoral programs in clinical psychology, comparable to those offered in the United States, any Indian university would permit the registration of a candidate for the Ph.D. in clinical psychology if he works under a university-approved supervisor who had had pertinent post-graduate qualifications, experience, and publications. A few candidates have already started doctoral work at the All-India Institute for Mental Health, Bangalore, and at the universities of Calcutta, Bihar, Mysore, Madras, and Lucknow.

Mysore University, Mysore, grants a postgraduate diploma in medical and social psychology to candidates undergoing a two year full-time training at the All-India Institute of Mental Health, Bangalore, started by the Government of India in 1954. Candidates with a Master's degree in psychology are eligible for admission to the course. A similar two year postgraduate diploma program was started by the Government of India in 1962 at the Hospital for Mental Diseases, Kanke, Ranchi.

Of the 45 universities, the following provide mainly theoretical training in clinical/abnormal psychology or in an allied branch, e.g., psychoanalysis, at the M.A. level: Agra; Aligarh; Allahabad; Banaras; Baroda; Bihar (Muzzaffarpur); Bombay; Calcutta; Delhi; Gujarat (Ahmedabad); Kerala (Trivandrum); Lucknow; Madras; Mysore; Patna; Poona; Punjab (Chadigarh); Ranchi; S. V. University, Tirupati.

Major clinical centers providing supervised practicum or intern training facilities include: Mental Hospital, Bangalore: All-India Institute of Mental Health, Bangalore; Hospital for Mental Diseases, Kanke, Ranchi; Mental Hospital, Loombini Park, Calcutta Psycho-Analytical Society; Christian Medical College Hospital, Vellore.

In the major center of postgraduate training, Mysore University, and the affiliated All-India Institute in Bangalore, trainees in clinical psychiatry and psychology function as a team and learn to work on a collaborative basis. Most mental hospitals have an inadequate number of posts for clinical psychologists; this may be because psychiatrists, who are mainly dependent on physical forms of treatment, are not very enthusiastic about or familiar with the methods of clinical psychology. There seems to be growing evidence of professional rivalry between psychiatrists and clinical psychologists; the former, however, are in a decidedly better position in status and financial aspects.

Among the applied branches of psychology, clinical psychology seems to have established itself firmly in India, with two Government-of-India sponsored institutes providing training and research facilities. The number of fellowships awarded for trainees in this subject, although inadequate for the whole country, is much greater than that available in other specialties. While no particular pattern of clinical practice has yet emerged, it appears that the determining influence is most likely to come from clinical psychologists working in areas outside the mental hospitals and clinics.

Correspondent: *N. N. Sen,* Bangalore

Indonesia

Indonesia has made great strides in clinical psychology. There is an active graduate training program at the University of Indonesia in Djarkarta. This program is directed by Dr. Slamet Inam Santoso, a psychiatrist who also directs the psychiatric ward of the university hospital. Members of his staff have received doctorates from European universities. Their techniques include European and American tests which have been, in part at least, standardized on Indonesian populations. Other universities offering work in psychology include Gadjah Mada in Jogjakarta and medical schools in Bandung and Surabaya. There is also some concern with psychological research at the Institute for Pedagogical Research at the University of Padjadjaran in Bandung.

The armed forces of Indonesia employ a number of psychologists, at least one of whom has taken some training in the United States. Their testing program makes use of tests developed by the Dutch. There have been a number of modifications of these tests since independence.

Psychologists in Indonesia have experienced difficulty obtaining journals and instruments from abroad because of severe currency restrictions. In spite of these difficulties they have maintained serious efforts to continue psychological research. They have been alert to the question of the appropriateness of foreign psychological techniques and theories when applied to Indonesian problems.

Correspondent: *George M. Guthrie,* University Park, Penna.

Japan

Already well established in the thirties, Japanese psychology has responded most actively to the post-World War II stimulus from the United States. There are twenty universities awarding Ph.D. degrees (usually five years after the B.A.). While experimental and educational psychology still predominate, social, clinical, and industrial psychology are receiving support.

As of December 1962, no Japanese university offered a systematic graduate training program in clinical psychology, although some students may major in this field and select clinical topics for their M.A. or Ph.D. theses. At the B.A. level, psychologists are usually trained in traditional academic psychology with few clinical courses. Since minimum academic qualifications for psychologists in hospitals and clinics are at the B.A. level, most aspiring clinicians learn their skills on the job. (Note: In the old educational system, the B.A. was regarded as the equivalent of the present M.A.)

Japan has not yet developed the kind of accredited intern training program established in the United States. Only the training offered at the National Institute for Mental Health (Konodai, Ickikawa, Chiba-ken, Japan), is regarded as the equivalent of graduate school credit. Other major training centers include the Central Training Institute of Correctional Officers, Diakan-cho, Chiyoda-ky, Tokyo, and the Research and Training Institute of the Family Court, Fujimi-cho, Chiyoda-ky, Tokyo.

Correspondent: *Keiichi Mizushima,* Tokyo

Malaya and Singapore

The University of Malaya in Singapore, like the University of Hong Kong, offers some training in psychology oriented to teacher training. There is a Malaysian Social Research Institute, but it is concerned primarily with topics outside of the distinct domain of psychology. The Chinese community in Singapore recently opened a new university, Nanyang University, with plans to offer instruction in Mandarin and English. As of 1960 there was no offering in psychology.

The Federation of Malaya built a new university in Kuala

Lumpur but as of 1960 no work was being offered in psychology. There appears to be a good deal of interest in the Ministry of Education in problems of measurement.

Correspondent: *George M. Guthrie,* University Park, Penna.

Pakistan

When independence came to the Indian subcontinent, Pakistan emerged as a new state, divided into two parts, East and West Pakistan, separated by more than 1,000 miles. Of the six universities in Pakistan (two in the East, four in the West), only the University of Peshawar does not have a Department of Psychology. The recently established University of Sind in Hyderabad, West Pakistan, and the University of Dacca in East Pakistan have psychology departments in which philosophy and psychology courses are still interwoven. The other three Pakistani universities, Karachi, Panjab (Lahore), and Rafshahi, have had psychology departments for some years. Panjab University plans a Department of Applied Psychology and has a Child Guidance Center, administered by the psychology staff of the Government College affiliated with the university.

Although there is no formal graduate program in clinical psychology, the M.A. and Ph.D. degrees in psychology are offered by the universities. Most graduate study is at the M.A. level, often in applied areas; the Ph.D. is usually required only for university teaching or research positions.

At the time of partition, Pakistan received as her share two government mental hospitals, one in each sector. There is a third hospital which has just been opened in West Pakistan. The total capacity of these hospitals is about 6,000 beds. They do not have the services of clinical psychologists or psychiatric social workers. The methods employed are more drug-oriented than psychotherapeutic.

Correspondent: *S. K. Ahmad,* Bloomington, Indiana

Philippines

Although long associated with the United States, which granted independence in 1945, the Philippines have an educational system that appears to be more privately than publicly oriented. There are several hundred colleges and universities. The large number arises from the fact that it has been found a profitable and prestigeful enterprise to establish universities. Many of these are owned by single families and serve only a few hundred students. The national government maintains one large university, the University of the Philippines, located in Quezon City on the outskirts of Manila. This is patterned after an American state university, both in courses offered and in structure and staffing. The other important universities in Manila include Santo Tomas, established about 1600; the Ateneo which has a graduate school with very high academic standards; the Philippine Women's University, which is owned by the Benitez family; Far Eastern University and the University of the East which are privately owned; and the Philippine Normal College. Each community of any size has two or three colleges; very much the same pattern is followed in high schools, with over half the high school education provided by private facilities.

Within this context, psychology is not well established and there are not many psychologists working in Philippine universities, even though a fair number of psychology courses are offered. The head of the department at the University of the Philippines is Alfredo Laymay (Ph.D., Harvard, in experimental psychology). Another well-known psychologist in Manila is Dr. Estafania Aldaba-Lim (Ph.D., University of Michigan) who teaches at the Philippine Women's University and has been most active in the area of mental health and counseling. Generally, American textbooks are used, since there are only one or two psychology books written by Filipinos.

While there are no special courses in clinical psychology, colleges and universities offer B.A., B.S., M.A., and Ph.D. programs in general psychology. As in the United States, the B.A. or B.S. usually requires four years after high school. The Master's generally takes a year plus a written thesis. At least an additional two years are needed for the Ph.D., plus defense of a research dissertation. Among the few Ph.D. level psychologists in Manila, some teach at the universities; others work in counseling facilities, including an outpatient clinic maintained by the U. S. Veterans Administration.

Supervision of practicum training is directed by the departments of psychology in the universities and colleges, usually in their respective guidance centers. Clinical training and experience in a psychiatric setting are available at the University of the East, Ramon Magsaysay Memorial Medical Center; Neuro-Psychiatry Department, the V. Luna General Hospital; Philippine Veterans Memorial Hospital; the National Mental Hospital; and the Philippine General Hospital Psychiatric Section. The objective is to prepare students to assume professional responsibilities for diagnostic testing and to understand adequately patient-psychologist relations, as well as all the functions of psychologists in collaborating with other members of the clinical team. American tests predominate and research to develop pertinent norms is urgently needed.

Correspondent: *Belen L. Garcia,* Quezon City and Trenton, N. J.

Taiwan

A Department of Psychology was established at National Taiwan University in 1949. Research and student interest has concentrated on measurement of ability and of personality. Projective techniques have been used in studies of aboriginal groups on Formosa. There has also been an extensive effort in testing of aptitudes and achievement in the armed forces. Mental health activities and guidance programs have been established.

At Taiwan Normal University there is considerable interest in child development and an extensive training and research program has been initiated. At both of these universities American influences are quite apparent, as is true in the armed forces.

Correspondent: *George M. Guthrie,* University Park, Penna.

Thailand

No Thai university offers a major in any kind of psychology, either on the graduate or undergraduate level.

Somdej Chao Mental Hospital together with the affiliated Child Guidance Clinic and the Hospital for Nervous Disorders (Rongphyabahn Prasat) has potential for internship training under quite good psychiatric supervision.

At present all personnel in the psychological-psychiatric field have been trained abroad and little research has been done to relate to Thai cultural norms. On a per capita income basis, Thailand is probably the best endowed nation in Southeast Asia, offering many opportunities for development.

Correspondent: *Frederic L. Ayer*, Bangkok

Vietnam

The division of Viet Nam resulted in the loss of the principal educational resources which were located in Hanoi. There is some interest in psychological problems on the part of persons concerned with education in Saigon. The French influence remains strong and is not particularly congenial to American testing traditions. United States aid programs are bringing many Vietnamese to the United States for training.

Correspondent: *George M. Guthrie*, University Park, Penna.

AUSTRALASIA

Australia

Two universities offer postgraduate training in clinical psychology, the University of Western Australia, Nedlands, and the University of Sydney, New South Wales. Others, including the University of Melbourne, Victoria, and the University of New South Wales offer professional-type courses in the third or fourth year of the degree course and may extend these into postgraduate programs.

The University of Western Australia has been the forerunner in Australia in providing professional courses beyond the B.A. degree level. The early beginnings were in 1949 when Dr. E. A. Morey who had received her Ph.D. at the university of California (Berkeley) and Dr. P. Petnoy initiated a one-year postgraduate course in psychodiagnostic testing, projective methods of assessment, and case study of emotional problems in children. This course developed until in 1956 it was expanded into the Diploma in Clinical Psychology. This now constitutes a three-year postgraduate program. Each year has seen considerable revision, as staff lecturers and internship opportunities become available, and as experience is gained.

In its present form, the program does not subscribe to any over-all theoretical orientation. There is, rather, a variety of professional and academic models represented in the university staff and field supervisors. The teaching in general psychology and research is taken by a staff member who comes from the British, and particularly Eysenckian orientation; the testing program follows a more American pattern, with the ego psychoanalytic approaches of Rapaport and Schafer emphasized; while a child psychotherapist trained under Anna Freud at the Hampstead Child Therapy Center takes the area of children's disorders and treatment.

Exposure to these varied orientations, while facing the student with considerable conflict, and also posing problems of integrating opposing concepts and techniques, does mean that both the academic scholarship tradition of psychology and the practitioner service model are emphasized. Frequent staff and staff/ supervisor meetings are held where opposing viewpoints are aired and where the teaching in different areas of the course is evaluated, and changes are made in the light of each year's experience.

There does not exist in Australia a system of accrediting institutions for practicum training comparable to those on the British and American scenes. Where a supervised internship exists, as in Western Australia, the main determinants in using a particular agency are the availability of adequately trained supervisors and the type of psychological duties that can be undertaken. At Western Australia, the shortage of supervisors and teaching staff has restricted each year's intake to about four students.

The internship makes up half the week during term time and continues throughout the second and third years. By the time of entry to the practicum setting, the student has completed the first-year courses on general theory, cognitive assessment, and psychopathology, and is expected to be capable of contributing to the work of the unit, with responsibilities increasing in line with his course program.

A rotation system has been developed among four agencies: a

child guidance clinic, a children's general hospital, an acute treatment unit for adult neurotic and psychotic disorders, and a day-hospital unit run along therapeutic community lines. Each supervisor will be responsible for, at the most, two students at a given time. Dr. Bownes acts as coordinator of the practicum program and frequently visits the various agencies. Supervisors in turn have regular meetings with the university staff, every eight weeks at least, for student evaluation.

The content of the practicum includes supervised training in diagnostic testing, report writing, and observation and interviewing, and at the later stages some contact with psychotherapy, usually in a group setting. Emphasis is also placed on the assessment of the organizational and social structure of the agency, the roles and functions of its personnel, and the interprofessional issues and problems that arise. The question of professional fields for the clinical psychologist that may develop beyond the traditional ones of diagnosis, therapy, and research is kept before the student.

This program of a supervised practicum, while yet inadequate (particularly in its shortage of supervisory staff and its lack of variety of specialists at each agency), does represent a big forward step. Prior to it, the new graduate entering these agencies found himself assigned to a psychiatric team with his role undefined and his task confined by a psychiatrist to diagnostic testing or psychometric routine. Putting the control of supervision and the allocation of the intern's duties into the hands of the staff psychologist meant that the medical and other professions had to reassess the psychologist's status and professional contribution.

In other Austrialian states, supervised practicum facilities are also being developed. Professor J. Clark, head of the School of Applied Psychology, University of New South Wales, reports that in the fourth year of the B.Sc. in Applied Psychology students undertake supervised practical work at the university teaching hospitals. These institutions are now being staffed by full-time clinical psychologists who will also be involved in teaching and supervision. The Associate Professor of Clinical Psychology in the School of Applied Psychology is also Director of Clinical Psychology in the teaching hospitals of the university. Correspondent: *A. F. Bownes* and colleagues, Nedlands

New Zealand

There are four universities in New Zealand—Auckland, Victoria (in Wellington), Canterbury (in Christchurch), and Otago (in Dunedin)—all of which offer graduate courses in psychology. The course at Otago does not go beyond the first year but a chair is soon to be established and then Otago will doubtless offer a bachelor's degree in psychology as the other universities do.

While the University of Canterbury offers a postgraduate diploma in clinical psychology, standards meeting British or American criteria have still to be established. The Department of Psychological Medicine in Otago cannot as yet offer any postgraduate training in psychology or psychiatry; however, together with certain other facilities in Dunedin, it constitutes the only center in New Zealand where clinical work in psychology approaches anything that would be academically recognizable elsewhere.

Correspondent: *Harold Bourne*, Dunedin

THE AMERICAS

Canada

Some three dozen colleges and universities in Canada have departments of psychology. In most of those which are large enough to undertake the graduate training of M.A. or Ph.D. candidates, provision is made for the training of clinical psychologists. The pattern of such training varies from those departments which emphasize the acquisition of clinical skills to those where the emphasis is on clinical research. The differences are so wide that students contemplating graduate training in clinical psychology in Canada should secure and study the respective curricula with care.

The following universities offer graduate training in clinical psychology. Degrees granted, special emphasis, and centers for supervised intern training are stated in brackets.

Dalhousie University, Halifax, Nova Scotia. [M.A.; Ph.D.; emphasis on experimental; Nova Scotia Hospital, Dartmouth, N.S.; DVA Hospital, Camp Hill, Halifax; Hospital for Nervous and Mental Diseases, St. John's, Newfoundland.]

Université Laval, Cité Universitaire, Ste-Foy, Quebec. [License and doctorate, equivalent to M.A. and Ph.D.; essentially clinical; Hôpital St.-Michel-Archange, Quebec; unspecified departments of psychiatry in general hospitals.]

University of Montreal, Montreal, Quebec. [License and doctorate, equivalent to M.A. and Ph.D.; essentially clinical; Training Center in Applied Psychology of the Institute of Psychology; unspecified outside clinics.]

McGill University, Montreal, Quebec. [M.Sc. (applied); Ph.D.; research oriented; Montreal Children's Hospital; Montreal General Hospital; Queen Mary Veterans Hospital; Jewish General Hospital; Verdun Protestant Hospital; Allan Memeorial Institute; Montreal Day Nursery.]

University of Ottawa, Ottawa, Ontario. [M.A.; M.Ps. (added courses plus practical training in lieu of thesis); Ph.D. (clinical or child clinical;) clinical cum educational; Guidance Center and Child Guidance Center of the School of Psychology and Education; Royal Ottawa Sanatarium; psychiatric units of Ottawa General and Ottawa Civic Hospitals.]

University of Toronto, Toronto, Ontario. [M.A.; Ph.D.; basic theory, method and research; Toronto Psychiatric Hospital; Ontario Hospital, New Toronto; Toronto General Hospital; Hospital for Sick Children, Toronto; Sunnybrook (DVA) Hospital, Toronto; Thistledown Hospital (for disturbed children), Thistledown; Crippled Children's Treatment Center; Institute of Child Study of the University of Toronto; twelve of the Ontario Hospitals and Ontario Hospital Schools (for 4-month summer internships); etc.]

Queens University, Kingston, Ontario. [M.A.; Diploma in Clinical Psychology M.A. (courses plus one-year practicum and added courses *sans* research project); Ph.D.; applied experimental; Kingston General Hospital, Ontario Hospital, Kingston (for nervous and mental disorders); Hotel Dieu Hospital,

Kingston; Kingston Rehabilitation Centre; Ontario Hospital, Smith Falls (for the mentally defective).]
 University of Alberta, Edmonton, Alberta. [M.A. general, with specific work in clinical; Ph.D. (clinical); University Hospital, Edmonton; other unspecified guidance clinics, mental hospitals, rehabilitation centers, research centers.]
 University of British Columbia, Vancouver, B.C. [M.A.; unspecified provincial mental hospitals, DVA and general hospitals.]

"Bursaries" for graduate training in clinical psychology are available under the National Health grants and are offered by provincial health departments to those who undertake a subsequent period of service in the province's mental hospitals, psychiatric units or mental health clinics. In 1961-62 about 38 students were receiving such assistance in Canada.

Correspondents: *C. Roger Myers,* Toronto, Ontario
Craig M. Mooney, Ottawa, Ontario

LATIN AMERICA

The development of clinical psychology in Latin America has been greatly stimulated by the increasing communication fostered by the Interamerican Society of Psychology, founded in December 1951 at the International Congress of Mental Health in Mexico. The first Interamerican Congress of Psychology was held two years later, in December, 1953, in the Dominican Republic at the University of Santo Domingo, the oldest university in the Americas. In viewing Latin America, it should be noted that information is not always readily obtainable and diverse details need to be properly understood in terms of prevailing trends and conditions.

First, there are the psychiatrists who work in mental hospitals almost exclusively and have a largely "non-dynamic" orientation. Although not directly involved in psychological training, they participate to some extent in practicum supervision.

Secondly, there are physician-psychologists who are MD's with experience in psychoanalysis or psychotherapy and who sometimes also have additional training in the behavioral sciences. They are one of the dynamic forces behind the training of clinical psychologists. Among the analysts there are some Ph.D. psychologists who play a very similar role and identify themselves as medical psychologists.

Thirdly, there is a small group of academic psychologists who are very rarely concerned with training for professional work. Harking back to a European psychology of over thirty years ago, they are deeply involved with theoretical contributions while rarely interested in statistical research design or systematic methodological efforts.

Fourthly, there are the "educationalists" who constitute another segment of the dynamic forces in clinical psychology training. Led by a relatively few Ph.D.'s in educational settings, they train a large number of students, many of whom obtain certification at what might be equivalent to an M.A. degree in the United States.

Leadership for clinical training has long been under the aegis of the physician-psychologists but is presently contested by the educationalists. Since the more traditional psychologists do not take much interest in clinical programs, the directions and goals of training frequently differ from the U.S. standard of endeavoring to produce a well-rounded psychologist with a research orientation as well as professional skills.

One of the major problems faced by the universities in staffing departments of psychology is the fact that many of the department heads and most of the faculty were trained in other disciplines, such as psychoanalysis, psychiatry, and philosophy. Only a few staff members in the departments of psychology received some training in the United States and that usually at the Master's level. Some others trained in Europe and immigrated to Latin America before World War II.

With the establishment of many new governmental agencies, there is an ever-growing need for professional personnel. Most of the students are young women (85 to 90%). They usually obtain an equivalent of a B.A. or Master's degree with little emphasis on research or methodology. After completing their training with a good deal of practicum experience, obtained in a variety of clinical settings, they are certified as psychologists and work under the direction of either a physician-psychologist, a medical psychologist, or an educationalist.

At this writing, the certified psychologists on the B.A. or M.A. level are very much concerned about their professional standing and independence. Their struggles are reminiscent of the efforts of clinical psychologists in the United States who twenty years ago tried to discover their role in society. For example, psychotherapy is a major issue in most Latin American countries. The physician-psychologists, who have a leading role in clinical training, by and large do not want to give the subdoctoral professionals the right to do psychotherapy. However, efforts have been initiated to establish doctoral level clinical psychology training programs in several countries, generally following the U.S. model and requiring five years of training, but with less emphasis on methodology and statistics.

While the educationalists appear more willing to permit young professionals to do psychotherapy, they are also involved in upgrading training programs, hopefully toward the Ph.D. degree, emphasizing professional rather than academic preparation. It should be noted, however, that the actual number of students who have so far graduated from these Ph.D. programs is very small (compared with some U.S. universities), while hundreds of students obtain certifiable psychological training on the lower levels.

In view of these remarks, descriptions of clinical training in Latin countries must be read with caution. In some instances they reflect only one of several forces acting upon clinical training and may not be representative of the entire situation in that country. Beyond these professional differences, each university takes much pride in differing significantly from all others in its training curriculum and goals. In the absence of widely accepted standards, the following reports represent an important aspect but not the total picture.

Correspondents: Ernst Beier, Salt Lake City, Utah
Victor D. Sanua, New York, N.Y.

Argentina

In the Argentine Republic, departments of psychology and courses in clinical psychology have been in existence since the 1957 establishment of the six national universities: Buenos

Aires, La Plata, Literal (Rosario), Cordoba, Cuyo (San Luis) and Tucuman. Instead of a Ph.D. degree, each branch of science confers its own doctorate, i.e., Dr. in Law, Dr. in History, Dr. in Psychology, etc. The doctorate in psychology usually requires seven years of university studies.

The Argentine degree of "Clinical Psychologist" is a regular university degree, similar to the Doctor of Medicine. It is authorized to be conferred by the University of Buenos Aires, the National University of La Plata, and the National University of Litoral (Rosario). While each institution of higher education, including private ones, has its own program of clinical psychology training, all require approximately seven years for completion.

Supervision of practicum training is directed by the psychology departments in the universities. Facilities for clinical training include the newer psychiatric hospitals of Buenos Aires, La Plata and Rosario; children's psychiatric services in pediatric hospitals; hospitals attached to the medical schools of national universities; and selected centers for working with delinquent, retarded, and difficult children, often in school settings. The goal of training is to prepare students for professional work in mental hygiene, psychodiagnosis, and personality analysis.

The Center of Child and Adolescent Psychology and Psychopathology of the Unversity of Buenos Aires offers a program in clinical psychology, psychotherapy, and child psychiatry to psychologists and psychiatrists. Students from other Latin American countries also apply to this center for training.

Correspondent: *Fernanda Monasterio*, La Plata

Brazil

At the college level in Brazil, psychology is generally taught in the faculties of philosophy, sciences, and letters. Courses created especially for the study of clinical psychology were introduced in 1953. At the graduate level, psychologists are usually in the faculties of philosophy, which number well over one hundred, with proportionately the greatest number located in Sao Paulo State. Instruction is primarily in theory, with limited opportunity for laboratory courses or research.

Advanced psychology curricula are rare in Brazil despite the expansion of private and state universities and public interest. While graduate students can major in psychology in departments of education and philosophy, specific psychology programs were developed only a few years ago. Courses in clinical psychology are given at Sao Paulo Catholic University, Rio Catholic University, Porto Alegre University, and University of Minas Gerais. The Ph.D. degree, based on a psychology thesis, has been granted almost exclusively at the State University of Sao Paulo. About ten degrees had been awarded by early 1963.

Practicum facilities were originally established in private clinics, but, to speed training, clinics were reorganized as annexes to the universities. Emphasis is on theory, diagnosis, and therapy, with the scope of the work differing in each of the Brazilian universities.

Correspondent: *Arrigo L. Angelini, São Paulo*

Chile

The University of Chile in Santiago has started a regular program in psychology under the chairmanship of Dr. Manuel Poblete. Dr. Carl Hereford of Texas University has been appointed by the Interamerican Society of Psychology as chairman of a committee to study standards of education, training and professional psychology. A well-known figure in the field of psychology in Chile is Dr. Carlos Nassar, who teaches abnormal psychology and mental hygiene at the university.

Correspondent: *Victor D. Sanua, New York, N.Y.*

Colombia

The National University in Bogota has a faculty of psychology where, following a four- or five-year program, students obtain a Master's degree in psychology (Licencia de Psicologia). This license is a general license and does not represent specialization in any branch of psychology. A new two-year program in clinical psychology was initiated in 1963. Students divide their time between university classes and practicum experience.

The Catholic University Javeriana in Bogota also has a Department of Psychology which offers special courses in industrial, clinical, and school psychology.

With the introduction of graduate training in clinical psychology at the university, the Clinica Neuro-Psiquiatrica Santo Tomas in Bogota and other leading clinics in the country provide opportunities for supervised practicum experience.

Correspondent: *Guido Wilde*, Bogotá

Cuba

Before 1959, four Cuban universities offered graduate training in psychology, with opportunities for specialization in clinical psychology. These were: University of Habana, 23 y L, Vedado; University of Vilanova, Reparto Biltmore, Habana; University Central de las Villas, Santa Clara; and University de Oriente, Santiago de Cuba. Habana University gave a Ph.D. while a "Doctor of Psychology" was granted by the other three universities.

Since 1959 the University of Vilanova has been closed and its buildings used for other training. Areas of study and standards for specialization have been changed in all the universities, with many students admitted directly from primary schools.

While there has never been an accredited intern training program in Cuba, supervised extern facilities for work with children and adults were available at the Dispensario San Lorenzo Marianao, Habana; Casa de Beneficencia, Habana del Este, Habana; and at several primary and secondary schools. Most of this training has been discontinued.

Correspondent: *Ines Segura Bustamante*, Miami, Florida

Ecuador

A School of Psychology is connected with the University Central del Ecuador. The Faculty of Judicial and Social Sciences publishes a journal, *Archives of Criminology, Neuropsychiatry, and Related Disciplines,* under the editorship of Dr. Julio Endara.

Correspondent: *Victor D. Sanua,* New York, N.Y.

Guatemala

As of March 1963, Guatemala had nine applied psychologists, three with Ph.D.'s and six at the Licentiate level. While the Psychology Department at San Carlos University has only been recently established, the number of students in the four-year program is rapidly increasing. Practicum facilities are available at private and state clinics. Attainment of a university degree is required for professional practice.

Correspondent: *Elisa Fernandez B.*, Guatemala City

Mexico

The present psychology program at the National University of Mexico, located in Mexico City, demands 3½ years of study beyond the junior college level and a dissertation for the degree of psychotechnician. An additional year of courses heavily loaded with teaching techniques, plus a thesis, is needed for the M.A. degree. Two further years, either beyond the psychotechnician level or beyond the Master's level, and a dissertation are required for the Ph.D. Previous to 1959, only M.A. and Ph.D's were granted.

As of 1963, there are over 1,000 students enrolled in the Psychology Department of the National University of Mexico, (Director: Dr. José Luis Curicl.) Women exceed men by a ratio better than two to one. The major problem at the university is the part-time faculty; of the 59 faculty members, only one is full-time and three are half-time. The others give one to three courses each but do not participate in student programs or committee work. Consequently, it is practically impossible for more than a few students to obtain adequate direction of their dissertations and to complete work for advanced degrees. The composition of the faculty is also unusual. Psychiatrists, psychoanalysts (Freudian and Frommian), lawyers, philosophers, educators, engineers, and a handful of psychologists give courses. Their philosophical approaches range from Thomism and existentialism to neo-empiricism, through various forms of eclecticism.

In former years the problem of the superabundance of individuals without a formal degree was resolved by granting a certificate of *pasantes*, indicating that a person has completed all academic requirements for a degree except his dissertation and final examination. As a result there is an almost infinite variety of combinations of training and experience which will have to be considered before criteria can be accepted on how to define a psychologist in Mexico.

From approximately 1953 to 1959, psychoanalysts and psychiatrists dominated the Psychology Department. Of the large number of psychologists produced, many underwent a form of private psychoanalytic training, which often consisted only of personal psychoanalysis. This has produced psychoanalyzed clinical psychologists who are only *pasantes* as well as psychoanalyzed psychotechnicians, and masters and doctors in Psychology.

In the last three years the Department of Psychology has become more role conscious and the doctorate in psychology is now offered in the fields of clinical, educational, industrial, social and vocational guidance, all of which require field placements. Supervised practicum experience of varying quality is usually arranged in conjunction with medical centers, state hospitals, and juvenile facilities. The doctorate in clinical psychology requires a dissertation focused on some pertinent aspect, which further enhances research in the field.

Correspondent: *Rogelio Diaz-Guerrero,* Mexico City

Panama

As of 1962 there were three professional psychologists in Panama, two of them with a doctorate. There is no psychological association and no efforts have been made toward legislation. While the University of Panama has no graduate psychology program, plans have been initiated to develop a seven-year curriculum for the doctorate degree, and another of four years for the Licentiate degree. Practicum facilities are available but seldom used.

Correspondent: *Carlos M. Malgrat,* Panama City

Peru

Ph.D. degrees with specialization in psychology are awarded by San Marcos University and by the Pontifical Catholic University, both located in Lima. Training programs are developed by the respective department heads, with practicum facilities provided by private and state agencies. The university degree is required for professional practice, teaching, and guidance positions in school systems. One of the leading figures in the Interamerican Society of Psychology is Prof. Dr. Carlos Alberto

Seguin, who is presently head of the Department of Psychiatry at the Hospital Obrera. He is trained both as a psychiatrist and psychologist, as is Dr. A. Cano, who teaches at the Catholic University.

Correspondent: *Miguel A. Sardon*, Lima

San Salvador, Uruguay, and Venezuela

A five-year program in psychology is offered by the Faculty of Humanities at the University of El Salvador.

The Uruguayan Society of Psychology is a member of the International Union of Scientific Psychology. Prof. Magda Louzan is president, and teaches child psychology and testing methods at the Instituto Normal of Montevideo.

The Department of Psychology at the Central University of Venezuela was reorganized in 1958. Some clinical psychology is taught at the National Institute of Pedagogy under the directorship of Father Manuel Montaner. Dr. Francisco del Olmo, who works for the Creole Petroleum Corporation, teaches measurement at the Department of Education of the Central University of Caracas and has been developing new techniques for use in Venezuela.

Correspondent: *Victor D. Sanua*, New York, N.Y.

Summary

Based on information from correspondents, a brief survey is presented of opportunities for graduate training in clinical psychology in fifty-seven countries outside the United States. Following an overview, the reports are arranged alphabetically within major geographic areas. It is recognized that the material is incomplete, and readers are invited to send us additional comments for future editions.

Collection of source material followed Benjamin Wolman's invitation to contribute a chapter on "International Trends" to the *Handbook of Clinical Psychology*, to be published by McGraw-Hill in 1965. The information elicited from fifty-seven countries far exceeded space allotments, and was published as a separate monograph on *International Resources in Clinical Psychology*, (McGraw-Hill, 1964). Aspects of training abroad are summarized in the *Sourcebook* and a survey of professional roles and issues will appear in the *Handbook*. Preparation of this chapter was facilitated by the New Jersey State Department of Institutions and Agencies. Special thanks are expressed to the Human Ecology Fund for its continuing efforts.

CORRESPONDENTS

Abramovitz, Arnold. University of Cape Town, Rondebosch, Cape Town, South Africa.

Ahmad, S. K. University of Indiana, Bloomington, Indiana, U.S.A.

Angelini, Dr. Arrigo L. Univ. of São Paulo, Rua María Antonia 294, São Paulo, Brazil.

Ayer, Dr. Frederic L. Business Research Ltd., 35 Suriwongse Rd., Bangkok, Thailand.

Barendregt, Dr. J. T. University of Amsterdam, Binnengasthuis, Amsterdam, Netherlands.

Beier, Dr. Ernst G. University of Utah, Salt Lake City, Utah, U.S.A.

Berntsen, Karen. Violvej 8, Gentofte, Denmark.

Bourne, Dr. Harold. University of Otago Medical School, Dunedin, C.I., New Zealand.

Bownes, A. F. University of Western Australia, Nedlands, W.A., Australia.

Bustamente, Dr. Ines Segura. 1566 Coral Way, Apt. 3, Miami 45, Florida, U.S.A.

Cansever, Dr. Gökçe. Bakirköy Mental Hospital, Istanbul, Turkey.

Choynowski, Dr. M. Psychometrical Laboratory, Polish Academy of Sciences, Warsaw, Poland.

Cohen, Dr. Irvin. Trenton State Hospital, Trenton, N. J., U.S.A.

Cowen, Dr. Emory L. University of Rochester, Rochester, New York, U.S.A.

David, Dr. Henry P. World Federation for Mental Health, 1 Rue Gevray, Geneva, Switzerland.

Diamant, Dr. J. Psychiatric Clinic, Ke Karlovu 11, Prague 2, Czechoslovakia.

Diaz-Guerrero, Dr. Rogelio. Georgia 123, Mexico 18, D.F., Mexico.

El-Meligi, Dr. Moneim A. N.J. Neuropsychiatric Institute, Princeton, New Jersey, U.S.A.

Falik, Mrs. Edith. 6 Weisel Str., Tel-Aviv, Israel.

Fernandez, B., Prof. Eliza. University of San Carlos, Guatemala City, Guatemala.

Ferracuti, Dr. Franco. Social Science Research Center, University of Puerto Rico, Rio Piedras, Puerto Rico, U.S.A.

Franks, Dr. C. M. N. J. Neuropsychiatric Institute, Princeton, New Jersey, U.S.A.

Föbärj, Dr. Gösta, Hjo, Sweden.

Garai, Mrs. Margareta. Södersjukhuset, Stockholm, Sweden.

Garcia, Dr. Belen. Trenton State Hospital Trenton, New Jersey, U.S.A.

Gravestein, A. Valeriuskliniek, Amsterdam, Netherlands.

Guthrie, Dr. George M. Pennsylvania State University, University Park, Pennsylvania, U.S.A.

Hla Thwin, Dr. University of Rangoon, Rangoon, Burma.
Hiltmann Prof. Dr. Hildegard. University of Freiburg, Freiburg i. Br., Germany.
Hoskovec, Dr. J. Charles University, Hradcanske Nam. 5, Prague 1, Czechoslovakia.
Killingmo, Bjorn. University of Oslo, Lokkeveien 7, Oslo, Norway.
Kopatic, Nicholas. Vineland State School, Vineland, New Jersey, U.S.A.
L'Abate, Dr. Luciano. Emory University Children's Clinic, 1317 Clifton Road, N.E., Atlanta 7, Georgia U.S.A.
Leal, Maria Rita Mendes. Hospital Miquel Bombarda, Lisbon, Portugal.
London, Dr. Ivan. Institute for Political Psychology, Brooklyn College, Brooklyn 10, New York, U.S.A.
Luria, Prof. A. R. 13 Frunze Street, Apt. 29, Moscow 19, U.S.S.R.
Malgrat, Dr. Carlos M. University of Panama, Panama City, Panama.
McKenna, Dr. John. University College, Dublin, Ireland.
Meschieri, Dr. Luigi. Istituto Nazionale de Psicologia, Rome, Italy.
Mizushima, Keiichi. 1300 Mure, Mitaka, Tokyo, Japan.
Monasterio, Dr. Fernanda. National University of La Plata, La Plata, Argentina.
Mooney, Dr. Craig M. Dept. of National Health and Welfare, Ottawa, Ontario, Canada.
Myers, Dr. C. R. University of Toronto, Toronto, Ontario, Canada.
Nuttin, Prof. Joseph R. University of Louvain, Louvain, Belgium.
Østergaard, Lise. University of Copenhagen, Copenhagen, Denmark.
Pinillos, Dr. Jose L. University of Valencia, Valencia, Spain.
Pluzek, Dr. Zenomena. Babinski Hospital, Krakow, Poland.
Priester, Dr. Hans J. Child Guidance Center of Mercer County, 253 Nassau Street, Princeton, New Jersey, U.S.A.
Rabinowitz, Dr. William. Pennsylvania State University, University Park, Pennsylvania, U.S.A.
Ruoppila, Isto. Jyväskylä Kasvatusopillinen, Jyväskylä, Finland.
Sanua, Dr. Victor D. Yeshiva University, 110 West 57 Street, New York, New York, U.S.A.
Sardon, Prof. Miguel A. National Psychopedagogic Institute, Lima, Peru.
Schmid, Dr. Fred. Freiestrasse 155, Zurich, Switzerland.
Sen, Dr. N. N. All-India Institute of Mental Health, Bangalore, India.
Shapiro, Dr. M. B. Institute of Psychiatry, Maudsley Hospital, London S.E. 5, England.
Soloyanis, Dr. George. Office of the Planning Commission, P.O. Box M76, Accra, Ghana.
Takala, Dr. Martti. Center for Educational Research, Jyväskylä, Finland.
Vassiliou, Dr. Vasso. 17 Yannarou Str., Kalamaki, Athens, Greece.
Wallace, John L. Box 713, St. Cloud, Minnesota, U.S.A.
Wickes, Dr. Thomas A. Office of the Premier, Institute of Administration, Enugu, Nigeria.
Wilde, Dr. Guido. Apartado Aereo 11228, Bogotá D.E., Colombia.
Wohl, Dr. Julian. University of Toledo, Toledo, Ohio, U.S.A.

The Crisis in Training
Viewed by Clinical Alumni

KARL E. POTTHARST
ARTHUR KOVACS

Introduction

For a variety of reasons, the field of clinical psychology is not overrun with those possessing a sense of history. We are more apt to plot our course into the future using extrapolations from ever fresh appraisals of our present confusion. This may give us a sense of being free from the influences of the past, but it may also let us fall into that particular kind of unwisdom that perpetuates the mistakes of the past by ignoring or not recognizing them.

Of course, the history of training programs in clinical psychology is not long—nor is the history of clinical psychology itself—but it is exceedingly complex. The last fifteen years have brought many confusing changes. Many sons of science have become clinical grandfathers, and some who started out clinical students have become full professors. Some scientists who are still trying to become professional are busy discrediting professionals who have not given up trying to become scientists. While today clinical activity in psychology seems to have clearly survived the danger of becoming identified by society with those institutional settings (academic and medical) which orginally nurtured it, it appears still more in danger of failing to outgrow certain limitations which it acquired in those settings and which it has now made its own. It has steadily expanded beyond the wards and clinics where it originally began doing too much diagnosis, not enough therapy, and token research, out into community settings and downtown offices where it often is too busy for diagnosis, takes on too much under the name of psychotherapy, and shuns a confrontation with the necessity of re-

278

searching the many problems that have thereby become its own. Also during this period, research activity has come out of the attic and the temporary building, has acquired a glamorized image and a sizeable financial empire, and now we are saying the same self-deceiving things about project research meeting our mental health needs as we were saying fifteen years ago about training more clinical people to meet those same needs.

Because of these and other confusing changes, one aim of the point of view reflected in this chapter is to feed back into the growing discussion on issues in clinical training certain appraisals, forecasts, warnings, and reminders that come out of the effort by clinical alumni to look ahead clearly, after having remembered back thoughtfully, and to try to see the problems in clinical training as they stand in relation to the fundamental aims of the science and profession of psychology.

This chapter has two parts. The first presents a statement of the current problems and trends in clinical training as seen by a group of forty clinical alumni from the University of Michigan. These alumni,* with from five to fifteen years' retrospective view on their training experiences in one of the country's foremost programs, are not in this statement primarily evaluating their own training experience. Many of them are psychologists who formerly did, or still do, actively participate in clinical training as instructors, supervisors, or administrators in internship or academic settings across the country. All of them have been thoughtful observers of the clinical training scene as well as maintaining touch with developments in different programs. It is out of this diverse experience that the statement on the training crisis emerges.

In the second part I have selected for concentrated and expanded discussion what appear to me as the two key issues in

*Their names are: Marvin L. Aronson, Leslie Berger, Robert D. Boyd, John J. Brownfain, George Calden, Dorothy Twichell Chappell, Sidney Cleveland, Richard L. Cutler, Charles Dailey, Kenneth Davidson, Griffith Freed, Glen D. Garman, Victor Goertzel, Stanley Goldstein, Thomas C. Greening, Audrey Snyder Harding, Arthur Kovacs, Julia Bader Leonard, John G. Martire, A. Freda Milstein, Sherman E. Nelson, Donald M. Pollie, Karl E. Pottharst, David Rigler, Henry Samuels, Stanley F. Schneider, Sohan Sharma, Joseph Sheehan, Herbert Silverman, James S. Simkin, Robert Sinnett, Elizabeth Slocombe, Zanwil Sperber, Alan M. Townsend, Steven G. Vandenberg, Helen Wadsworth, Benjamin White, Jack Wilcox, Louise Winter, William Winter.

clinical training, the integration of academic with field training, and the problems in the research training of clinical psychologists. This second part grows naturally out of the first, because these two issues have been interwoven through my discussion and correspondence with the Michigan clinical alumni over the last three years. However, what I have to say on these issues does not necessarily reflect their thinking, and any mistakes or excesses I must acknowledge as my own.

The Michigan Alumni Statement

The Michigan alumni statement grew out of a feeling of deep concern, that has not since subsided, about recent developments in clinical doctoral training programs. On the basis of responses to an original letter, the statement was prepared by Arthur Kovacs and myself and distributed by us to all University of Michigan clinical Ph.D.'s and clinical faculty, APA's Education and Training Board (ETB), the Board's Committee on Evaluation, Division 12's Committee on Training, to many other segments of the national professional community responsible for policy and planning in clinical doctoral training, as well as to numerous other interested psychologists. In whole or part it was reprinted in Division 12's *Newsletter* (Fall, 1962 issue) as well as in the *Bulletin of the Psychologists Interested in the Advancement of Psychotherapy* (December, 1962). Thus, what began as an effort to provide feedback to one university department from its clinical graduates on matters affecting the future of clinical training has had some larger effects in stimulating discussion at many levels of the basic issues underlying what many people see today as the crisis in clinical training.

The statement consists of three sections. The first describes certain changes in training programs indicative of a decline and attenuation in clinical training, a second section seeks to identify factors contributing toward this situation, and, finally, in a third section, specific remedial proposals are made. The statement follows.

Clinical Alumni Statement on Doctoral Training

A feeling of deep concern about developments in clinical doctoral training programs has spread through groups of psychologists who are in touch with university training programs across the country and whose memories are long enough to recall earlier aspirations set for ourselves and commitments made or implied to society.

1. The recurrent dismaying observation is made that doctoral clinical training is gradually being de-emphasized in universities across the country. There are many different indications of this, as well as problems traceable to it. The number of graduated Ph.D.'s has not increased with the social need, clinical elements in training programs have become attenuated, and some training universities have moved into positions of openly or implicitly questioning the principle of the universities' responsibility for providing clinical training.*

A. Coming out of the *Miami* Conference, our policy-makers on training urged increased use of sub-doctoral clinicians to meet the increasing demands society continues to make of us. Although university training programs have not responded on any scale to implement this recommendation by developing master's level clinical programs, neither have they responded to the recognition given at *Miami* to the rising social need for psychological knowledge and skills by expanding or strengthening clinical doctoral training in existing programs.

B. Candidates for the Ph.D. seeking valuable predoctoral training experiences are increasingly asked to defer clinical training until after the doctorate. Academic departments seem to dislike the fact that such clinical training makes the attainment of the Ph.D. degree in clinical psychology a longer process than the attainment of the degree in some other sub-specialty. Universities often seem to have an interest in turning out as many degrees in as short a time as possible. When the clinical student attempts to absorb the fruits of certain valuable predoctoral clinical experiences, he is often told that it is not the university's goal to make him into an accomplished clinician. He is asked to

*See Chapter 5, (Eds.)

defer some of his training and to secure adequate clinical training postdoctorally. It is felt that this is an unrealistic rejoinder. Postdoctoral training positions are not in great supply and vary markedly in quality. They do not offer a stipend that a family can live on without outside help. Good ones add three more years to the eight or ten years that a student often needs to prepare himself for his profession. This bids fair to make us the oldest if not the best trained profession.

Faced by internal economic pressures, society's demands for service, and the higher financial and status rewards for accepting a position, the new Ph.D. typically succumbs and launches himself into his career regardless of how well trained he is at that point. Many even seek the rewards of independent private practice. But who is to protect society against even larger numbers of more poorly trained clinicians that will result from further de-emphasis of clinical training?*

The decline in strength and quality of clinical doctoral training is already promising to provide a boost to postdoctoral training, but this effect requires a careful appraisal. Increasing numbers of psychologists after their first one or two years' experience in community and institutional settings have been recognizing their need for more and better clinical training than they were graduated with. There is reason to doubt that this recognition has stemmed from the new, perplexing and challenging clinical problems that have arisen, and to which they feel unequal. There is more sobering reason to believe it has stemmed rather from deficiencies in training programs in providing needed basic skills.

As pointed out by Martin Mayman (*Jour. Proj. Techniques,* Sept. 1962), over the same period we have seen a rapid proliferation of postdoctoral training programs. This trend is also reflected in a marked increase of journal papers and convention programs concerned with postdoctoral training. No systematic appraisal is available to tell us what proportion of this increase in postdoctoral training activity has taken place in the area of advanced or specialized postdoctoral training and what proportion has taken place in the area of deferred internships or brief, intensive, specialized workshops. However, we know a certain

---

See Chapter 4.

large proportion of the increase has been in the latter types of activity. For example, many professional organizations like the Los Angeles Society of Clinical Psychologists offer inservice supervision and postdoctoral training programs.* With nominal university affiliation, these programs have provided excellent seminars and supervision staffed by well-qualified people. However, the response from newly graduated Ph.D.'s saturated with eight to ten (undergraduate and graduate) years of steady instruction is often understandably weak.

An inevitable effect of the weakening of doctoral training takes the form therefore of a change in the role of postdoctoral training from that of developing truly advanced or specialized training programs for those who have completed doctoral clinical training (practica plus the internship), into the role of taking up the slack in doctoral training by providing deferred internships. Already in some of the thinking and policy regarding postdoctoral training, a confusion prevails about the purpose of such training as distinct from the aims of doctoral training. This confusion is evident, for example, in the thinking of those planning postdoctoral training for the Los Angeles Society of Clinical Psychologists. (L.A.S.C.P. Report of Ed. Planning Committee, May 1961).

Martin Mayman makes the vital discriminations between postdoctoral training that is in fact advanced and specialized and that which in effect consists of a deferred doctoral internship. However, his realism (or pessimism, whichever you prefer) when confronting the kind of issues brought forth in this chapter, leaves him with no other alternative but to propose postdoctoral training as the method of insuring basic clinical competence, because "graduate departments more and more eschew the responsibility of looking after the students' progress toward the professional-practitioner ideal."

If this is the only effective alternative open to us, it is hard to see how certain further undesirable consequences can be avoided. If clinical training is allowed to become a postdoctoral enterprise and if the universities allow the clinical curriculum to converge increasingly toward the academic curriculum for all

---

*See Chapter 13 for the contributions of professional organizations to clinical training. (Eds.)

Ph.D.s in psychology, it is clear that more of the clinical course work and clinical training will have to be accomplished post-doctorally, thus lengthening out the total period of professional education by additional years. We will then find ourselves inadvertently approximating the "residency" model of combined specialized and clinical training undergone by physicians to become psychiatrists, which they have told us in candid moments is a mistake as it is superimposed upon several years of earlier non-functional medical training. We do not think this model serves them very well and it is doubtful, if we do not deceive ourselves, that it will serve us any better.

C. The more the graduate departments move toward the research-scientist Ph.D. model in predoctoral training, the more the professional organizations of clinicians will move to counterbalance this postdoctorally and to keep alive and advance the clinical-practitioner half of their identity. This has already begun, as mentioned above, through the formation of post-doctoral internships, through the creation of institutes, study groups, training clinics and other arrangements for supervision and clinical instruction sponsored or provided by their organizations. Considerable force in this postdoctoral direction has in recent years already gathered momentum particularly in large metropolitan areas. As constructive and desirable as this move is in some ways, two notable effects will increasingly work against us. One effect is to produce a total learning experience where the clinical or practical learning is deferred and then superimposed upon rather than increasingly integrated with the theoretical. The other effect will work against us in recruitment through further lengthening out preparation for careers in our field, making it even less attractive than it already has become to prospective students.

For the past ten years we have been experiencing a continuing struggle and controversy in psychological associations at all levels around the issues of professionalism, legislation, standards for private practice, etc. It is true there are growing and vocal minorities of clinical practitioners who have strong divisive inclinations, whose major commitments are exclusively to private practice or psychotherapy.

However, it is also true that unless clinical psychology can achieve for all of psychology full social recognition of its rights to provide services and to study and to observe responsibly and collaboratively, but, if need be, sometimes independently, in clinics, hospitals and private professional settings, scientific psychology and the behavioral sciences will be the losers.

We cannot exercise our prerogative to observe, conduct research studies, or revise theory as scientists in these areas of human relations and problems of living unless we achieve and maintain society's full recognition as independent, responsible professionals. We cannot achieve this recognition unless we have clinical skills and professional prerogatives commensurate with those that prevail. Viewed in this perspective, maintenance of vigorous clinical training programs at high levels of excellence serves the vital purpose of scientific psychology as much as it serves those of professionalism.

D. Psychologists in touch with students making career choices note that those interested in becoming service-oriented clinicians are turning to the other disciplines for career training. When approached by young people for recommendations on opportunities in our field, we often hear ourselves and our colleagues encouraging them to enter psychiatry, social work or another field with a shorter educational requirement, one less conflicted about service commitment or training in needed skills. Are we selling our own field short or are we being realistic?

The Kelly and Goldberg study (*Psychol. Monographs,* 1959, 73, No. 482) of clinical graduates ten years after entering training shows that a surprising proportion—two out of five Ph.D.'s —indicate disillusionment with their profession to the extent they would make a different choice if they had their lives to live over again.

There are a variety of reasons for students' disenchantment with clinical psychology. We might mention briefly the trend toward longer and longer educational commitments noted above. Further, there is the familiar schism within our professional organizations, from the national to the local levels, between academic and research psychologists on the one hand and service-oriented clinical psychologists on the other—a schism which has great impact on students. This division is inevitably reflected within the university and the resulting identity cleavage shows up not only in power alignments between faculty groups but in conflicts and torn allegiances within students. Finally, the realistic difficulty in securing adequate clinical training is an additional factor which takes its toll in discouraging career choices in clinical psychology.

We are going through a period when the whole of psychology and the behavioral sciences are facing increasingly stiff competition from the more glamorous space technologies and hard sciences in recruiting students to their ranks. Even some medical schools are sending recruiting teams to high schools to interest graduates in medical careers. If our training programs and the prospects of a career in clinial psychology do not have an appeal and do not provide the incentives that are competitive with other fields, we will no longer be selecting from the best but from the second-best.

E. A disquieting attitude of strained tolerance has been noticed among those conducting clinical training, an attitude viewing it as a half-necessary nuisance. Efforts to recruit young clinical graduates for service positions are met in some instances by indifferent or discouraging attitudes on the part of training faculty. Such attitudes drive students increasingly to supervisors in the field or internships for help with clinical problems. This development further accentuates the failure to integrate theory and research with clinical work that already assails our field.

2. A divergent point of view prevailed among some of the Michigan alumni group concerning the contemporary scene in training. They point out that we are witnessing not a dilution of clinical elements in training but rather a broadening in the aims and skills the universities are trying to impart. These colleagues feel strongly that the *generalist* is the proper identity model for the clinician and that it would be a mistake to solidify around any one function of diagnosis, teaching, therapy, research or administration. They observe that universities are constantly experimenting and modifying clinical training programs to anticipate changing needs in our complex, rapidly developing society, and that if we were to pour graduate students into a "rigid mold" we would be in danger of extinction.

Certainly more thinking is needed on this whole issue. It is hoped that both training and practicing clinicians in the near future will find more adaptive and compelling professional alternatives than a) the generalist model, or b) the research (and teaching) clinician model toward both of which most university training programs seem to aim, or c) the practitioner of psychotherapy model that monolithically dominates the private practice scene. In the instance of the generalist model, it appears that some degree of happy congruence has been attained between the needs of one segment of the profession, the institutional clinical psychologists, and the output of one segment of the training programs, the segment that does its training on this model. As will be seen later on, there is serious question whether those trained on the research-clinician model meet the realistic research needs and whether they are equipped to step into the realistic research opportunities of the profession. And certainly we are aware that the expectations of the profession directed toward training programs for more intensive preparation for careers in psychotherapy are frustrated by those trained after the generalist and research-clinician models.

In some ways many training programs seem stalled in the sticky alternative of prolonged identity diffusion while the profession often seems headbent on the alternative of premature identity crystallization. The oft-cited facts that 1) ours is a complex and changing society and that 2) our science is making rapid advances (even though not as rapid as we would like to believe in such contexts) require that a certain adaptive fluidity, receptivity to significant change, capacity for revision of old and for development of new methods, etc., be built into our professional identity. However, this is no justification for indefinitely forestalling in training a clear commitment to certain basic essentials in human and social values (our code of ethics), in scientific method (our research training) and above all in theoretical outlook and useful clinical skills about which some consensus prevails.

Goals of training conferences and papers are replete with "shoulds" and "oughts" describing the ideal clinician and prescribing the ideal training program that would produce him. The time is overdue for professional associations of clinicians in institutional and community practice to define clearly the minimum levels, as well as the specific workable combinations of skills, professional attitudes, etc., found to be necessary to accomplish what has been required of them in their work and practice. The first generation of clinicians in institutions and communities has not yet done this. Those in institutional settings stay too close to highly localized "position descriptions." Those practicing in the community venture no further than statements of requirements for membership in professional associations, where the formula is "The Ph.D. plus X number of years' (supervised) experience."

3. The group was unanimously agreed, however, that there is a continuing social need for greater numbers of clinical psychologists than are being produced, at higher levels of clinical competence than the training programs are setting their sights on. Diagnosticians and psychotherapists are in chronically short supply in every geographical area and in every variety of clinical setting. It would be regrettable if these areas of activity were forfeited to the other professions. Not that we have any monopoly on excellence, but we have seen often enough what kind of stereotyped, rote-learned, clinical applications of authority-given techniques prevail in segments of our sibling professions.

4. Significant research contributions can grow, in an immediate and vital way, only out of actual contacts with people. We feel strongly that clinical training and continued clinical experience are necessary not only to those who serve but indispensable to those who observe and convey the observations to the profession and to society. We are disturbed by the *Boulder* to *Miami* shift in training model from equal emphasis on practice and research to the research-scientist model. We feel strongly that the professional full-time researcher, regardless of how well selected and how sophisticated his training, divorced from specific areas of clinical interest in therapy, whose thought is unshaped by the many available lines of clinical evidence, is unlikely to produce any significant research contributions, although he may produce many research publications.

Some believe that clinical psychology has earned a greater share of scientific recognition and deserves more academic support than it has been given for its efforts to introduce a creative research attitude in the use and interpretation of instru-

ments even where it is not producing publications on the reliability and validity of instruments, for its efforts to construct
research rationales for innovation in clinical techniques where it
is not validating or invalidating the technique itself, for its efforts
to formulate hypotheses testable through relevant clinical application of their implications in single cases rather than through
control of conditions affecting many cases.

Others believe that although the clinical service contributions
of clinical psychology are close to full acceptance by society, its
research contribution lags far behind and is open to serious
question. We need to ask, how is its research contribution to be
appraised? By number of research publications? By number of
dogmas of diagnosis, theory or psychotherapeutic technique that
have been joltingly confronted with unimpeachable clinical or
scientific facts? By number of colleagues in other professions
persuaded to positions more open to their own observation, more
questioning of their own theory, more aware of divergent theoretical views? By number of unpublished papers presented and
discussions participated in during professional meetings? Many
scientifically productive clinicians whose status or salary are not
enhanced by publication share their findings and open their work
to their peers' critical scrutiny at annual meetings nonetheless.
Are they less scientific on this account? It used to be often
asserted that the clinical Ph.D. had a unique vital contribution to
make to science and to society, and that neither the research-
scientist Ph.D., nor the people in the other mental health professions make this contribution. The Michigan group holds that this
unique contribution consists far less in the external behaviors of
diagnostic testing or teaching or research than it does in seeking
to combine the methods of field and laboratory, in building the
two-way bridge between clinical situations and theoretical-
experimental thinking.

5. Several forces are recognized as contributing toward the
problems in clinical doctoral training outlined above.

A. Clinical work in diagnosis and therapy now as always
produces anxiety within us. Some of us find research and teaching less anxiety-producing. Because of this anxiety, some clinical
students leave clinical work; others go into personal therapy in

order to remain in clinical work; some experimental and theoretical people are drawn to clinical problems but remain at a distance because of this anxiety. However, while this is true, it is no truer now than it was fifteen years ago.

It is noted however, that since fifteen years ago one change has taken place that in effect has lowered the prestige as well as the economic reward once almost exclusively associated with clinical work in psychology. That is the current glamorization of research activity, both in contemporary society at large and in academic settings in particular. The "sputnik neurosis," as Fritz Redl terms it, in educational and professional circles generally revives and reenforces the latent bias in our field for theoretical and research activity over service or applied activity. The great quantities of money now available, from both private foundation and government sources, for research undertakings and the increasing numbers of research positions open in convention placement offices attest to this.

We believe this trend has specific adverse effects on the viability of clinicians as clinicians in university training and teaching positions. To advance or achieve security in academic settings, frequent research publication admittedly has high priority. However, significant research growing out of clinical work consumes long stretches of career time, does not produce certain results, and involves skills difficult and again time-consuming to acquire. Moreover, clinical instruction and supervision lend themselves best to small group or one-to-one relationships, while other forms of graduate teaching are effective in large seminars or classes. In number of publications and of graduate students, therefore, the teaching clinician is at a disadvantage when it comes to security and advancement.

B. Clinical psychology's adolescent identity problem is invoked by some as a symptom, by others as cause, of what ails us. At least there is general agreement that clinicians suffer an incomplete professional identity. Clinical psychologists form what professional identity they have later in their careers than any other profession, that is postdoctorally. At least psychiatrists have an earlier identity as physicians to which they cling tenaciously.

Some of the Michigan group, looking to the broader social

scene, predict our identity-conflicts will continue as long as certain familiar problems remain unresolved: psychological vs. extra-psychological (medical, psychiatric, etc.) determination of the need for psychological services; unstable intraprofessional consensus regarding needed uniform socially recognized standards of service and training; uneven legislative expression of the principle of direct and open availability of psychological services to all segments and levels of society. Others of the group, looking back at our educational and training origins, note that not enough strong clinical people are retained in academic settings to enable students to crystallize their professional identity predoctorally. They note that early in training students often crystallize their identity around a particular skill or technique, most often psychotherapy, and later cement this "technique identity" as psychotherapist within a guild loyalty to the interdisciplinary or private practice setting where this skill is practiced. To the larger image of clinical psychology they remain uncommitted, and as a result this larger image remains diffuse and impotent.

C. A large segment of the group reports the continuation of strong tensions between clinical and academic psychologists in department faculties. Expectations that energy bound up in these tensions, as we saw them in the period immediately after World War II, would be eventually and creatively released in a common effort have proven naive. Instances recur where academic faculties "make it tough" on both faculty and students expressing interest in clinical work. Very few full professors are actually dedicated clinicians. Clinical program administrators are rarely active themselves in any way in clinical work. The recurring observation is made that insufficient avenues for advancement in academic rank are open to clinical faculty comparable to those open to non-clinical faculty. Clinical teaching continues largely to be done by the "younger" members of the graduate teaching staff, who may not have established department tenure nor gained professional or scientific recognition. The persistence of this situation year after year in certain settings tells us something of the power structure prevailing in departments where clinical programs, although managing to survive, never seem to develop vigor.

As a result, it is not surprising that the embryo professional identity within the university training programs continues to drift away from that of the clinician and toward that of the "research-clinician." The contraction in clinical commitment and the shift in function of clinical programs not only affects students already in programs, but also the selection of students who seek to enter programs, and particularly affects those psychologists who are doing the clinical teaching and training in the universities.

6. Several specific recommendations and proposals grow out of the group's appraisal:

A. Graduate training in clinical psychology should be increasingly custom-tailored to the needs and proclivities of the individual student. If a student is empathic and clinically perceptive, he should be so encouraged and his training supplemented with training in research and its evaluation as an adjunct. If a student demonstrates primary interest and skill in research endeavors, this should be cultivated but he should receive continuing exposure to clinical practice to sensitize him to the drama of live research problems. Individual student needs can be met and potentials realized within a wide range of variation and the choices made can still be kept within limits set by academic standards and professional requirements.

B. Clinical, theoretical and experimental training should be synthesized throughout the period of graduate study—not left as an after-thought to be achieved in an internship. Those who teach, whether in a place of internship or in a university, should take positions that actively bridge the gap between "research" and "clinical," instead of passively entrenching on either side of it.

C. The clinical curriculum should be enriched with larger doses of the humanities and social sciences. Anyone who must work closely with people needs to be steeped in the history and cultures of mankind as much if not more than he needs to be steeped in research methodology, mathematics, and the hard sciences.

D. As much as possible, predoctoral training should be removed from medical and psychiatric settings. These engender role diffusion and conflict, particularly in early and middle phases of training. Young psychologists should be trained by experienced psychologists in psychological settings. Here they will have an opportunity to identify with those within our profession who have managed to master their own identity problems. Interdisciplinary clinical supervision and training would best come in the later stages of doctoral or postdoctoral training.

E. The university naturally has a right to offer whatever curriculum in clinical psychology it feels best expresses its judgment as to what kind of product society needs. However, the university also has a responsibility to convey fully and explicitly to the public, to the profession, as well as to prospective candidates for graduate work, just what its philosphy is. Too often students reading course descriptions or statements in catalogues cannot tell what they will encounter upon acceptance.

F. Departments should not give lip-service only to providing a clinical training program, but need to evaluate what personnel are available to supervise or instruct in the light of their strengths and weaknesses. Better to avoid a course or seminar than to offer one taught by a person who has little interest or experience with a given type of material simply because the offering would "round out the program."

G. Ways need to be found to provide avenues for academic advancement and security for the clinical faculty comparable to those provided for the non-clinical faculty. Again, ways need to be found to attract and keep the more experienced, capable clinicians on the faculty, and to make them available to the clinical candidates in the early stages of graduate training.

H. Clinical graduates have a continuing responsibility to their own graduate department and to all graduate departments. This responsibility is to report back to the "manufacturers" information which we as the "consumers" of clinical training programs have accumulated on the effectiveness, defects, strong points, and shortcomings of the "product."

The formation of corresponding committees of clinical alumni is proposed for the purpose of maintaining communication in an organized way with the clinical faculty and psychology departments that trained them. The task of these committees will be to offer comments, suggestions and constructive criticism. The faculties, in turn, would keep the alumni informed of departmental policies, conflicts, and anticipated changes in curriculum or philosophy. Those of both groups attending APA or other conventions could meet for a couple of hours to exchange ideas and make suggestions. It would be acknowledged that decision-making continues in faculty hands. But both groups should welcome the opportunity to confer and to share reactions.

The formation is also proposed on a local or regional basis of committees within professional psychological associations to maintain similar liaison with clinical training programs in the area, as the corresponding committees would maintain with their own graduate departments. In addition, these local committees could cooperate in the solution of such mutual problems as: university policy on community employment of interns while in training; recruitment of students and clinical faculty; upgrading of internships and field placements; psychotherapy for graduate students; striking a balance between doctoral and postdoctoral clinical training, etc.*

I. Joint research projects are feasible, such as a survey of attitudes and perceptions of what should constitute a model Clinical Training Program. Analysis of possible discrepancies 1) between faculty and alumni and 2) between early and late graduates might be highly provocative and have real implications for curriculum planning.

A sizeable portion of the group expressed concern that the time for corrective action is upon us; that the situation is rapidly moving in a direction where many envision independent professional schools devoid of any integration with departments of psychology.

Two Key Issues in Clinical Training

In the controversial dialogue on issues in clinical training in psychology, one hears the charge from one side that although selected and trained to produce research and contribute to knowledge, the clinical Ph.D.'s have done little or nothing in this direction. (Leon Levy, *The American Psychologist,* May 1962). From the other side, one hears the criticism that univer-

*In an effort to deal with such issues, the Division of Clinical Psychology in 1962 organized the Committee on Relations with Local Clinical Groups. (Eds.)

sity training programs are reneging on clinical training, turning out clinical Ph.D.'s who need a postdoctoral clinical internship or residency-equivalent before they can even function competently. The theme of this second charge has been spelled out through the early pages of this chapter, as it has elsewhere (Michigan Clinical Alumni Statement on Training, David Grossman's 1960 letter in The L.A.S.C.P. *Newsletter,* Leonard Blank and Henry David's article in *The American Psychologist* April, 1963).

However, the issues of the ambiguous role of the clinical psychologist in research and of the paucity of research and theoretical contributions by clinical psychologists need to be examined in relation to goals in research training for the clinical field.

To begin with, the clinical field in psychology has a peculiar, almost obsessive preoccupation with the image of research, to the neglect of, and sometimes even in substitution for, the substance of research. Research is a magic word with which to consecrate new programs, a lure to attract people into new positions and new settings, a credit card honored in the respectable scientific world. It is invoked to prove our uniqueness as a profession and then laid aside to prove our dedication to our patients. We all lay claim publicly to being interested in research, but few of us privately invest in it any great or sustained passion.

It is difficult to think of another field that resounds with as many pronouncements on research as clinical psychology. Certainly no other field has attempted in such a self-conscious way to make a vocational or professional specialization out of research methodology, turning out people overtrained in the how of research but undertrained in the why and uncommitted to the what of research—its substantive content. No other field has so thoroughly confused skill in the mechanics of research (proficiency in the arts of methodology, grantsmanship and publication) with the elusive vitals of scientific creativity. Our persistent overvaluation of formal research training to the detriment of allowing people to become intrigued with persistent problems or infected with inquiring attitudes, our making a shibboleth of research for its own sake instead of research for the sake of discovery, our mistimed overemphasis on critical and challenging research attitudes appropriate to an anti-authoritarian phase of historical scientific development during a period in our own field marked by a dearth of strongly held or widely supported indigenous points of views in technique or theory—these all attest to our confusion.

From the standpoint of training, we have need of sharper, more functional definitions of research activity for clinicians than we have had. There are at least four distinguishable models of research activity after which most clinicians seem to be trained.

1. The professional (clinical) researcher on a research project financed by government or private funds, often interdisciplinary in nature, in a setting with an institutional (hospital, university, or teaching clinic) affiliation or sponsorship.

2. The academic clinical researcher—usually doctoral research with classroom or laboratory subjects conducted on a team basis with senior (faculty) and junior (student) members.

3. The administrative or "research-and-development" clinical researcher. He is the "applied" researcher, often teamed up with a clinical administrator. Selection, screening, outcome or criterion studies are his forte, with refinement of procedures, techniques or tests in the interest of management or administration, as well as the development of new procedures and adaptation of existing procedures to diverse groups. He enhances know-how in the "arts of practice."

4. The clinician who cannot forget how to be scientist, who actively and independently revises theoretical formulations and initiates research enterprises growing out of the impact of his own clinical experience to which his mind remains open despite its commitments to viable theory and workable technique. He may do this alone or with others. The setting is a clinical one: hospital, clinic, or consultation room.

The research training phase of clinical programs follows the first, second and third models of reasearch activity; it neglects the fourth model, or considers it insufficiently. Clinical research training seems based on the assumption that most clinical psychologists either will be "consumers of research" or will produce research on the model of the professional researcher, project researcher, or academic researcher.

There are certain premises in the philosophy of research training for clinicians in graduate programs that continue to be silently accepted by clinicians who should be appalled by them. These premises can be phrased as follows: 1) that new knowledge and new theory will come only from the research of laboratory and classroom, from project research, and academic research, 2) that no new knowledge or observations forcing revisions in old knowledge will come from the translations of knowledge into technique and from the returning impact of the applications of clinical techniques on theory, 3) that it is somehow unscientific or ethically wrong to apply or use knowledge until it is tested out, proven, or validated by experimental or correlational method, or integrated thoroughly into existing theory, within the framework of research activity following the first three models, and 4) that it is impossible to contribute to knowledge *and to apply* knowledge and still function at the top level of each endeavor. Although these premises are not based on fact, they perpetuate the image of the clinician as a "practitioner of the arts," as a "consumer of research," and, if he takes them seriously, guarantee the impotence of the scientist portion of his professional identity. (For a pertinent, well-stated but naive definition of the clinical psychologist as "pure practitioner," *see* Kahn and Santostefano, *The American Psychologist,* April 1962).

Perhaps, curriculum sequences in our training programs could be thought through again with these considerations in mind. Some programs may be ready to experiment. The medical school faculty at Western Reserve University, several years ago, began to break down the traditional distinction between basic science years and clinical years, offering opportunity for clinical experience from the beginning. Certainly the broad spectrum of philosophy of training should include more programs wherein clinical skills and procedures together with theoretical orientations are taught early, at a time when students selected as clinical candidates are still highly motivated toward social service or clinical social action.

Research methodology and scientific procedures for the challenge and revision of established theories, and for exploration of the limitations of techniques and shortcomings of programs, could be taught and applied later in training or given a secondary (or at least not more than a collateral) emphasis in training. The student should first acquire some skill, become familiar with established theoretical alternatives, and later become aware of their inherent limitations and recurrent problems. Such a shift in sequence or emphasis would restore what seems to be the natural order of those complex learnings and identifications that have to take place in training.

Our preoccupation with the conflicting requirements of the science and the profession in training can lead us to overlook the needs and requirements of those who come for training. It is a common observation that graduate work in psychology attracts young adults who are not only extremely bright, competitive, verbal, conceptually quick, but whose make-up includes strong emotional attitudes of non-conformity toward established ways of thinking and doing things, attitudes highly critical and questioning toward social convention and toward the educational and intellectual equivalents of parental authority. In addition, the younger students come for their graduate training when the emancipation thrust in their post-adolescent lives is moving them away from parental, family, and religious authority—away from the authority of their origins. For both these reasons, our field with its emphasis on applying scientific method to social and human problems naturally has a high valence for them.

Equally potent is the fact that these same bright young adults have a *high motivation to do something about the human condition and to prove their capability and social worth in doing it.* They seek this in social interaction with others, whether in discussion where new intellectual contents, new attitudes toward people, new habits of thought are exchanged and conveyed, or in clinical work where life goals are reexamined, human relationships reworked, etc. Our field, therefore, has a high valence for young students because it offers skills like teaching, counseling, and psychotherapy which they can use in this vital business of doing.

Conclusions

If clinical programs select students with various combinations of both of these complex needs and characteristics, as they must necessarily do, and yet expect them to defer serious training that would satisfy the second need while overtraining them in ways that meet the first need, we can expect two results. The first is that some students will emerge overcommitted to the ideology of the professional researcher, more interested in the tools of methodology than in the substance of psychological phenomena, preoccupied with problems of design rather than human problems, and will not likely pursue clinical training. The second is that those students who will finally obtain clinical training will over-identify in the role of the practitioner and therapist, retaining their research skill as an unused appendage, overcommitted to the "clinical ideology," and hyperreceptive to philosophical and only tangentially scientific beliefs about man. To get away from this familiar bimodal output of clinical training programs, we must continually reevaluate and reshape our selection and training efforts, aware of the dual attraction that our field exerts upon the needs of students who enter it for training.

Furthermore I believe there is urgent need for development of a unitary professional ethos or ideology for psychologists that does not set the values of research and theoretical inquiry above the values of alleviating human distress and conflict. Without this we will continue to fail to do in fact what we have resolved to do and exhorted each other to do so many times in so many conferences and publications—to integrate academic with field training, research and theoretical with clinical orientation.

Such an ideology needs to be developed in teaching and training at the universities, in the policies and outlook of the professional associations, and most important in the very fiber of our methodology and our orientation in all our activities, whether in clinic, classroom, laboratory or consultation room.

The continuing impact of human anguish, conflict, and confusion on those who are professionally in the clinical role creates within them a powerful need for a set of workable beliefs about human life and human behavior. This is true whether they are engaged in what is primarily a research inquiry on meaningful human problems or whether they are relieving human distress and conflict in a clinical setting. Only an integrated ethos or ideology based on a synthesis of scientific and humane values can rightly fill this need. We do not have this at the present time.

If we do not develop—not eventually but rapidly—such a unitary ideology, clinical psychology will turn more and more into an enterprise that, in the absence of scientific knowledge that can be humanely applied, thrives on philosophies and systems of belief about human behavior that are taken on faith and are applied by intuition, and that while not totally segregated from scientific psychology will not achieve any fruitful integration with it.

REFERENCES

1. Bolgar, Hedda, Clinical psychology—looking ahead. *Los Angeles Society of Clinical Psychologists News,* January, 1962.
2. Blank, Leonard, and David, Henry P., The crisis in clinical psychology training. *Amer. Psychol.,* 1963, *18,* 216-219.
3. Grossman, David, From the president—a note of pessimism to start the year off. *Los Angeles Society of Clinical Psychologists News,* September, 1960.
4. Education for research in psychology. *Amer. Psychol.,* 1959, *14,* 695.
5. Kahn, Marvin W., and Santostefano, Sebastian, The case of clinical psychology—a search for identity. *Amer. Psychol.,* 1962, *17,* 185-189.
6. Kelly, E. Lowell, and Goldberg, L. R., Correlates of later performance and specialization in psychology. *Psychological Monographs,* 1959, No. 482, 73.
7. Levy, Leon, The skew in clinical psychology. *Amer. Psychol.,* 1962, *17,* 244-249.
8. Loevinger, Jane, Conflict of commitment in clinical research. *Amer. Psychol.,* 1963, *18,* 241-251.
9. Mayman, Martin, Postdoctoral training for clinical competence. 1962. *26,* 305-309.
10. Michigan Clinical Alumni Statement on Training. *Division 12 Newsletter,* Fall, 1962, *15,* 2-3., *APA.*
11. Redl, Fritz, Crisis in the children's field. Presidential addres, American Orthopsychiatric Association, Los Angeles, 1962.
12. Report of the Education and Training Committee, Los Angeles Society of Clinical Psychologists, May, 1961.
13. Summary of Michigan Clinical Alumni Statement on Cinical Doctoral Training, *Bulletin of the Society for Psychologists Interested in the Advancement of Psychotherapy,* December, 1962.

13

Conclusions and Implications

LEONARD BLANK

HENRY P. DAVID

In the last seventeen years, the conception of the role and training of clinical psychologists has been in a state of flux. The reports issuing from the *Shakow* Committee and the conferences at *Boulder, Stanford, Miami,* and *Princeton* have demonstrated both a progressive delineation of issues and, at times, a rather pusillanimous confrontation of these very issues. But clinical psychologists are persevering and optimistic if they are anything. Thus, the 1962 and 1963 Annual Conferences of Chief Psychologists in State Mental Health Programs devoted part of their program to training. Similarly, the 1963 annual meeting of Division 12 Committee on Relations with Local Clinical Groups had Training in Psychotherapy as its theme. Another national conference on training is being planned by the Division of Clinical Psychology for the spring of 1965. This is but a sample of the activity caused by the critical state of logistics in clinical psychology.

Logistics

In 1963, President Kennedy[14] requested an increase of mental health workers from 45,000 in 1960 to 85,000 by 1970. All of the pertinent specialties, however, are suffering acute shortages of qualified recruits.[1] In 1961, only somewhat over 300 Ph.D.'s were granted in clinical psychology.[2,4] In addition to the demand for mental health workers, there is an increasing drift towards private practice, and more and more demand for clinical psychologists for faculty, government positions, and private agencies. The report of the Joint Commission on Mental Illness and

Health that "an estimated 17,000,000 persons in the United States suffer some form of psychological disturbance" is not likely to be significantly qualified for years to come.[6] Raimy points out that, "Despite all the money poured into training in clinical psychology since the war, the number of Ph.D.'s to be graduated with a concentration in clinical psychology in the coming years will be no larger than the number turned out annually, starting 1952." [18] Meanwhile the population steadily increases.

This, then, is the frame of reference within which we must view the training and roles of clinical psychologists as they are now and as they must be modified. In fact, and irrespective of the imperatives, roles are changing. Thus, Tryon[22] notes that 1962 is the first year in which Ph.D.'s in non-academic positions outnumbered the academicians. From 1948-1960, the professional psychologist has increased three times as much as the academic psychologist. A recent survey of Division 12 indicated that 86% of the Division have the Ph.D. and that more than half received their highest degree since 1949. Thirty-seven percent have the ABEPP (43% in full-time positions that are not clinical in function).[17] Nevertheless, as Tryon[22] comments, "Presently most graduate curricula and research are designed to fulfill the false image that all graduate students will become 'pure' scientists and scholars. Actually, the majority will probably wind up in professional work outside the colleges" (p. 141). Tryon believes that this split exerts a demoralizing influence on students and faculty which worsens when the clinical psychologist discovers how inadequately prepared he has been for his life's work. His further comments on the etiology and treatment of the "schizoid" training have been quoted in Chapter 9. Nevertheless, Tryon's primary thesis is that a research-trained and research-based clinical psychologist makes the most positive contribution and at the same time maintains his status (pp. 138-139). (That is, Tryon would resolve the split by broadening the scope of research training but not by encouraging professional preparation.)

Winder[23] takes a different view of the matter:

"There is a strategy which might be implied. . . and which is clearly championed by many faculty members of training universities. This is the basic research strategy. In essence, it is proposed that university psychology departments should contribute to the mental health field only by doing research and by training researchers. This program was not the one which attracted support from our society, e.g., via the VA and the USPHS. The program which did attract that support was an embodiment of the strategy calling for the training of clinical psychologists who, as a group or as individuals, would make contributions to the mental health field in a variety of ways.

"If there are individuals or training departments which want to concentrate on basic research and the training of basic researchers, many would applaud their honesty and conviction, if only they would declare themselves publicly and without ambiguity."

"It would seem that if this is a time for rallying around, the standard might best be excellence in whatever we choose to do, including any research, basic or otherwise." (p. 70)

Albee's[1] comment that the answer to professional manpower shortage is dedication fairly exclusively to research is debated by Greening[9] who suggests that professional practice can, does, and should be compatible to meaningful research.

The Kelly and Goldberg report[13] and feedback from clinical alumni (Chapter 12) dramatized the dissatisfaction of many clinical psychologists with their professional work. The latter underscore their unhappiness with clinical training. Even more important is the fact that the traditional one-to-one approach in diagnosis and treatment cannot meet the almost limitless need for these services. Recently, behavior therapy has been earning more and more attention. Even if such techniques prove effective, and although they are purported to be relatively short-term in application, the dyadic approach is not obviated.[3,8] The focus on the individual will always be a concern of the highly trained clinician and it is indispensable for training. Learning about idiosyncratic thinking (which is the essence of psychopathology) and how one person relates to another, can best be demonstrated when dealing with individuals. The clinical psychologist must utilize his skills with other mental health workers and lesser trained personnel so as to reach the broadest segment of the populace. The foregoing chapters have suggested where innovations may be made in research, diagnosis, treatment, consultation, and in training itself.

Research

Phillips (Chapter 9) argues the necessity of alternatives to the apprentice role and the traditional postdoctoral research fellowships. He believes it is important to place the suitable clinical research aspirant in an ongoing program of research, in contact and collaborating with colleagues in various specialties, in a clinical setting, and functioning with a high degree of autonomy.

Holzberg (in Finn and Brown[7]) begins research training in nature similar to the Phillips plan. However, Holzberg believes that research should be initiated more vigorously during the internship. He encourages the intern to utilize every third or fourth week for research and supervises this work in the same manner as psychodiagnosis and psychotherapy.

Such recommendations, valuable as they are, may not meet the challenge of the vast gaps in our knowledge of individual maladjustment as well as of interpersonal and social aberrancies. Perhaps the laboratory ought to be more in the family or university populations; in the schools and playgrounds rather than in institutions. The issue would seem to be the pertinence of the education and experience of the research trainee to the demands for answers and opportunity for appropriate settings presented to him.

Diagnosis

L'Abate (Chapter 7) advocates the "laboratory method" in diagnosis. He would have the Ph.D. psychologist master a wide spectrum of tests and techniques, train technicians in utilizing narrow but appropriate bands of these skills, as applicable to groups of people as is feasible, and reserve the time and talent of the doctorate for interpretation and other suitable professional responsibilities. Schofield (Chapter 4) recommends a "total impact" two-year Master's program to train diagnostic technicians. He believes that such personnel, in addition to freeing the time and energy of the Ph.D. for broad functions, would be at least as competent diagnosticians, and many more of them could be trained.

Innovations of any sort probably will not solve the dilemma of vast *numbers* of psychodiagnosticians required. It has been estimated that 250,000 physicians actually practiced medicine in the United States in 1960 (Kubie[15]), while *total membership* in the APA was 18,000 in 1960 and 21,000 in 1963. It may be argued that medical problems are more general and exigent, and that prophylactic measures are more easily carried out by physicians. Nevertheless, the people urgently requiring psychological services are legion, and the scope of psychological prophylaxis is vast. We need only consider the implications for education, for utilization of skills in the complex vocational world, and for the rate of divorce, crime, and addiction. If we assume, most generously, that two thirds of the APA membership are applied psychologists involved someway in diagnosis,* then we arrive at a figure of 14,000, or one potential psychodiagnostician per 13,000 of population (in contrast to roughly one physician per 700 of population). Even if we think in terms of group techniques (and we cannot do so exclusively) as does L'Abate, or in terms of technicians as does Schofield, we must concern ourselves with producing vastly larger numbers of personnel trained to perform psychodiagnosis than we are currently turning out. Later in this chapter we will consider the alternatives this issue presents to us.

Psychotherapy

The quality of training as well as the social controls and internal and external conflicts experienced by the profession of psychology are far more controversial in the area of psychotherapy than in research or diagnosis.

Lubin,[17] in his survey of the members of Division 12, reports that two thirds of the respondents in full-time psychotherapy practice with children had less than one year of supervised experience. Of those doing full-time psychotherapy with adults 87% had this supervision. (The erratic nature of psychotherapeutic training throws doubt on the meaning of the many papers pur-

---

*Kelly and Goldberg[13] in their follow-up of 1948 VA clinical students found that a very small percentage of these psychologists were involved in psychodiagnostic work.

porting to evaluate the results of psychotherapy, since often the criterion cited for qualification as psychotherapist is merely graduate student, training, or staff status.) More than one half of Lubin's respondents who had had supervised experience in psychotherapy with adults received most of their training at the Ph.D. level, either in their work setting, by private arrangements, or through postdoctoral programs for training in psychotherapy. Major sources of training in group psychotherapy with adults were the internship and postdoctoral programs. With children, the major sources were at the postdoctoral level at universities or during the internship. For group psychotherapy with adults and children, supervision was provided by mostly psychologists and for individual psychotherapy for adults mostly by psychiatrists.

Cognizant of the erratic supervision, leaders in clinical psychology recently have spearheaded several types of programs. First, there is the development of postdoctoral training programs in psychotherapy, such as at New York University and Adelphi (*see* Chapters 6 and 8). Secondly, there are postdoctoral programs sponsored by particular facilities, regional associations, and the APA Postdoctoral Institutes (*see* Chapter 6). Local associations have also sprung to the fore. In 1961, the Los Angeles Society of Clinical Psychologists presented a detailed program for postdoctoral psychotherapy training including plans for a clinic and training center, administrative details, curriculum, supervision, etc. (Siegel *et al.*,[21] which includes bibliography in postdoctoral training for psychotherapy.)

Professional degree

With all of this ferment, there is little standardization of training. Kubie[15,16] some time ago underscored the peril of the lack of standards for psychotherapy training of clinical psychology (Schofield discusses standards in Chapter 4.) Kubie suggested there be a profession of medical psychology, with a fairly specific curriculum within a medical school. The advantages were thought to be particularly with respect to standardization of training and control of practice. Such a profession, it would seem, would largely replace the current one of psychiatry while absorbing those psychologists, social workers, and educators especially interested in psychotherapy and diagnosis. It would, by no means, be congruent with the current specialty of clinicial psychology. A major criticism, in addition to the problem of stepping on the toes of psychiatists and university psychologists, might be raised: such training in psychotherapy would be strait-jacketed into whatever medical concept is current while there are loud and pervasive objections to the woeful lack of knowledge about psychotherapy, medically and otherwise. (Kubie's recommendation of spicing the faculty with sociologists, educators, etc., would not alter the basic medical recipe for training.)

Recently, a conference was held among leaders in psychotherapy training in psychoanalysis, psychiatry, psychology, and social work.[12] The purpose was to discuss a profession of psychotherapy. The proceedings have not been published as yet, but the discussions were so stimulating as to result in almost all of the participants electing to serve on a committee to deliberate further on the possibilities of translating their recommendations into action.

On a more general basis, the consensus of the *Princeton* conferees was to experiment with professional schools.[4,5] Tryon[22] suggests that psychology departments should maintain close ties between university staffs and professional personnel in field training institutions. Research, theses, and curricula would be pitched towards "professional reality" (e.g., the professional student in clinical psychology would have training in medicine, physiology, pediatrics, and social welfare). Perhaps, suggests Tryon, a Ph.D. in clinical psychology or one in child psychology (and so on) would result.

There is no doubt that change is afoot. The powerful catalyst of social need, the maturity of the specialty of clinical psychology, and the clamoring of the local associations and individual practitioners are combining to bring the issue to a head.

Role

Even more fundamentally, the role of the clinical psychologist is being exposed to self-criticism. Raimy[18] makes three suggestions:

1) Take our own field serious without apologies to anyone. All fields of psychology are so limited that it is foolish to say, 'First a psychologist and *then* a clinical psychologist.' To be apologetic about interest in psychopathology because psychiatry got there first is as ridiculous as the idea that we must pursue only those activities which make us truly unique. 2) Clinical psychology is a broad field which draws only to some extent upon other fields of psychology—laboratory research and clinical investigation are not the only means to advancement of knowledge. Forego dichotomy that basic research in personality is good but research in applied psychopathology is 'bad,' that statistical manipulation of even poor data is good but intelligent pondering of real problems is not good. 3) Curriculum for clinical psychology should be organized around problems of clinical psychology. Problems of adjustment or psychopathology should be central to the curriculum. Exposure to learning theory, perception, and motivation should be in the context of people, not rats, and with major reference to the field of abnormal psychology or psychopathology.

Hobbs[10,11] stresses the need to develop patterns of consultation in psychology, as well as other mental health disciplines, that will permit the specialists to work through other less well trained persons. The psychologist must change his traditional one to one relationship. He must train other mental health workers, and offer consultation to various groups and agencies within the community. And he must be able to synthesize knowledge and be a critical and discriminating interpreter of the findings produced by others.

Rioch[19] and her coworkers experimented in tapping the large reservoir of talent among middle-aged women (applicable to retired people as well). The study focused on training for psychotherapy. "This differentiates it from training for social work, psychology, and psychiatry. Members of all three professions engage in psychotherapy but their education includes many other things." The aim was to select applicants who in a very short time could qualify to perform psychotherapy. "If such people as our trainees can perform useful service to patients—and in their first year of training they have done just that—then it should be possible for departments of psychiatry, psychology, or social work to offer a sub-curriculum something like this one, with emphasis upon practical work, which would train people in psychotherapy." (p. 687)

The VA, which has been one of the most influential factors in stimulating the growth and quality of training in clinical psychology, is illustrative of innovations in training (*see* Chapter 3). VA psychologists are being trained to work in units of hospitals, in milieu and open-ward therapeutic situations, in day-care treatment centers, and so on. The clinician is being mixed with the social and experimental psychologist.

The view is held by many[20] that "the way to attack mental illness is not through the treatment of adults but through prevention at the level of the child and his interactions with his parents." (p. 4). The holders of this view stress that developmental information is central to clinical child psychology, clinical psychology, and, in fact, to the field of psychology in general. The Section on Child Psychology has prepared a report recommending specialized training for child psychologists, including the possibility of a doctoral degree in this area and postdoctoral training programs. This report will probably influence the deliberations at the national conference of psychology training to be held in the Spring of 1965.

REFERENCES

1. Albee, G. W., Psychology in the sixties. *Amer. Psychol.*, 1963, *18*, 90-95.
2. American Psychological Association, Report of the ad hoc committee on problems of practicum agency evaluation. Washington, D.C.: APA, 1961 (mimeo).
3. Beech, H. R., Some theoretical and technical difficulties in the application of behaviour therapy. *Bull. Br. Psychol. Soc.*, 1963, *16*, 25-33.
4. Blank, L., and David, H. P., The crisis in clinical psychology training. *Amer. Psychol.*, 1963, *18*, 216-219.
5. David, H. P., and Blank, L. *Manpower and Psychology: Joint responsibilities of states and universities.* Washington, D.C.: USPHS, 1963.
6. Ewalt, J., ed., *Action for mental health* (Final report of the Joint Commission on Mental Illness and Health). New York: Basic Books, 1961.
7. Finn, M. H. P., aand Brown, F., eds., *Training for clinical psychology.* New York: International Universities Press, 1959.
8. Franks, C. M., Behavior therapy, the principles of conditioning and the treatment of the alcoholic. *Quart. J. Studies Alcohol.*, 1963, *24*, 261-275.

9. Greening, T. C., Reaction to Albee, G. "Psychology in the sixties." *Amer. Psychol.*, 1963, *18*, 317-318.
10. Hobbs, N., Statement on mental illness and retardation. *Amer. Psychol.*, 1963, *18*, 295-297.
11. Hobbs, N., Strategies for the development of clinical psychology. *Newsl., Div. Clin. Psychol.*, 1963, *16*, no. 2, 24.
12. Holt, R. R., Report of a conference on "An ideal training program for psychotherapists." *Newsl., Div. Clin. Psychol.*, 1963, *16*, no. 3, 7-8.
13. Kelly, E. L., and Goldberg, L. R., Correlates of later performance and specialization in psychology. *Psychol. Monogr.*, 1959, no. 482.
14. Kennedy, J. F., *Mental illness and mental retardation.* Washington, D.C.: House of Representatives, 1963, no. 58.
15. Kubie, L. S., The pros and cons of a new profession: a doctorate in medical psychology. *Tex. Rpts., Biol. Med.*, 1954, *12*, 125-170.
16. Kubie, L. S., Need for a new subdiscipline in the medical profession. *Arch. Neurol. Psychiat.*, 1957, *78*, 283-293.
17. Lubin, B., Characteristics of clinical psychologists in various work settings. *Dis. Nerv. Syst.*, 1963, *24*, 1-4.
18. Raimy, V., The case for clinical psychology. Symposium: *Clinical psychology and public health training.* Annual meeting, APA, New York, 1961.
19. Rioch, M. J., et al., Training mental health counsellors. *Amer. J. Orthopsychiatry*, 1963, *33*, 678-689.
20. Ross, A. O., Report on clinical child psychology. *Div. Clin. Psychol.*, 1963 (mimeo).
21. Siegel, M., Small, L., and Michael, Ethel, eds., The development of a postdoctoral training program. Committee on Relations with Local Clinical Groups, *Div. Clin. Psychol.*, APA, 1963.
22. Tryon, R., Psychology in flux: the academic-professional bipolarity. *Amer. Psychol.*, 1963, *18*, 134-143.
23. Winder, C.L., Diversity for clinical training programs. *Amer. Psychol.*, 1963, *18*, 69-70.

Bibliography on Clinical Training 1955-1963

MARTIN MAYMAN

I. THE CLINICAL PSYCHOLOGIST: SCIENTIST OR PRACTITIONER?

Akutagawa, Donald, The clinical psychologist. *Amer. Psychol.,* 1959, *14,* 48.

Bookbinder, Lawrence J., *The psychologist as a psychotherapy practitioner and researcher: needs, problems, and future development.* Chicago: Midwestern Psychol. Assoc., May, 1962.

Cook, Stuart, The psychologist of the future: scientist, professional, or both. *Amer. Psychol.,* 1958, *13,* 635-644.

Cronbach, Lee J., The two disciplines of scientific psychology. *Amer. Psychol.,* 1957, *12,* 671-684.

Education and Training Board, *What is a psychologist—a sample of important opinions.* Washington, D.C.: APA, 1957.

Ericksen, Stanford C., The place of thinking in an ideal university. *Amer. Psychol.,* 1962, *17,* 763-771.

Frank, Lawrence K., Research for what? Kurt Lewin Memorial Address, Washington, D.C.: APA, September 3, 1957.

Hackman, Ray C., and Ross, Sherman, Hypothesis testing and hypothesis producing research. *Amer. Psychol.,* 1955, *10,* 828.

Hathaway, Starke R., A study of human behavior: the clinical psychologist. *Amer. Psychol.,* 1958, *13,* 257-265.

Holzberg, Jules D., The clinical and scientific methods; synthesis or antithesis?. *J. Proj. Tech.,* 1957, *21,* 227-242.

Holzberg, Jules D., Research training during the internship. In *Training for clinical psychology.* M. H. P. Finn and F. Brown, eds. New York: International Universities Press, 1959, 120-138.

Holzberg, Jules D., The role of the internship in the research training of the clinical psychologist. *J. Consult. Psychol.,* 1961, *25,* 185-191.

Kinder, Elaine F., Areas of training and their specific implementation; research, therapy, testing. In *Training for clinical psychology.* M. H. P. Finn and F. Brown, eds. New York: International Universities Press, 1959, 31-49.

Koch, Sigmund, Psychological science versus the science-humanism antinomy: intimations of a significant science of man. *Amer. Psychol.,* 1961, *16,* 629-639.

Levy, Leon H., The skew in clinical psychology. *Amer. Psychol.,* 1962, *17,* 244-249.

311

Oppenheimer, Robert, Analogy in science. *Amer. Psychol.*, 1956, *11*, 127-136.

Richman, Joseph, Reactions to Albee's 'Psychology in the sixties'. *Amer. Psychol.*, 1963, *18*, 317.

Rodnick, Eliot H., Training for research in the mental health field. In *Psychology and mental health.* Charles R. Strother, ed. Washington, D.C.: APA, 1957, 93-109.

Rogers, Carl, Persons or science? A philosophical question. *Amer. Psychol.*, 1955, *10*, 267-278.

Rogers, Carl, A personal view on some issues facing psychologists. *Amer. Psychol.*, 1955, *10*, 247-249.

Rychlak, Joseph F., Clinical psychology and the nature of evidence. *Amer. Psychol.*, 1959, *14*, 642-648.

Sargent, Helen D., and Mayman, Martin, Clinical psychology. In *Handbook of Amer. Psychiatry.* New York: Basic Books, 1959, 1711-1732.

Snyder, William U., Professional training for clinical psychologists: synthesis of a symposium. *J. Clin. Psychol.*, 1962, *18*, 243-248.

Stein, Arthur, On research in clinical psychology. *Amer. Psychol.*, 1959, *14*, 527-528.

Towbin, Alan P., The way to professional maturity. *J. Clin. Psychol.*, 1961, *17*, 115-119.

Tryon, Robert C., Psychology in flux: the academic-professional bipolarity. *Amer. Psychol.*, 1963, *18*, 134-143.

Tyler, Forrest B., Integrating scientific and professional training at the graduate level. *J. Clin. Psychol.*, 1963, *19*, 116-120.

Ullmann, Leonard P., The clinician as behavior scientist. *J. Clin. Psychol.*, 1961, *17*, 119-122.

Winder, Clarence L., Diversity for clinical training programs. *Amer. Psychol.*, 1963, *18*, 69-70.

Symposia:

Training for research in psychology. APA, New York City, September 3, 1957 (Leonard Carmichael, Chairman).
   a. Underwood, Benton J., Research training for experimental psychology.
   b. Bayton, James A., Research training for applied psychology.
   c. Garmezy, Norman, Research training for clinical psychology.
   d. McKeachie, Wilbert J., Research training in the graduate curriculum.

Professional training for clinical psychologists. APA, New York City, September 2, 1961 (Joseph R. Sanders, Chairman).
   a. Mensh, Ivan N., Academic and other training and the facts of life.
   b. Moore, Bruce V., What will be the relation of the science of psychology to the profession of psychotherapy?
   c. Holt, Robert R., Would a special degree for psychotherapists be desirable?

d. Snyder, William U., An appraisal of research training for clinicians.

e. Mayman, Martin, Postdoctoral training in clinical psychology.

II. ON THE NATURE AND THE PRACTICE OF CLINICAL PSYCHOLOGY

Blatt, Sidney J., The objective and subjective modes: some considerations in the teaching of clinical skills. *J. Proj. Tech.*, 1963, *27*, 151-157.

Carson, Robert C., The status of diagnostic testing. *Amer. Psychol.*, 1958, *13*, 79.

Clark, Kenneth E., *America's psychologists: a survey of a growing profession*. Washington, D.C.: APA, 1957.

Ekstein, Rudolf, and Mayman Martin, On the professional identity of the clinical psychologist. *Bull. Menninger Clin.*, 1957, *21*, 59-61.

Fine, Harold J.,The status of the clinical psychologist. *J. Clin. Psychol.*, 1961, *17*, 107-110.

Frank, George, On the nature of clinical psychology. *J. Gen. Psychol.*, 1963, *69*, 119-124.

Freeman, Frank S., On the teaching of psychological tests and testing. *Amer. Psychol.*, 1957, *12*, 154-155.

Hauck, Paul A., Psychological testing policies in seventeen midwestern state hospitals. *Amer. Psychol.*, 1959, *14*, 522-523.

Hauck, Paul A., Testing in state hospitals. *Amer. Psychol.*, 1960, *15*, 269.

Jacobson, Frank N., Rettig, Salomon, and Pasamanick, Benjamin, Status, job satisfaction, and factors of job satisfaction of state institution and clinic psychologists. *Amer. Psychol.*, 1959, *14*, 144-150.

Kahn, Marvin W., and Santostefano, Sebastian, The case of clinical psychology: a search for identity. *Amer. Psychol.*, 1962, *17*, 185-189.

Kelley, Noble H., Sanford, Fillmore H., and Clark, Kenneth, The meaning of the ABEPP diploma. *Amer. Psychol.*, 1961, *16*, 132-141.

Kelly, Everett L., Clinical psychology—1960: report of survey findings. *APA Division of Clinical Psychology. Newsletter*, 1961, *14*, 1-11.

Kelly, Everett L., and Goldberg, Lewis R., Correlates of later performance and specialization in psychology. *Psychol. Monogr.* 1959, No. 482.

Klopfer, Walter G., The role of diagnostic evaluation in clinical psychology. *J. Proj. Tech.*, 1962, *26*, 295-298.

Lesser, Erwin, Popularity of Rorschach training in the United States. *J. Proj. Tech.*, 1961, *25*, 179-183.

Leventhal, Theodore, et al., The utilization of the psychologist-patient relationship in diagnostic testing. *J. Proj. Tech.*, 1962, *26*, 66-79.

Lindemann, Erik, The nature of mental health work as a professional pursuit. Appendix A, *Psychology and mental health*. Charles R. Strother, ed. Washington, D.C.: APA, 1957, 136-145.

Mayman, Martin, Style, focus, language and content of an ideal psychological test report. *J. Proj. Tech.*, 1959, *23*, 453-458.

Moss, C. Scott, and Clark, J. F., Role satisfaction of psychologists in state hospitals. *Amer. Psychol.,* 1961, *16,* 523-528.

Riegel, Lyman M., and Spern, Raymond A., Psychologists' concept of their role in institutions housing the 'criminally insane.' *Amer. Psychol.,* 1960, *15,* 160-163.

Rosenwald, George C., Psychodiagnostics and its discontents. *Psychiatry,* 1963, *26,* 222-240.

Shoben, Edward J., Jr., Conflict and identification in the training process. In *Training for clinical psychology.* M. H. P. Finn and F. Brown, eds. New York: International Universities Press, 1959, 66-73.

Sines, Lloyd K., On Carson's comment regarding diagnostic testing. *Amer. Psychol.,* 1958, *13,* 601-602.

Small, Leonard, Toward professional clinical psychology. *Amer. Psychol.,* 1963, *18,* 558-562.

Sundberg, Norman D., The practice of psychological testing in clinical services in the United States. *Amer. Psychol.,* 1961, *16,* 79-83.

Towbin, Alan P., The way to professional maturity. *J. Clin. Psychol.,* 1961, *17,* 115-119.

Wohl, Julian, Traditional and contemporary views of psychological testing. *J. Proj. Tech.,* 1963, *27,* 359-361.

Woods, James E., Testing in state hospitals. *Amer. Psychol.,* 1960, *15,* 268-269.

Symposia:

Clinical psychology: the second generation's perspective and prospectus. APA, Chicago, September 1, 1960 (Harold J. Fine, Chairman).
    a. Ullmann, Leonard P., The clinician as behavioral scientist.
    b. Zimet, Carl N., Psychologist first, clinician second: slogan reconsidered.
    c. Towbin, Alan, Toward professional maturity.
    d. Fine, Harold J., How smug are we?

The self-image of the psychodiagnostician: role and ideal. APA, New York City, September 2, 1961 (Martin Mayman, Chairman).
    a. Schachtel, Ernest, On self-doubt and self-esteem in the practice of psychodiagnostics.
    b. Piotrowski, Zygmunt A., Why diagnose at all?
    c. Harris, Robert A., The implications for psychoanalytic theory and psychotherapy of diagnostic testing: a positive value for clinicians.
    d. Rosenwald, George C., Sources and consequences of ambivalence toward testing.

Testing and the psychology student. APA, New York City, September 1961 (Howard B. Lyman, Chairman).
    a. Sappenfield, Bert R., Training students in testing.
    b. Hamilton, Sidney, Communicating test results.
    c. Marquart, Dorothy, Suitable goals for testing.
    d. Hoffmann, Banesh, Examining the tester.

III. Psychotherapy Training for the Clinical Psychologist

Blanck, Gertrude, *Education for psychotherapy: a guide to the major training facilities in the field of psychotherapy in the United States.* New York: Institute for Psychoanalytic Training and Research, 1962.

Ekstein, Rudolf, and Wallerstein, Robert S., *The teaching and learning of psychotherapy.* New York: Basic Books, 1959.

Holt, Robert R., *Proceedings of the conference on an ideal training program for psychotherapists.* Ardsley-on-Hudson, N.Y., March 1963. Unpublished. (Contributions by: John Warkentin, Edward Stainbrook, Jerome Cohen, Bernard Kalinkowitz, Milton Rosenbaum, Robert Wallerstein, Starke Hathaway, Zoltan Gross, David Shakow, Arthur Mandelbaum, David Rubinfine, Arthur Leader, Esther Schour, Margaret Rioch).

Lubin, Bernard, Survey of psychotherapy training and activities of psychologists. *J. Clin. Psychol.*, 1962, *18*, 252-256.

Rogers, Carl, Training individuals to engage in the therapeutic process. In *Psychology and mental health.* Charles R. Strother, ed. Washington, D.C.: APA, 1957, 76-92.

Schlesinger, Herbert J., Qualifications for psychotherapists. *Amer. J. Ortho.*, 1956, *26*, 57-65.

Schonbar, Rosalea A., and Shoben, Edward J., Jr., Postdoctoral training in psychotherapy. *Amer. Psychol.*, 1957, *12*, 280.

Symposia:

The psychologist's identity as a psychotherapist. APA, Philadelphia, August 30, 1963 (Irving A. Alexander, Chairman. Contributions by James F. T. Bugental, Max Hutt, Gerald Gurin).

Teaching and supervision in psychotherapy. APA, Philadelphia, August 31, 1963 (Harold J. Fine, Chairman. Contributions by Irving H. Frank, Laurence Hemmendinger, Irving Schulman, Ernst Prelinger).

IV. Clinical Training for A Subdoctoral Degree

Ansbacher, Heinz L., A training unit in individual testing at the undergraduate level. *Amer. Psychol.*, 1957, *12*, 151-153.

Beck, Harry S., Subdoctoral psychologists? *Amer. Psychol.*, 1957, *12*, 165-166.

Education and Training Board Committee on Subdoctoral Education, The training of technical workers in psychology at the subdoctoral level. *Amer. Psychol.*, 1955, 10, 541-545.

Education and Training Board Task Committee, Report on the role of the Master's degree in doctoral training. *Amer. Psychol.*, 1959, 14, 501-503.

Kahn, Theodore C., M.A. versus Ph.D. for psychologists. *Amer. Psychol.*, 1957, *12*, 516.

Raimy, Victor, 'Submasteral' psychologists. *Amer. Psychol.*, 1957, *12*, 516-517.
Ryckman, Marjorie, Graduate training in psychology: the trend in specialization at the Master's level. *Amer. Psychol.*, 1962, *17*, 143-145.
Wallin, J. E. Wallace, Comments on the report of the Committee on Sub-Doctoral Education for Psychological Technicians. *Amer. Psychol.*, 1957, *12*, 37.

Symposia:
Training of technical workers at the sub-doctoral level, Southeastern Psychological Association, April 29, 1956 (Bruce Moore, Chairman).
   a. Dashiell, John F., Historical orientation and basic elements of sub-doctoral training in psychology.
   b. Penningroth, Paul W., The technical elements of training at the sub-doctoral level.
   c. Walsh, Merrick K., Supervised practicum training at the sub-doctoral level.
   d. Harlow, J. E., Jr., Appropriate areas for sub-doctoral technical training and the counseling of students in regard to them.
The training and utilization of M. A. psychologists. Southwestern Psychological Association, Galveston, March 24, 1960 (Frances Carp, Chairman. Participants: Sadie Aaron, Robert G. Smith, James W. Layman).

V. IMPLEMENTING THE OBJECTIVES OF TRAINING
IN A DOCTORAL PROGRAM IN CLINICAL PSYCHOLOGY

Blank, Leonard, and David, Henry P., The crisis in clinical psychology training. *Amer. Psychol.*, 1963, *4*, 216-219.
Brody, Benjamin, Psychoanalytic psychologists evaluate their academic training. *Amer. Psychol.*, 1955, *10*, 29-31.
Bugental, James F. T., Lasko, Alvin A., and Greening, Thomas C., The university and internships. *Div. of Clin. Psychol. Newsletter*, 1963, *16*, 10-11.
Calabresi, Renata A., Structuring the training situation. In *Training for clinical psychology*. M. H. P. Finn and F. Brown, eds. New York: International Universities Press, 1959, 24-30.
Clark, Kenneth E., and Moore, Bruce V., Doctoral programs in psychology: 1957-1958. *Amer. Psychol.*, 1958, *13*, 631-633.
Dawson, Joseph G., A practicum training program. *Amer. Psychol.*, 1957, *12*, 532-535.
De Palma, Nicholas, and Drake, Raleigh M., Professional ethics for graduate students in psychology. *Amer. Psychol.*, 1956, *11*, 554-557.
Derner, Gordon F., The university and clinical psychology. In *Training for clinical psychology*. M. H. P. Finn and F. Brown, eds. New York: International Universities Press, 1959, 55-65.

Education and Training Board, Criteria for evaluating training programs in clinical or in counseling psychology. *Amer. Psychol.*, 1958, *13*, 59-60.

Education and Training Board Ad Hoc Committee, Donald W. Taylor, Chairman, Education for research in psychology. *Amer. Psychol.*, 1959, *14*, 167-179.

Ericksen, Stanford C., The core curriculum is a dependent variable. *Amer. Psychol.*, 1958, *13*, 56-58.

Fine, Reuben, Pre-doctoral training in psychotherapy. *Pcdg. and summaries*, New York State Psychological Association, 1960, 16-20.

Ford, Donald H., and Urban, Hugh B., The training of clinical psychologists. 1961. Unpublished.

Goldstein, Fred J., Guidelines and obstacles in training for the profession of clinical psychology. *J. Clin. Psychol.*, 1962, *18*, 248-252.

Grossman, David, Clinical psychology: comments and suggestions. *Amer. Psychol.*, 1963, *18*, 568-570.

Gustad, John W., The core curriculum is an *in*dependent variable. *Amer. Psychol.*, 1958, *13*, 655-656.

Heron, Alastair, Common problems of training. *Amer. Psychol.*, 1958, *13*, 547.

Kennelly, Thomas, The selection of psychological interns. In *Training for clinical psychology*. M. H. P. Finn and F. Brown, eds. New York: International Universities Press, 1959, 9-23.

Kovacs, Arthur L., and Pottharst, Karl E., A vacuum of responsibility. *Division of Clin., Psychol. Newsletter*, 1963, *16*, 10.

Languth, William, Psychotherapy and the intern. In *Training for clinical psychology*. M. H. P. Finn and F. Brown, eds. New York: International Universities Press, 1959, 139-160.

Luchins, Abraham S., *A functional approach to training in clinical psychology*. Springfield, Illinois: Charles C Thomas, 1959.

McCary, James L., et al., Psychology internship training: panel discussion. *J. Clin. Psychol.*, 1955, *11*, 114-126.

Moore, Bruce V., Policies and standards for evaluating intern training in clinical psychology. In *Training for clinical psychology*. M. H. P. Finn and F. Brown, eds. New York: International Universities Press, 1959, 161-168.

Pope, Benjamin, Supervisory functions and relations in internships. In *Training for clinical psychology*. M. H. P. Finn and F. Brown, eds. N.Y.: International Universities Press, 1959, 74-85.

Raimy, Victor, and Pepinsky, Harold, A reply to the report of the Ad Hoc Committee of Departmental Chairmen of 'Evaluation and accreditation of clinical psychology training programs.' 1958. Unpublished.

Roe, Anne, et al., eds., *Graduate education in psychology*. (The Miami Conference Report), Washington, D.C.: APA, 1959.

Shakow, David, The improvement of practicum training and facilities.

Psychology and Mental Health. Charles R. Strother, ed. Washington, D.C.: APA, 1957, 53-75.

Slockbower, Edward W., Problems of communication in the training situation. In *Training for clinical psychology.* M. H. P. Finn and F. Brown, eds. New York: International Universities Press, 1959, 102-119.

Snyder, William U., Professional training for clinical psychologists. *J. Clin. Psychol.,* 1962, *18,* 243-248.

Stafford, John, The university in clinical psychology. In *Training for clinical psychology.* M. H. P. Finn and F. Brown, eds. New York: International Universities Press, 1959, 50-54.

Van de Castle, Robert L., and Eichhorn, Oscar J., Jr., Length of graduate training for experimental and clinical psychologists. *Amer. Psychol.,* 1961, *16,* 178-180.

Whitmer, Carroll A., and Beier, Ernst G., A training plan for first year graduate psychology students in a Veterans Administration hospital. *Amer. Psychol.,* 1959, *14,* 600-601.

Zeichner, Abraham, Psychodynamics of the supervisor-intern relationship. In *Training for clinical psychology.* M. H. P. Finn and F. Brown, eds. New York: International Universities Press, 1959, 95-101.

Zimet, Carl N., Clinical training and university responsibility. *J. Clin. Psychol.,* 1961, *17,* 110-114.

Symposia:

Preparing the clinical psychologist for his chosen profession. APA, New York City, September 3, 1957 (Robert G. Bernreuter, Chairman).
  a. Hildreth, Harold, What will he do?
  b. Heiser, Karl F., What should he know academically?
  c. Houtchens, Max, What constitutes practical training?

Graduate education in psychology: philosophies and research strategies. APA, New York City, September 4, 1957 (Robert Leeper, Chairman. Participants: Stanford Ericksen, Donald Marquis, Abraham Maslow, Michael Wertheimer, Robert White).

The process and goals of supervision in clinical psychology. APA, Cincinnati, September 3, 1959 (Robert S. Morrow, Chairman).
  a. Bernstein, Leonard, Supervision as perceived by those who are being supervised.
  b. Kalinkowitz, Bernard, Training and supervision in psychotherapy.
  c. Halpern, Florence, Training and supervision in diagnostic testing.
  d. Roe, Anne, Supervision as perceived by the training supervisor and university consultant.

Major phases of internship training. Southwestern Psychological Association, Galveston, March 26, 1960 (John Gladfelter, Chairman. Participants: Irwin J. Knopf, William Seeman, Sanford Goldstone, James L. McCary, Phillip Worchel, B. Maker, Austin Foster).

Current characteristics of practicum instruction in clinical, counseling, industrial and school psychology. APA, Chicago, September 5, 1960 (Thomas M. Magoon, Chairman).

a. Pumroy, Donald K., Clinical psychology practicum instruction.
b. Magoon, Thomas M., Counseling psychology practicum instruction.
c. Katzell, Raymond A., Industrial psychology practicum instruction.
d. McCandless, Boyd R., School psychology practicum instruction.
The role of the internship in pre-doctoral clinical training. Eastern Psychological Association, Philadelphia, April 7, 1961 (Harold Basowitz, Chairman. Participants: Jules D. Holzberg, Julius Wishner, Justin L. Weiss, Gordon Derner).
What responsibility should training departments take for preparation of the psychologist for practice? APA, Philadelphia, August 31, 1963 (Starke R. Hathaway, Chairman. Participants: Kenneth Clark, Bernard F. Riess, Lloyd G. Humphreys).

VI. POSTDOCTORAL TRAINING IN CLINICAL PSYCHOLOGY

Bennett, Chester C., Post-academic clinical internships. *Div. Clin. Psych. Newsletter*, 1963, *16*, 9-10.
Cook, Stuart W., Beyond law and ethics: a proposal for collaboration in psychological practice. *Amer. Psychol.*, 1957, *12*, 267-272.
Frank, George H., Post-doctoral training in clinical psychology. *Psychol. Rep.*, 1957, *3*, 219-220.
Mayman, Martin, Post-doctoral training for clinical competence. *J. Proj. Tech.*, 1962, *26*, 305-309.
Raimy, Victor, Should clinical internships be post-doctoral? *Div. Clin. Psych. Newsletter*, 1963, *16*, 1-2.
Santostefano, Sebastian, Post-doctoral training in clinical psychology: A preliminary report by an interest group. *Amer. Psychol.*, 1960, *15*, 213.

Symposia:

Postdoctoral training needs and programs in psychology. Western Psychological Association, San Diego, April, 1958 (James F. T. Bugenthal, Chairman. Participants: David B. Klein, James A. Waites, Launor F. Carter, Edward M. Glaser).
Postdoctoral training in clinical psychology. Western Psychological Association, San Jose, April 1960 (Keith Sward, Chairman. Participants: Hedda Bolgar, Irving E. Alexander, Thomas C. Greening, Stewart B. Shapiro).
Postdoctoral training programs in clinical psychology. APA, Chicago, September 3, 1960 (Leslie Phillips, Chairman).
a. Bibace, Roger, Post-doctoral programs: past and present.
b. Garmezy, Norman, Post-doctoral programs and their relation to graduate education.
c. Korchin, Sheldon U., Post-doctoral training as a future direction in clinical psychology.

VII. OTHER CURRENTS IN CLINICAL TRAINING

Albee, Gordon W., American psychology in the sixties. *Amer. Psychol.,* 1963, *18,* 90-95.
Bordin, Edward S., Clinical psychology at the crossroads. APA, *Division of Clinical Psychology Newsletter,* 1963, *16,* 2-3.
Education and Training Board, Anticipations of developments during the next decade which will influence psychology. *Amer. Psychol.,* 1956, *11,* 686-688.
Garmezy, Norman, The training program of the National Institute of Mental Health. *Amer. Psychol.,* 1958, *13,* 37-40.
Hobbs, Nicholas, Strategies for the development of clinical psychology. *Div. 12 Newsletter,* 1963, *16,* 3-6.
Holt, Robert R., Report of a conference on an ideal training program for psychotherapists. *Amer. Psychol.,* 1963, *18,* 677-679.
Jones, Marshall R., and Levine, David, Graduate training for community clinical psychology. *Amer. Psychol.,* 1963, *18,* 219-223.
Kelly, Everett L., The reaction of psychology to the Joint Commission on Mental Illness and Health recommendations. APA, Philadelphia, August 31, 1963.
Mensh, Ivan, Clinical psychology in transition. *Div. Clin. Psych. Newsletter,* 1960, *13,* 9-10.
Strother, Charles R., ed. *Psychology and mental health,* Washington, D.C., APA, 1957 (Contributions by: Robert H. Felix, Jerry W. Carter, Jr., Victor C. Raimy, David Shakow, Carl R. Rogers, Eliot H. Rodnick, Neil D. Warren, Charles R. Strother, and Erich Lindemann).
Von Felsinger, John M., and Klein, Donald C., A training program for clinical psychologists in community mental health theory and practice. In *Psychology and Mental Health,* Appendix B, Charles R. Strother, ed. Washington D.C.: APA, 1957, 146-150.
Warriner, Clell C., and Gatch, Vera, Workshop. *Amer. Psychol.,* 1963, *18,* 162.

Symposia:
The impact of the mental health orientation on the future of clinical psychology. Eastern Psychological Association, Atlantic City, March 23, 1956 (John M. von Felsinger, Chairman. Participants: Chester C. Bennett, Donald C. Klein, Samuel Waldfogel).
Clinical psychology and public health training. APA, New York City, September 1, 1961 (A. J. Bindman, Chairman).
   a. Bell, John E., The need for public health trained clinical psychologists: An overview.
   b. Conners, J. Edward, Training in public health for clinical psychologists.
   c. Raimy, Victor C., The case for emphasis on clinical psychology training.

d. Reid, Melvin P., Clinical psychology and public health training: How applicable?

Implications of community mental health for the training of clinical psychologists. APA, New York City, September 1, 1961 (Ira Iscoe, Chairman).

a. Bobbitt, Joseph M., The changing national scene.
b. Rodnick, Eliot H., Community mental health research and psychology.
c. Wellin, Edward, Social science.
d. Plaut, Thomas F. A., Public health.

Prospects for a new mental health profession— report of an interdisciplinary conference on an ideal training program for psychotherapists. APA, Philadelphia, August 29, 1963 (Robert R. Holt, Chairman. Contributions by: William U. Snyder, Eliot H. Rodnick).

Appendix A

UNIVERSITY PROGRAMS

Since many of the requirements for training are the same in both clinical
and counseling psychology, they are treated together, with the differences
noted.

I. Staff

The quality of the staff is the most important factor in any doctoral
program. There must be a minimum of seven qualified (Ph.D. or Diplomate) persons on the staff.

1. Basic staff. At least four different persons must contribute to graduate
nonclinical and noncounseling teaching, and their total time assigned to
this teaching must be the equivalent of at least 2.0 full-time graduate
teachers.

2. Clinical or counseling Staff: a) Three persons for regular teaching
of graduate students in clinical (or counseling) psychology. One of these
must be primarily in clinical or in counseling psychology and cannot be
counted for both, and must be on the department budget for at least
half-time. b) Their combined graduate teaching load is the equivalent
of not less than one full-time graduate teacher in clinical or in counseling
psychology.

II. Content Areas

This is not a list of courses, and it is liberally interpreted when applying it in an evaluation of a program.

1. General psychology: a) General, physiological, and comparative
b) History and systems or theory, c) Developmental or child psychology
d) Social psychology.

2. Psychodynamics of behavior: a) Theory of personality and motivation, b) Psychopathology.

3. Diagnostic methods.

4. Psychotherapy and counseling: a) Psychotherapeutic theory and
methods, or b) Techniques of guidance and counseling.

5. Research methods: a) Experimental psychology, b) Advanced statistics and quantitative methods, c) Research in dynamic psychology, d
Dissertation, preceded by master's thesis or a research project.

322

6. Related disciplines. Not all of the following are necessary, but it is expected that the graduate program in psychology will be a part of a strong graduate school with graduate studies in supporting areas, such as: a) Physiological sciences, b) Study of social and economic environment, including occupational information—this is important for counseling psychologists, c) Cultural anthropology, d) Philosophy of science.

III. Facilities and Equipment

1. Offices and classrooms for effective instruction and personal conferences.

2. Laboratory space and equipment with shop for repairs and construction of apparatus; calculators for statistical work.

3. Practicum facilities: a) Ongoing clinic on campus or nearby for experience under intensive supervision at laboratory and clerkship levels; equipped with one-way vision observation rooms and recording equipment, b) Definite arrangements made for internships.

4. Library well-stocked for psychology and easily accessible to the students.

5. A student seminar or reading room and lounge where students can get together, educate each other, and learn to communicate.

IV. Overall Atmosphere of the Department

1. Faculty accessible to students, and the student-faculty ratio making it possible for the students to receive adequate counsel and supervision.

2. Ongoing research projects conducted by both faculty and by the students, providing an atmosphere that challenges the student to participate and undertake research; quality of research evidenced by list of research articles accepted and published in psychological journals.

3. Planning and growth in the department, giving evidence of vision and initiative on the part of the faculty, who do not wait for specific suggestions on what to do in order to develop a good department.

INTERNSHIPS

Standards for practicum training in clinical psychology were described in the *American Psychologist* (1950, Vol. 5, November, 594—609) and for counseling psychology in the *American Psychologist* (1952, Vol. 7, June, 182—188). These standards, with slight modification, will serve as criteria for evaluating internships or trainee assignments to be approved as adequate for doctoral training programs. These criteria are summarized briefly here to indicate what will be looked for; but persons applying for approval of an agency are urged to read the references cited above.

I. Staff

1. The student's work is planned with him and supervised by a psychologist who is qualified in clinical or counseling psychology as indicated by a diploma from ABEPP, or by a Ph.D. plus experience.

2. This supervisor or advisor must be regularly on the job at least half-time.

3. The supervision and guidance is supplemented by specialists from other professions and by a representative from the student's university.

II. Prerequisites of Students Accepted

1. The agency accepts only those students whose background of training is sufficient to enable them to incorporate and integrate their practicum experience in such a way as to further their own scientific and professional development.

2. Students at the intern level must have had some practicum training before being accepted as interns.

3. Interns may not be accepted for less than half-time in the formal internship or trainee assignment.

III. Content and Methods of Practicum Training

1. The student has contact with the whole variety of patients and clinical problems in the agency.

2. The student is informed of the purposes and the organization of the agency and is made acquainted with the special services of the professional personnel.

3. The student attends case conferences and teaching seminars, and he learns the theory and practice of the other professions.

4. The student is given supervised training in at least two of the three functions of diagnosis, therapy, and research, which include activities in: a) Observation and interviewing, b) The use of a variety of diagnostic testing procedures, c) Report writing, d) Counseling or psychotherapeutic procedures, e) Any other special treatment procedures used by psychologists, f) Research and validation studies.

IV. Facilities for Study and Research

1. A desk in a room with some privacy is provided for each student so he can study, write reports, work on research, and carrry on his professional work.

2. Recorders and other equipment for psychological work are available to the student.

3. A professional library with research publications is provided and serviced to keep it in usable condition.

4. Research projects are in progress by staff and students.

BRUCE V. MOORE
Education and Training Board

Reprinted in condensed form from the *Amer. Psychol.*, 1958, *13*, 59-60.

Appendix B

APA APPROVED DOCTORAL PROGRAMS IN CLINICAL AND IN COUNSELING PSYCHOLOGY, 1963

In the institutions listed the approved programs are directed by the department of psychology unless otherwise indicated. Only programs leading to the Ph.D. essentially in psychology are approved. Programs that have not requested evaluation and programs that have been evaluated but not approved are not included in the lists. (The criteria for evaluating these programs are reprinted in Appendix A.)

Inclusion of an institution indicates approval of doctoral programs in clinical psychology and in counseling psychology only. Inclusion or non-inclusion carries no implications for other graduate programs in psychology or for programs of graduate education in other disciplines.

Schools marked with a year have received interim approval in that year. All newly approved programs have this designation for at least a few years of further trial before full approval is given.

The institutions listed have been reported to the USPHS, to the VA, and to the Surgeon General's Office, Department of the Army, as conducting approved programs.

CLINICAL PSYCHOLOGY

Adelphi University, Garden City, New York
Alabama, University of, University, Alabama
Arizona, University of (1962), Tucson, Arizona
Boston University, Boston, Massachusetts
Buffalo, University of, Buffalo, New York
California, University of, Berkeley, California
California, University of, Los Angeles, California
Catholic University of America, Washington, D. C.
Chicago, University of, Chicago, Illinois
Cincinnati, University of (1963), Cincinnati, Ohio
Clark University, Worcester, Massachusetts
Colorado, University of, Boulder, Colorado
Connecticut, University of, Storrs, Connecticut
Duke University, Durham, North Carolina
Florida State University, Tallahassee, Florida
Florida, University of, Gainesville, Florida

Fordham University (1962), New York, New York

George Peabody College for Teachers, Division of Human Development and Guidance, with cooperation of Vanderbilt University, Nashville, Tennessee

Harvard University, Department of Social Relations, Cambridge, Massachusetts

Houston, University of (1959), Houston, Texas

Illinois, University of, Urbana, Illinois

Indiana University, Bloomington, Indiana

Iowa, State University of, Iowa City, Iowa

Kansas, University of, Lawrence, Kansas

Kentucky, University of, Lexington, Kentucky

Louisiana State University, Baton Rouge, Louisiana

Loyola University (1959), Chicago, Illinois

Massachusetts, University of, Amherst, Massachusetts

Michigan State University, East Lansing, Michigan

Michigan, University of, Ann Arbor, Michigan

Minnesota, University of, Minneapolis, Minnesota

Missouri, University of, Columbia, Missouri

Nebraska, University of (1959), Lincoln, Nebraska

New York University, Graduate School of Arts and Sciences, New York, New York

North Carolina, University of, Chapel Hill, North Carolina

Northwestern University, Evanston, Illinois

Ohio State University, Columbus, Ohio

Oklahoma, University of, Norman, Oklahoma

Oregon, University of, Eugene, Oregon

Pennsylvania State University, University Park, Pennsylvania

Pennsylvania, University of, Philadelphia, Pennsylvania

Pittsburgh, University of, Pittsburgh, Pennsylvania

Purdue University, Lafayette, Indiana

Rochester, University of, Rochester, New York

Southern California, University of, Los Angeles, California

Southern Illinois University (1962), Carbondale, Illinois

Stanford University, Stanford, California

Syracuse University, Syracuse, California

Teachers College, Columbia University, Department of Psychological Foundations and Services, New York, New York

Temple University, Philadelphia, Pennsylvania

Tennessee, University of, Knoxville, Tennessee

Texas, University of, Austin, Texas

Utah, University of, Salt Lake City, Utah

Vanderbilt University, with cooperation of George Peabody College for Teachers, Nashville, Tennessee

Washington State University, Pullman, Washington

Washington, University of, Seattle, Washington

Washington University, St. Louis, Missouri

Wayne State University (1961), Detroit, Michigan
Western Reserve University, Cleveland, Ohio
Wisconsin, University of, Madison, Wisconsin
Yale University, New Haven, Connecticut

COUNSELING PSYCHOLOGY

Boston University, Boston, Massachusetts
Buffalo, University of, Buffalo, New York
California, University of, Los Angeles, California
Catholic University of America, Washington, D. C.
Duke University, Durham, North Carolina
Florida, University of, Gainesville, Florida
George Peabody College for Teachers, Division of Human Development
    and Guidance, with cooperation of Vanderbilt University, Nashville,
    Tennessee
Illinois, University of, Urbana, Illinois
Iowa, State University of, Iowa City, Iowa
Kansas, University of, Departments of Education and of Psychology,
    Lawrence, Kansas
Maryland, University of, College Park, Maryland
Michigan, University of, Ann Arbor, Michigan
Minnesota, University of, Departments of Psychology and of Educational
    Psychology, Minneapolis, Minnesota
Missouri, University of, Departments of Education and of Psychology,
    Columbia, Missouri
Nebraska, University of (1959), Lincoln, Nebraska
Ohio State University, Columbus, Ohio
Oregon, University of, Departments of Education and of Psychology,
    Eugene, Oregon
Pennsylvania State University, University Park, Pennsylvania
Purdue University, Lafayette, Indiana
Southern Illinois University (1962), Carbondale, Illinois
Teachers College, Columbia University, Department of Psychological
    Foundations and Services, New York, New York
Temple University, Philadelphia, Pennsylvania
Texas, University of, Departments of Education and of Psychology,
    Austin, Texas
Utah, University of; Departments of Psychology and of Educational
    Psychology, Salt Lake City, Utah

SHERMAN ROSS
Education and Training Board

Reprinted in condensed form from the *Amer. Psychol.,* 1963, *18,* 309-10.

Appendix C

The training agencies listed meet the minimum standards stated in *Appendix A*. The Committee on Evaluation is currently reviewing a large number of additional agencies.

A revised formulation of the predoctoral internship in clinical and in counseling psychology was produced by the Ad Hoc Committee on Practicum Agency Evaluation of the ETB. This report (which is available on request) describes three types of internships: G, S, and U. The listing which follows includes only types G and S. Type G internship provides relatively broad training and experience with a wide variety of patients. Type S provides intensive and varied experience, but with relatively restricted clinical material. (Type U internship consists of two subclasses: the "captive" agency limiting its resources to students from a single university, and a group of agencies offering an organized pattern of rotations coordinated with a university training program.) The list is alphabetical by states and agencies.

California

S Kennedy Child Study Center, 1339 - 20th Street, Santa Monica.

G Langley Porter Neuropsychiatric Institute, University of California School of Medicine, Medical Center, San Francisco 22.

G Letterman General Hospital, Clinical Psychology Service, San Francisco.

S Los Angeles Psychiatric Service, 8770 West Whitworth Drive, Los Angeles 35.

G Metropolitan State Hospital, Norwalk.

G Mount Zion Hospital and Medical Center, Department of Psychiatry, 2255 Post Street, San Francisco 15.

G Napa State Hospital, Box A, Imola.

G Neuropsychiatric Institute, Department of Psychiatry, UCLA School of Medicine, Los Angeles 24.

S Pacific State Hospital, P. O. Box 100, Pomona.

S Reiss-Davis Clinic for Child Guidance, 9760 West Pico Boulevard, Los Angeles 35.

Colorado
G University of Colorado School of Medicine, Division of Clinical Psychology, 4200 East Ninth Avenue, Denver 20.

Connecticut
G Connecticut Valley Hospital, Psychological Laboratories, Middletown.
G Fairfield State Hospital, Newtown.
G Institute of Living, Department of Clinical Psychology, 200 Retreat Avenue, Hartford 2.
G Norwich State Hospital, Psychological Laboratories, Box 508, Norwich.

District of Columbia
S Child Center, Catholic University of America, Washington 17.
G Saint Elizabeth's Hospital, Washington 20.
G Walter Reed General Hospital, Clinical Psychology Service, Department of Neuropsychiatry, Washington 12.

Florida
G J. Hillis Miller Health Center, University of Florida, Gainesville.

Georgia
G Milledgeville State Hospital, Milledgeville.

Hawaii
G Hawaii State Hospital, Kaneohe.

Illinois
S Children's Memorial Hospital, 707 West Fullerton Avenue, Chicago 14.
G Galesburg State Research Hospital, Galesburg.
G Institute for Juvenile Research, 907 South Wolcott Avenue, Chicago 12.
G Neuropsychiatric Institute, University of Illinois College of Medicine, 912 South Wood Street, Chicago 12.
G Northwestern University Medical School, 303 East Chicago Avenue, Chicago 11.
G University of Chicago School of Medicine, Department of Psychiatry, 950 East 59th Street, Chicago 37.

Indiana
G Indiana University Medical Center, Section on Psychology, Department of Psychiatry, Indianapolis 7.
G Larue D. Carter Memorial Hospital, 1315 East Tenth Street, Indianapolis 7.

Iowa
S Des Moines Child Guidance Center, 1201 Pleasant Street, Des Moines.

Kansas
G Topeka State Hospital, Department of Psychology, Topeka.
G University of Kansas Medical Center, Department of Psychiatry, Rainbow Boulevard at 39th Street, Kansas City.
S Wichita Guidance Center, 3422 East Douglas, Wichita 8.

Kentucky
G University of Louisville Medical School, Department of Psychiatry, Louisville 2.

Louisiana
G Louisiana State University School of Medicine, 1542 Tulane Avenue, New Orleans 12.
G Southeast Louisiana Hospital, Mandeville.

Maryland
G Psychiatric Institute, University of Maryland School of Medicine, Baltimore 1.
G Springfield State Hospital, Sykesville.

Massachusetts
S Child Guidance Clinic of Springfield, Inc., 759 Chestnut Street, Springfield 7.
S Children's Hospital Medical Center, Division of Psychology, Department of Psychiatry, 300 Longwood Avenue, Boston 15.
S Judge Baker Guidance Center, 295 Longwood Avenue, Boston 15.
S South Shore Guidance Center, 1120 Hancock Street, Quincy 69.
G Worcester State Hospital, Department of Psychology, Box 57, Worcester 1.
S Worcester Youth Guidance Center, 2 State Street, Worcester 8.

Michigan
S Children's Center of Wayne County, 5475 Woodward Avenue, Detroit 2.
S Flint Child Guidance Clinic, 302 West Second Avenue, Flint 2.
G Lafayette Clinic, 951 East Lafayette, Detroit 7.

Missouri
S Community Child Guidance & Child Evaluation Clinics of Washington University, 369 North Taylor Street, Saint Louis 8.
G Greater Kansas City Mental Health Foundation, 2200 McCoy Street, Kansas City 8.
G Washington University School of Medicine, Division of Medical Psychology, Department of Psychiatry, 4940 Audubon Avenue, Saint Louis 10.

Nebraska
G Nebraska Psychiatric Institute, University of Nebraska College of Medicine, 602 South 44th Avenue, Omaha 5.
G Norfolk State Hospital and Out-Patient Clinic, Norfolk.

New Jersey
G New Jersey State Department of Institutions and Agencies, Trenton 25.

New York
G Albert Einstein College of Medicine & Bronx Municipal Hospital Center, Eastchester Road and Morris Park Avenue, Bronx 61.

G Bellevue Psychiatric Hospital, 30th Street & First Avenue, New York 16.
G Columbia-Presbyterian Medical Center, Division of Clinical Psychology, Department of Psychiatry, 722 West 168th Street, New York 32.
G Creedmoor State Hospital, Jamaica 27.
S Institute for the Crippled and Disabled, 400 First Avenue, New York 10.
S Jewish Board of Guardians, 120 West 57th Street, New York 19.
G Kings County Hospital Center, Division of Psychiatry, Brooklyn 3.
S New York University Medical Center, Institute of Physical Medicine and Rehabilitation, 400 East 34th Street, New York 17.
G St. Vincent's Hospital, 144 West 12th Street, New York 11.

North Carolina
G Duke University Medical Center, Division of Medical Psychology, Durham.
G North Carolina Memorial Hospital, University of North Carolina School of Medicine, Chapel Hill.

Ohio
G University Hospitals of Cleveland, 2065 Adelbert Road, Cleveland 6.

Oregon
G University of Oregon Medical School, Department of Medical Psychology, Portland 1.

Pennsylvania
S Child Study Center of Philadelphia, 110 North 48th Street, Philadelphia 39.
S Devereux Foundation, Institute for Research and Training, Devon.
G Norristown State Hospital, Psychology Department, Norristown.
S Pittsburgh Child Guidance Center, 201 DeSoto Street, Pittsburgh 13.

Rhode Island
S Emma Pendleton Bradley Hospital, Riverside 15.

Tennessee
G Gailor Hospital, University of Tennessee School of Medicine, Department of Psychiatry, 42 North Dunlap, Memphis 3.
G Nashville Mental Health Center, 2410 White Avenue, Nashville 4.

Texas
G Baylor University College of Medicine, Department of Psychiatry, 1200 Anderson Boulevard, Houston 25.
G University of Texas Medical Branch, Department of Psychology, Galveston.
G University of Texas Southwestern Medical School, Division of Psychology, Department of Psychiatry, 5323 Harry Hines Boulevard, Dallas 35.

Utah

G University of Utah College of Medicine, Department of Psychiatry, 156 Westminster Avenue, Salt Lake City 15.

Wisconsin

G University of Wisconsin Medical School, Department of Psychiatry, Madison.

SHERMAN ROSS
Education and Training Board

To be published in a future issue of the *American Psychologist*

Index

Academic vs. service orientation, 285-288
Accreditation and licensing, 40-41
  and the APA, 91-93.
  approved doctoral programs (table), 92
  attitude in university, 97-100
  defects, 112
  origins and procedures, 91-100
  of practicum agencies, 100-105
  purposes of, 87-89
  voluntary certification, 110
  see also Evaluation, Standards for clin-
    ical psychology, and individual con-
    ferences
Admission requirements to university programs, 121-123
Agencies. *See* Field agencies
Alumni statements, 280-294
American Association of State Psychology Boards, 110
American Board for Psychological Services, 104-105
American Board of Examiners in Professional Psychology (ABEPP), 88,
  104-108
  distribution of diplomates (table), 106
  grandfather diplomates, 106
American Psychological Association (APA)
  and accreditation, 91-93
  committee on evaluation, 93, 102
    approved internship agencies, 102-103
    report on standards, 94-96
  committee on graduate and professional
    training, 91
  committee on practicum training, 93
  committee on problems of internship
    evaluation
    predoctoral internships, 103
    approved internship centers, 328
  committee on relations with the social
    work professions, 37
  committee on training in clinical psy-
    chology (CTCP)
    and accreditation, 92
    plans for internships, 100-102

  standards, 90
  standards for practicum and intern-
    ship agencies, 100
  1947 report, 39
  education and training board (E & T
    Board), 93-96
  NIMH support, 46
  and psychology departments, 117
  and the VA, 64
  evaluation principles and practices,
    93-96
  and predoctoral internship, 99
  social control and legislation, 109
  subcommittee on graduate internship
    training, 90
  see also Division 12
Approved internship centers, 328
Argentina, 269
Armed services, training in, 82-85
  graduate psychology student program, 82
  Letterman General Hospital, 82
  Walter Reed General Hospital program,
    83-85
Australia, 262-265
Austria, 223

Belgium, 223
Boulder Conference, 2-3
  accreditation, 40
  field training, 18-20
  graduate program, 14
  internship 18-20
  psychotherapy, 31
  relations with other professions, 36
  selection of students, 38
  standards, 91
Brazil, 270
Burma, 253

Cameroons, 249
Canada, 265-267
Certification. *See* Accreditation

Chile, 271
China, 254
Clerkship, 13, 18, 20
Clinical doctorates, 7
Clinical faculty, 132-137, 293
Clinical psychologist
  academic vs. service orientation, 285-288
  number of, 1, 38, 89
  role of, 307-309
  use of term, 3, 4, 24
Clinical psychology, levels of non-academic training (table), 101
Colombia, 271
Columbia Law Review survey of legislation, 108
Committees of the APA. *See* APA
Committees of the NIMH. *See* NIMH
Congo, 249
Counseling Psychology
  and clinical psychology, 36
  Northwestern Conference, 29
  VA program, 64-65
Crisis in training viewed by clinical alumni, 278-300
CTCP, 92, 100-102
Cuba, 272
Curriculum in the university, 123
Czechoslovakia, 224

Denmark, 225
Developmental psychology, 164, 181
Diagnosis, 152-174, 304-305
Diagnostic methods
  Shakow recommendations, 11-12
Dissertation
  Miami recommendations, 34
  Shakow recommendations, 13, 33
Division 12 of the APA
  conference on clinical training, 144
  committee on training, 141
  postdoctoral institute program, 148
Doctoral programs, growth in number (table), 92
Draw a Person (DAP) test, 155

Ecuador, 272
Education and Training Board, 93-96
Egypt, 245
England, 242-244
Evaluation
  of programs, 86-89, 112
  levels, agencies, and methods of, 87, 88
  principles of the APA, 93-96
see also Accreditation, and Standards for clinical psychology

Experimental psychology, 32

Field agencies 17, 22, 25, 120-128
  approved list, 328
  attitudes towards interns, 3, 4
  NIMH support 47, 53-54
  standards for, 19
  see also Internship, and Field training
Finances of the NIMH, 55-59
Finland, 226
France, 227-229
Field training, 17-25
  and university, 17, 20-25, 126
  see also Field agencies, Internship, and individual conferences

General psychology, 8, 11
German Democratic Republic, 231
Germany, Federal Republic of, 229
Ghana, 250
Graduate program, 10-17
  see also University
Graduate training, 292-293
Graduate training abroad, 219-275
  see also individual countries
Graduate training in university. *See* University
Grandfather diplomates, 106
Grant procedures of the NIMH, 45-55
Greece, 232
Group testing, 154-156
Guatemala, 273

Holland, 234
Hong Kong, 255

Ideology, professional, 299
India, 255-257
Indonesia, 257
Integration of field and university training, 17, 20-25, 126
Intelligence testing, 166
Internship
  in armed services, 82-85
  centers. *See* Field agencies
  predoctoral vs. postdoctoral, 13, 23, 98, 147, 281-285
  shortage of candidates, 24
  standards, CTCP report on, 100-102
  supervision by university, 99
  timing of, 23, 98
  training and the NIMH, 53-54

training and university. *See* University
see also Field agencies, Field training, and individual conferences
Interpersonal Checklist (ICL), 155
Ireland, 232
Israel, 246-248
Italy, 233

Japan, 258
Joint Commission on Mental Illness and Health, 301-302

Kelly and Goldberg study 142, 285

Laboratory training, 18, 20, 160
Language and semantic analysis, 165
Legislation and non-statutory regulation, 108-110
    American Association of State Psychology Boards, 110
    AMA recommendations, 108
    APA report, 109
    Columbia Law Review survey, 108
    state regulations, 110, 111 (table)
Letterman General Hospital, 82
Licensing and Accreditation, 40-41, 88
Los Angeles Society of Clinical Psychologists, 148, 283

Malaya 258
Mexico, 273
Miami Conference, 5-6
    clinical faculty, 134
    field training, 21-24
    postdoctoral recommendations, 147
    research, 33
    subdoctoral training, 26
    training, 15, 115, 118-119
Michigan alumni statement, 280-294
MMPI, 115, 155, 159

National Advisory Mental Health Council, 45
National Institute of Mental Health (NIMH), 43-60
    philosophy of support, 44-47
    research fellowships, 58
    research grants, 49, 52, 59, 191
    and school psychology, 53
    statistics on finances, 55-59
    Training Branch, 45

training grants, 45-55
training program support, 55-59
    1962-1963 (table), 56
Netherlands, 234
New Jersey training program, 205-214
New York state legislation, 110
New Zealand, 265
Nigeria, 251
Non-doctoral training, 27
Non-statuatory regulation, 108-110
Northwestern Conference, 29
Norway, 235-237

Pakistan, 259
Panama, 274
Peru, 274
Ph.D., shortage of, 301
Ph.D. training, 23, 116-120
    and internship, 125
    in research, 127-129
Phillippines, 259-261
Physiological psychology, VA training in, 72
Poland, 237
Portugal, 238
Postdoctoral Institute, 148
Postdoctoral professional training, 140-150, 166-170
    fellowships, 140, 149
    list of programs, 146-147
    postdoctoral models, 145-149
    and psychodiagnosis, 166-168
    and psychotherapy, 129, 142, 145, 183, 306
    in research, 197
    see also Internship, and Michigan alumni statement
Practicum agencies, 17, 22, 25, 120-128
Practicum training in university. *See* University
Predoctoral training
    inadequacy of, 141-144
    and psychotherapy, 179-181
    scientific, 162-166
    see also Internship
Princeton Conference, 6-7
    field training, 24
    internship, 6, 24
Professional degree, 306
Program support by NIMH, 55-59
Projective techniques, 9
Psychodiagnosis, 152-174
    conventional training, 152-157
    innovations for training, 157-172

New Jersey program in, 207
postdoctoral training in, 166-168
report, 153, 170
technical aspects, 163
tests, 154-156. *See also* individual tests
see also Predoctoral and Postdoctoral
     training
Psychodiagnosticians, numbers required,
     305
Psychodynamics, Shakow recommenda-
     tions, 11
Psychological technicians, 170-172
Psychotherapy, training for, 30-32, 175-
     184, 305
  in armed services, 82-85
  curriculum, 181
  predoctoral training in, 179-181
  postdoctoral training in, 129, 142, 145,
     183, 306
  prerequisites, 176-180
  psychopathology training, 181
  research in, 130, 182
  and social psychology, 181
  in state program, 205-214
  techniques, 32
  university and professional program,
     102, 129, 175, 179
  with VA patients, 73, 75
  see also individual conferences
public health and mental health, 50

Relations with other professions, 36-37
Research training, 16, 32-35, 118-119, 185-
     203, 295-300, 304
  in armed services, 82-85
  contributions, 289
  and dynamic psychology, 33
  graduate training in, 187-197
  grants of NIMH, 49, 52, 59, 191
  Institute of Life Sciences, 199
  Michigan alumni view, 288-290
  models, 296
  opportunities for trainees, 78
  postdoctoral training in, 197
  in psychotherapy, 130, 182
  publication rate, 187-190
  in state program, 205-214
  in the VA, 61-81
  in Worcester State Hospital, 198-203
  see also Ph.D., University, and indi-
     vidual confereneces
Rorschach test, 154
Russia, 241
Rutgers training program, 205-218

San Salvador, 275
School psychology
  and NIMH, 53
  Thayer Conference, 29
Selection of students 37-40, 121
Semantic analysis, 165
Service vs. academic orientation, 285-288
Shakow Report, 2-3
  and CTCP report, 92
  emphasis on clinical training, 121
  field training, 17
  graduate program, 10-13
  internship, 10, 13, 17
  research, 32
  standards, 90
  undergraduate program, 8
Singapore, 258
Social control, 109
Social psychology
  and clinical psychology, 165
  and psychotherapy, 181
  VA training in, 65, 72
South Africa, 251
Spain, 239
Specialization in training, 4, 28-30
Staff training, 35
Standards for clinical psychology, 86-113
  APA principles, 92
  nature and purposes, 86-89
  specification of 112-113
  in state program, 207-211
  see also Legislation, Accreditation, and
     Evaluation
Stanford-Binet, 9
Stanford Conference, 3-4, 185, 194
  field training, 20
  specialization in training, 28
State legislation, 110
State training program, 205-218
  diversity of facilities, 206
  psychodiagnosis, 207
  Psychology Junior Fellows, 206
  psychotherapy, 208
  research, 208
  staff training, 213
  standards, 207-211
  training director, role of, 213
Subdoctoral training, 5, 26-28, 281
Support for graduate clinical programs,
     130, 132
Sweden, 239
Switzerland, 240

TAT, 154
Taiwan, 261

Technicians, 170-172
Tests, clinical, 154-156
    teaching of, 20
    see also individual tests
Thailand, 261
Thayer Conference, 29
Therapy. *See* Psychotherapy
Training abroad, 219-275
Training Branch of NIMH, 45
Turkey, 248

Undergraduate program, 8-10, 122
Union of South Africa, 251
United Arab Republic, 245
United Kingdom, 242-244
University, clinical psychology training in,
        115-139
    abroad, 219-275
    admission requirements, 121-123
    clinical faculty, 132-137, 293
    curriculum, 123
    and field training, 20-25
    internship, 125-127
    meaning of Ph.D., 116-120
    objectives, 118
    practicum training, 124
    and psychothcrapy, 102, 129, 179
    and research, 127, 129
    support for programs and students, 130,
        132
    see also APA, Michigan alumni state-

ment, and individual conferences
University responsibility, 281
Uruguay, 275
USPHS training, 131
USSR, 241

Venezuela, 275
Veterans Administration, training in, 6,
        61-81,148
    development of program, 61-66
    experiences with patients, 70-77
    projects in research 78, 79, 81
    psychological assistantship program, 68
    psychology trainees (table), 65
    social psychology, 65, 72
    stipend program, 68
    types of trainee appointments, 68
    vocational counseling, 64, 75
Vietnam, 262
Vocational counseling in VA, 64

WAIS, 155
Walter Reed General Hospital, 83-85
Wechsler-Bellevue, 9
Western Reserve University, 297
Worcester State Hospital training pro-
        gram, 198-203

Yugoslavia, 244